IMAGES
*of America*

# SOUTHWEST GARDEN

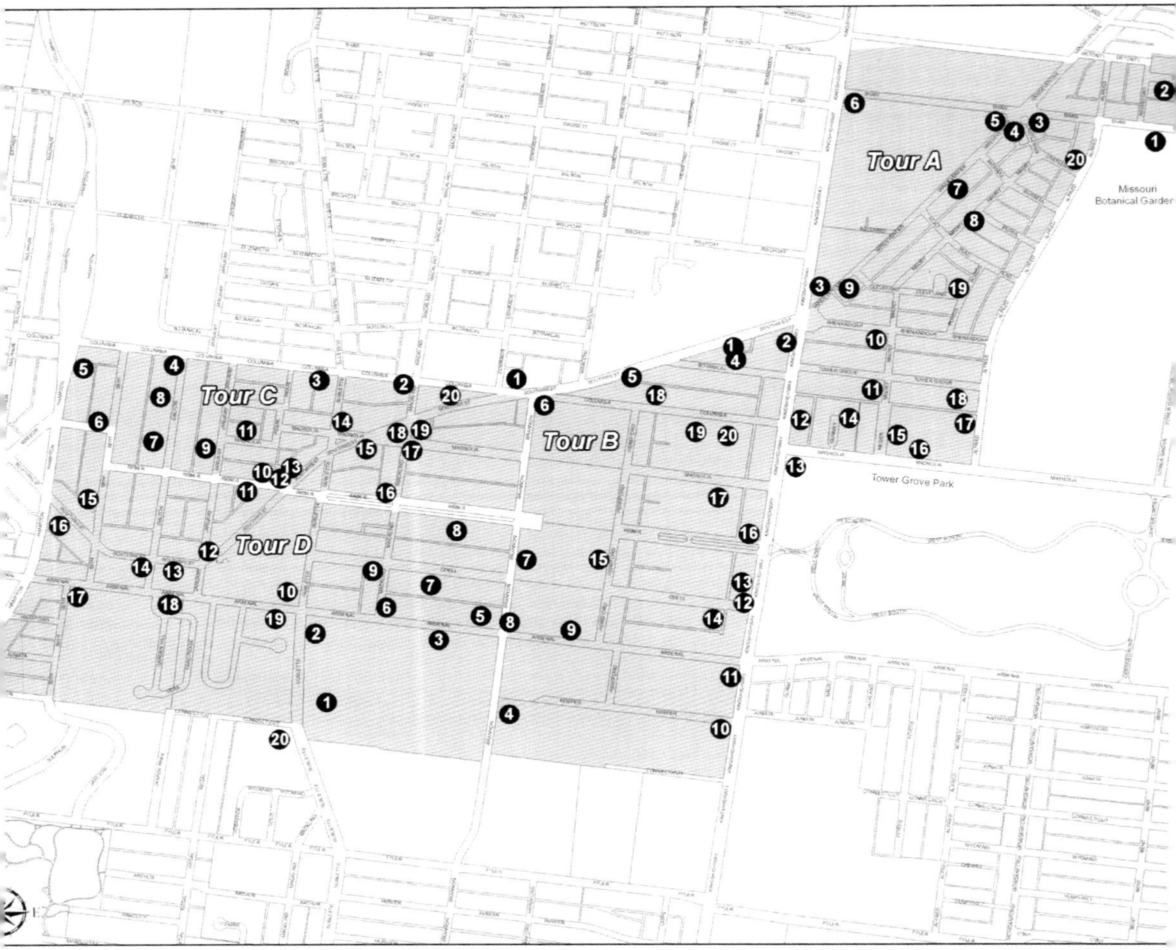


In celebration of its 30th anniversary, the Southwest Garden Neighborhood Association, which was founded in 1978, commissioned Edna Campos Gravenhorst to write a book to celebrate and preserve the neighborhood's history. The association represents approximately 3,000 households and was founded to help St. Louis with the redevelopment and revitalization of city neighborhoods. The association wishes to acknowledge Robert and Wanda Bowen, who reside and own the four-family residence on Alfred Avenue. Wanda was the first president of the Southwest Garden Property Owners Association. The Bowens moved here in the 1980s and were some of the first residents responsible for stabilizing the area. In the same block as the Bowens is the home of noted artist Charlie Houska. Houska converted his four-family home into two town houses and the garage into his artist's studio. These are the kinds of residents that make the Southwest Garden what it is today. The map pictured is by Shari L. Maxwell-Mooney. (Planning and Urban Design Agency City of St. Louis.)

*On the cover*: Please see page 92. (Jennifer Guidici collection.)

IMAGES
*of America*

# SOUTHWEST GARDEN

Edna Campos Gravenhorst

ARCADIA
PUBLISHING

ISBN 978-0-7385-6185-1

Published by Arcadia Publishing
Charleston SC, Chicago IL, Portsmouth NH, San Francisco CA

Printed in the United States of America

Library of Congress Catalog Card Number: 2008929034

For all general information contact Arcadia Publishing at:
Telephone 843-853-2070
Fax 843-853-0044
E-mail sales@arcadiapublishing.com
For customer service and orders:
Toll-Free 1-888-313-2665

Visit us on the Internet at www.arcadiapublishing.com

*To the residents of the Southwest Garden neighborhood who take pride in their community and its history, may we continue to make progress in preserving the history of the working-class people of St. Louis.*

# Contents

# ACKNOWLEDGMENTS

I would like to say thank you to the following people and organizations who, with their help and support, made this book possible: Floyd Wright, Judy Lewin, Barbara Anderson, Dana Gray, Southwest Garden Neighborhood Association and board members, Fr. Vincent Bommarito, Tony Meyers, JoAnn Vatcha, St. Louis Community Development Administration, Planning and Urban Design Agency City of St. Louis, 8th Ward alderman Stephen Conway, 10th Ward alderman Joseph Vollmer, Operation Brightside, Mary Lou Green, Southwest Bank, Becke Sigman, Zeis Group, St. Louis Public Library, Missouri History Museum in St. Louis, St. Louis Public Schools Record Center/Archives, St. Louis Mercantile Library at the University of Missouri–St. Louis, Missouri Institute of Mental Health Library, Christina Sullivan, Laurent D. Javois, Vicki Eichhorn, St. Louis City Hall, Missouri Botanical Garden, Andrew Colligan, Bob Herleth, Nick Ballta, Melinda Jackson, Steve Miller, Cheryl and John Fillion, Paul Simon, Lori Willis, Don Quante, Kathy Buckley, Bill Hart, Jeffery Krull, Shawn Phillip Burkard, South City Family YMCA, Carole Rulo, Robert Porter, and all the residents and friends of the Southwest Garden that took time to meet, communicate, and look for photographs and information for me, which enabled me to tell a more complete history of the neighborhood.

A special thank-you to my editor Anna Wilson and publisher John Pearson for believing in the history of the Southwest Garden and for their patience during the book process. The final thank-you goes to my husband, Ted, and my family and friends who understood and supported me while my focus was on completing the book.

# INTRODUCTION

During a walking tour of the Southwest Garden, one can view a building from the 1860s, another one from the 1870s, historic homes, two- and four-family dwellings, small to midsize apartment complexes, and community structures built from the 1880s to the 1930s. There are beautiful architectural details to discover. To experience the essence of the community, take time to visit the shops and cafés and to chat with the local residents.

The Southwest Garden and the Hill neighborhoods are partners in promoting their businesses and community. There are two business associations that cover the area, the Hill Business Association and the Tower Grove Business Association. Southwest Garden resident Carole Rulo, who works for the City of St. Louis, had a major role on the Neighborhood Stabilization Team and introduced the packet "A Landlord's Guide to Managing Rental Property." This has been a great tool for investors and developers.

The Southwest Garden Neighborhood Association, the Southwest Garden Property Owners Association, and the Southwest Neighborhood Improvement Association have been working with the Southwest Neighborhood Housing Corporation to secure the stabilization of this historic neighborhood. With the organizations working together since 1992 and with the leadership of their city alderman, Stephen Conway, many properties in the vicinity of the Missouri Botanical Garden have been developed with an emphasis on home ownership.

The Southwest Garden has done a great job of balancing the diversity in its residents and businesses. They have enhanced the neighborhood with new development and construction, while preserving its historic integrity.

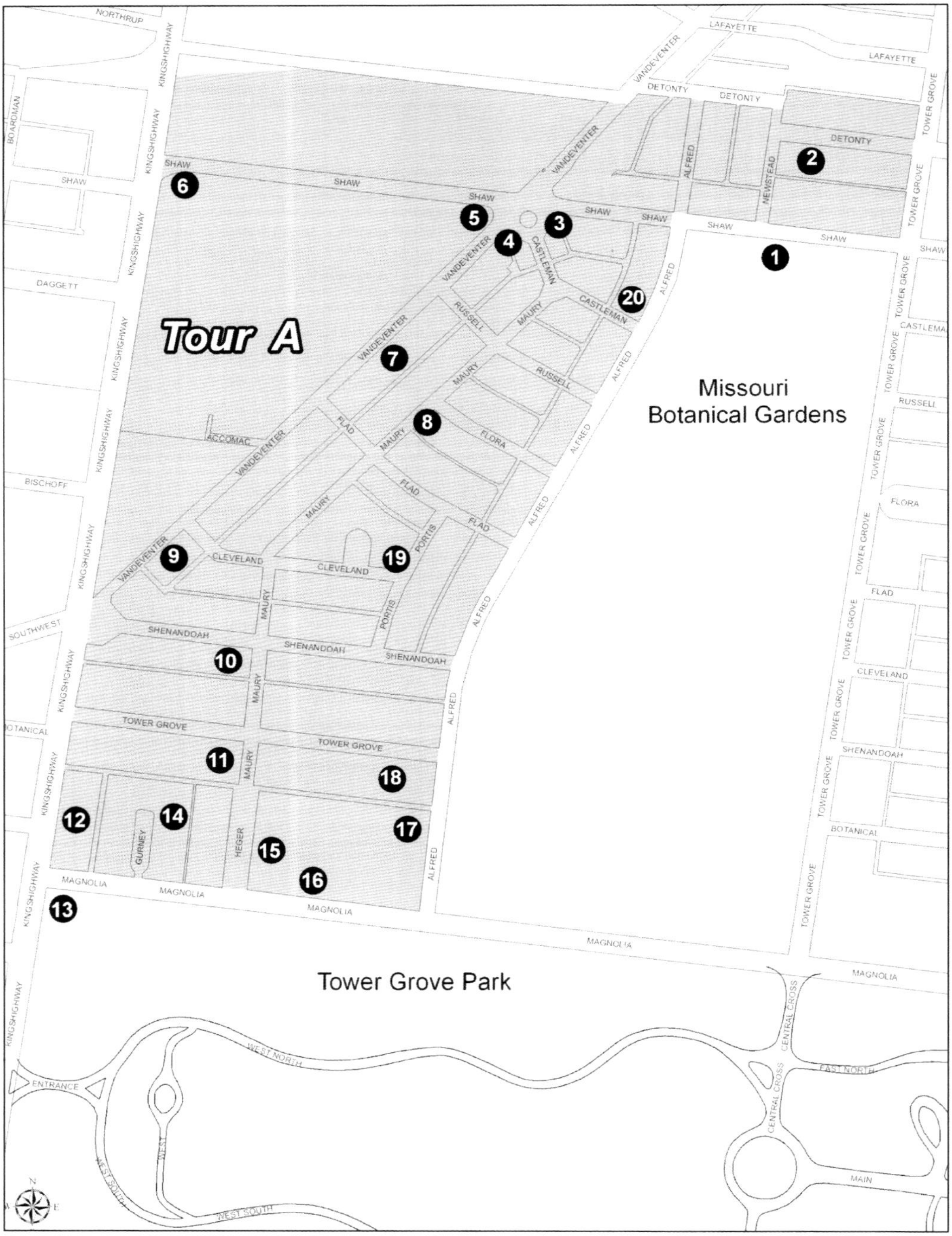


This is a map of Tour A by Shari L. Maxwell-Mooney. (Planning and Urban Design Agency City of St. Louis.)

# *One*

# Tour A

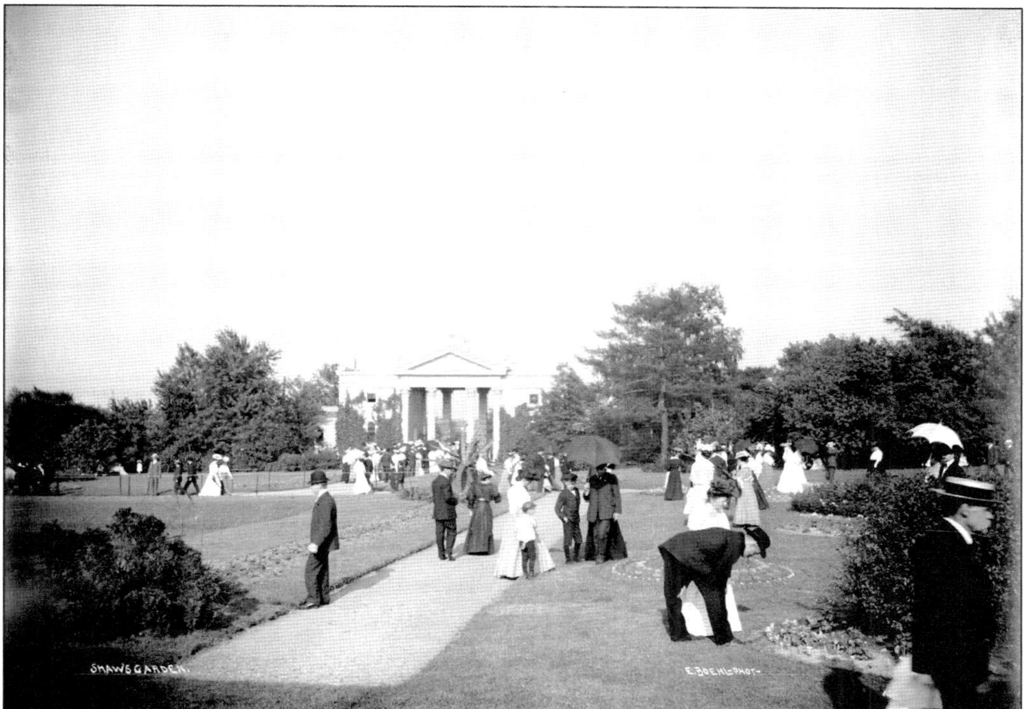


This 1890 photograph with a view to the east of the main gate gives a glimpse of how interested the visitors were in viewing the flower beds in the Missouri Botanical Garden. The garden opened to the public in 1859, and the original entrance was on Flora Avenue. Today the main entrance is on Shaw Avenue. The garden's manicured grounds cover 79 acres. It is the oldest continuously operating botanical garden in the country. (Missouri Botanical Garden Archives.)

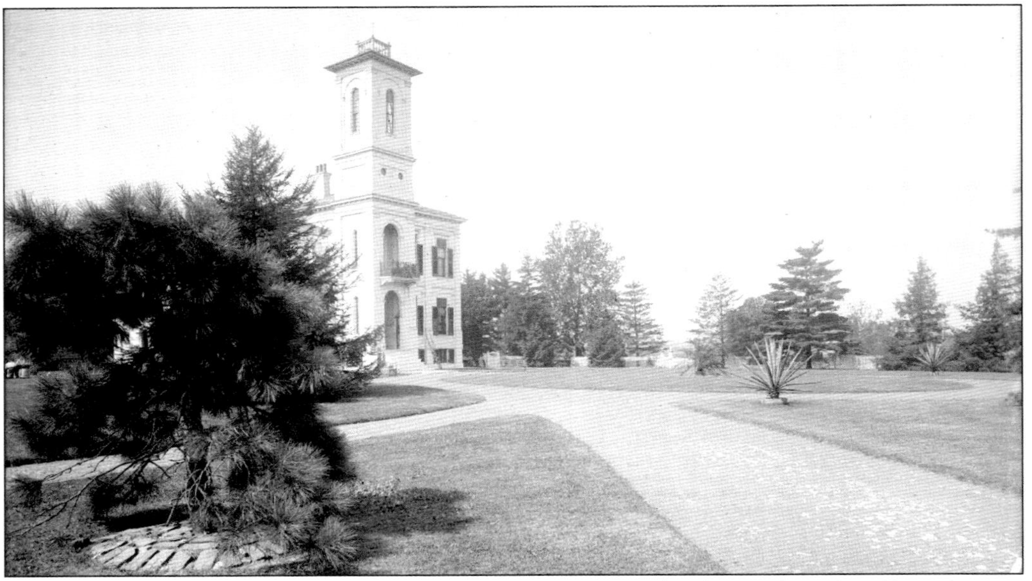

This is the Tower Grove House in the Missouri Botanical Garden (site A1) at 4344 Shaw Avenue around 1890. Formerly Henry Shaw's country home, it was located in the Victorian District and designed in 1849 by George I. Barnett. The two-story Italian-style villa became known as Tower Grove House because its tower could be seen above a grove of trees as visitors approached. Shaw's country estate included the house and the 80 acres surrounding it. (Missouri Botanical Garden Archives.)

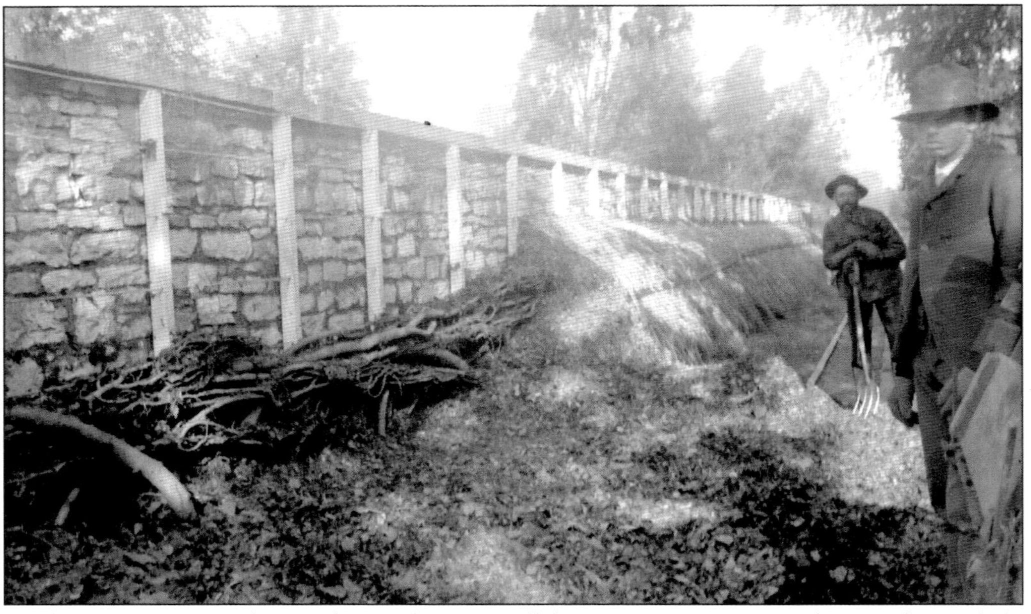

Workers are preparing fig trees lining the west wall for winter in 1891. For today's gardeners, help is available through the Kemper Center for Home Gardening. Those unable to attend classes and workshops can find information on the organization's Web site, where Chip Tynan answers gardening questions. He has answered more than 1,700 questions that are posted on the Web site. (Missouri Botanical Garden Archives.)

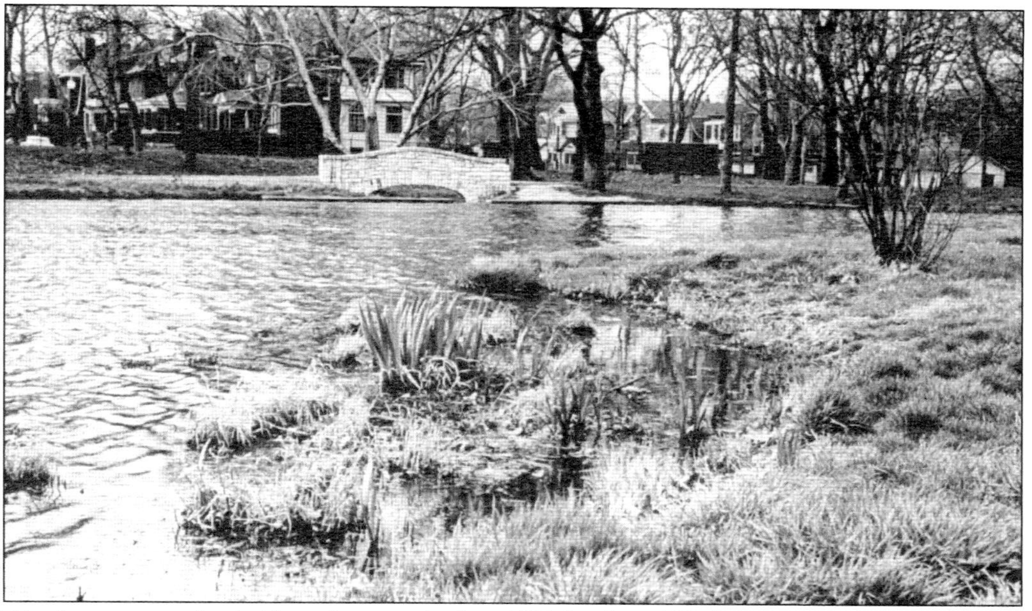

The Japanese garden bridge, photographed in 1975, borders Alfred Avenue and the Southwest Garden neighborhood. The garden is called Seiwa-en, meaning "garden of pure, clear harmony and peace." Visitors are encouraged to slow down and observe. This little piece of heaven in the midst of a busy city is the largest traditional Japanese garden in North America. The Japanese garden covers 14 acres and includes a lake that spans 4.5 acres. (Missouri Botanical Garden Archives.)

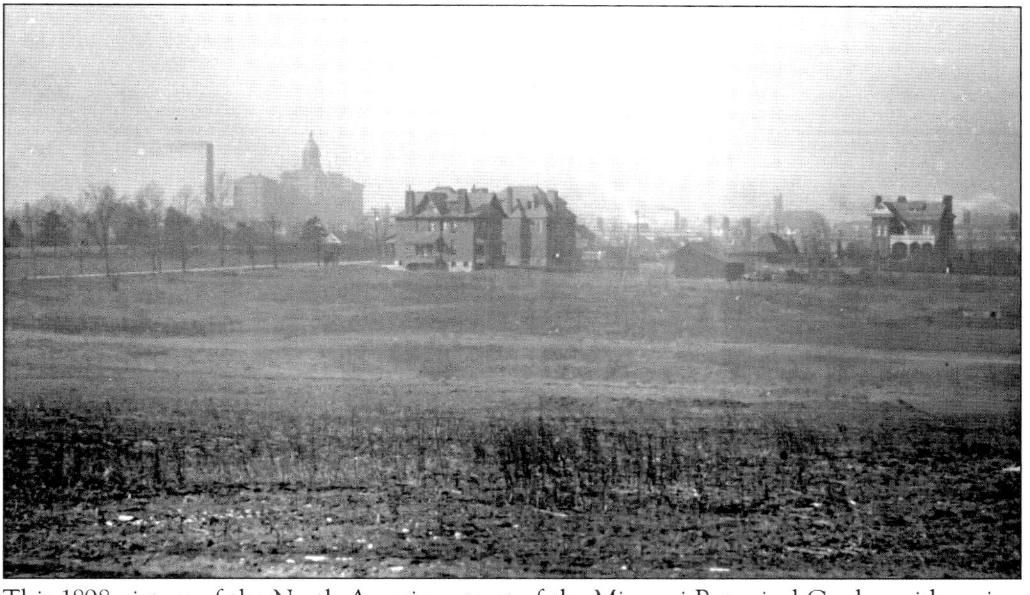

This 1898 picture of the North American tract of the Missouri Botanical Garden with a view to the west gives an idea of what the area looked like before the dawn of the 20th century. The state mental hospital that provided many jobs in the area is visible in the background. The northwest area bordering the garden was filled with Tudor-style houses in the 2600 block of Alfred Avenue in the 1920s. (Missouri Botanical Garden Archives.)

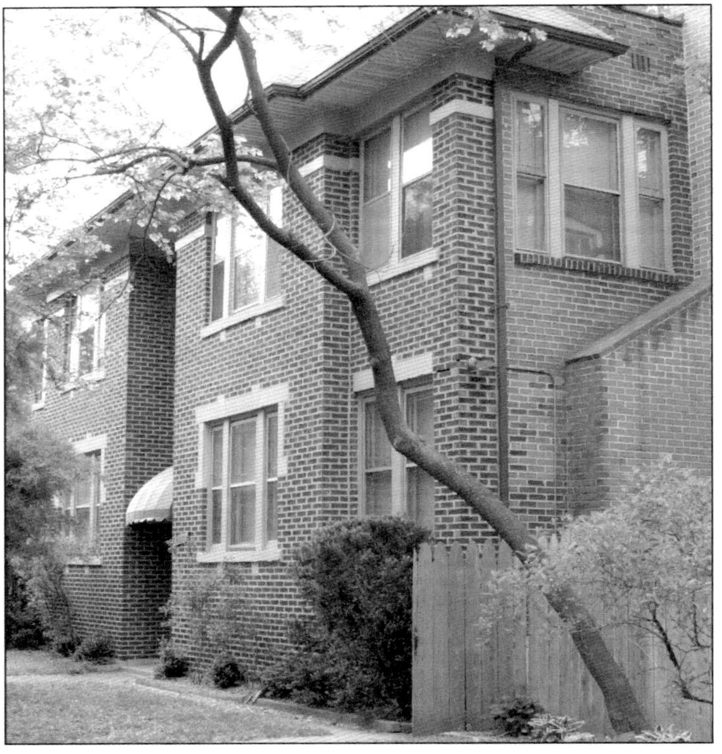

This four-family residence (site A2) at 4336 DeTonty Street was built for W. D. Lane by J. Moran in 1922 for $12,000. The Wright family moved to this block to help redevelop the area. Floyd Wright Jr. and his mother, Janie, live in a two-family on DeTonty that she and her husband, Floyd Wright Sr., purchased in 1978. The Floyd Wright family invested and developed the 4300 blocks of Shaw Avenue and DeTonty Street. (Derek Cadzow Photography.)

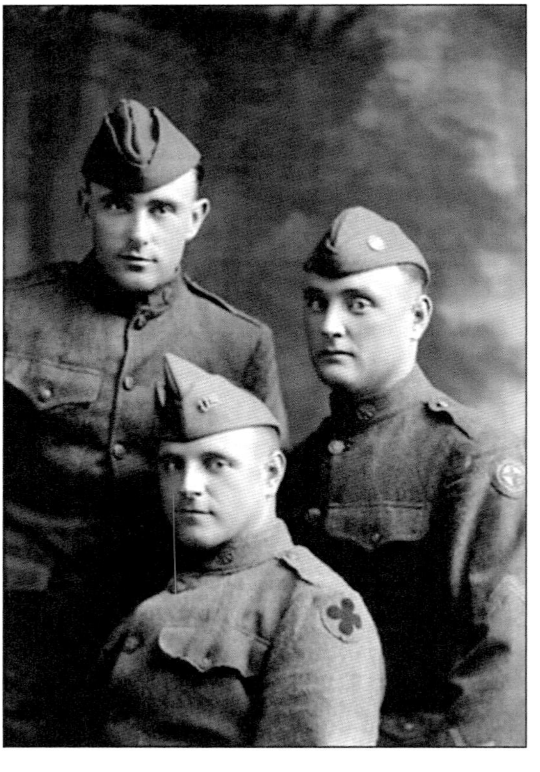

These World War I soldiers are, from left to right, Arthur, Henry, and George Owens. When the young men came back from the war, they needed places to live. The multifamily units on this city block were just right for the market when they were built in 1917. Most of them were built by the Modern Building and Alco Improvement Companies, Barru Realty and Investment, and H. A. Barrett. (Owens family collection.)

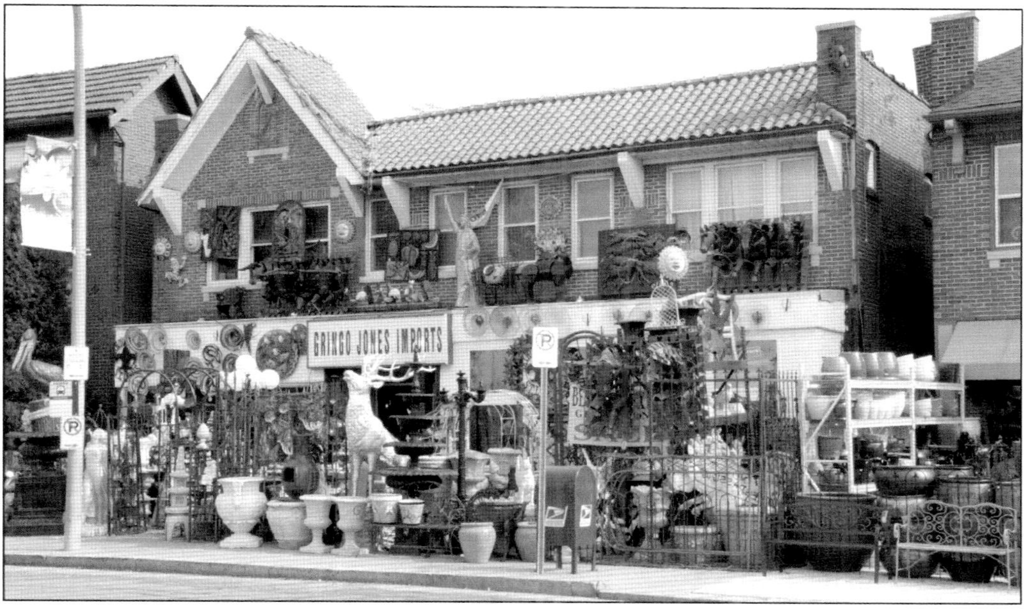


Gringo Jones Imports (site A3) at 4468–4470 Shaw Avenue started out as a restaurant, bakery, and apartment. The structure was built in 1924 for $15,000 by Charles W. Hehmann. In 1959, it was a dental laboratory, and in 1967, it was a film-stripping laboratory. Today it houses 8,000 square feet of home and garden accessories ranging from mantels to fountains, handbags, and glass art. Many items are imported from Mexico. The owner, Archie Leon Jones, lives on Shaw Avenue. (Derek Cadzow Photography.)

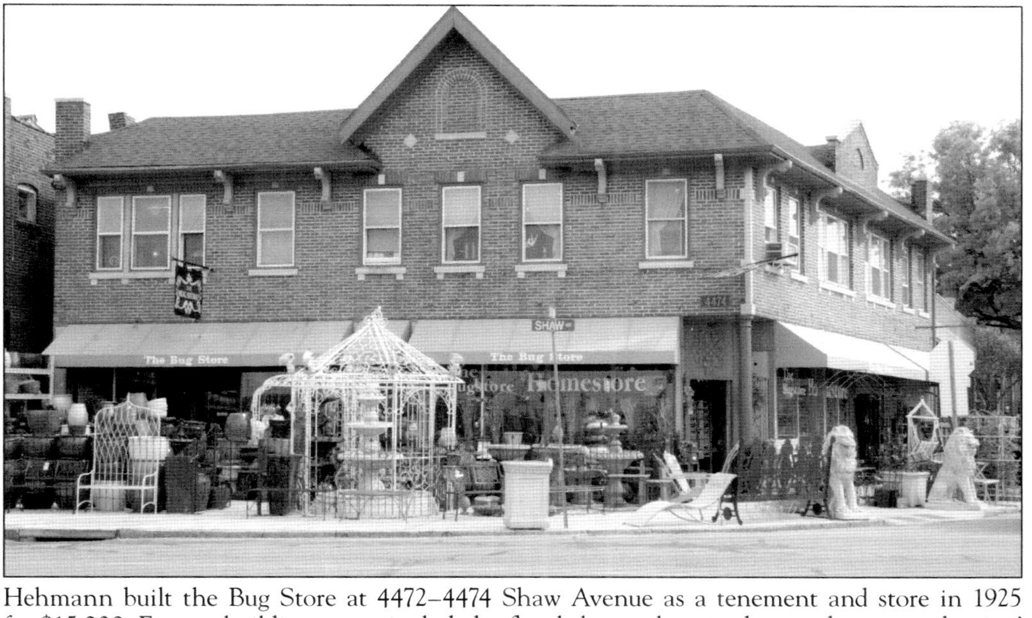


Hehmann built the Bug Store at 4472–4474 Shaw Avenue as a tenement and store in 1925 for $15,000. Former building usage included a floral shop, a beauty shop, a drugstore, dentists' and physicians' offices, and apartments upstairs. In 1947, it was the Metropolitan Ice Cream Company, and in 1970, it was a full package and sundry tavern. The current owner, Shaw Building, bought the property in 1991. (Derek Cadzow Photography.)

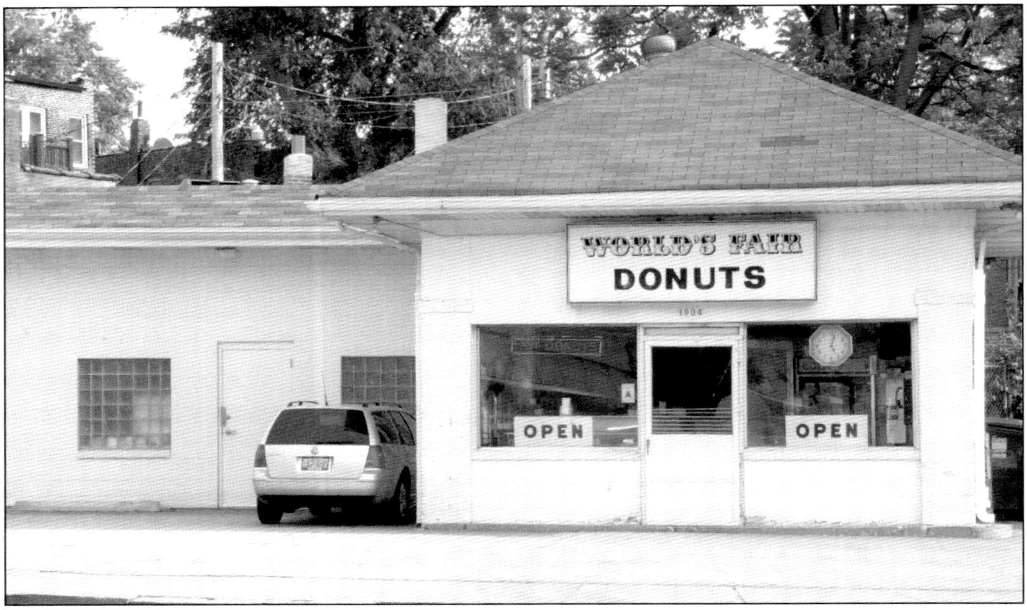


World's Fair Donuts (site A4) at 1904 Vandeventer Avenue was built in 1928 by the Puritan Oil Company as a filling station at a cost of $1,000. In the early 1920s, this area was used for billboards. In the 1930 city directory, this address is listed as the Independent Service Station. An addition was built to the station in 1938. In 1976, J. C. Clanton turned the old filling station into a doughnut shop. (Derek Cadzow Photography.)

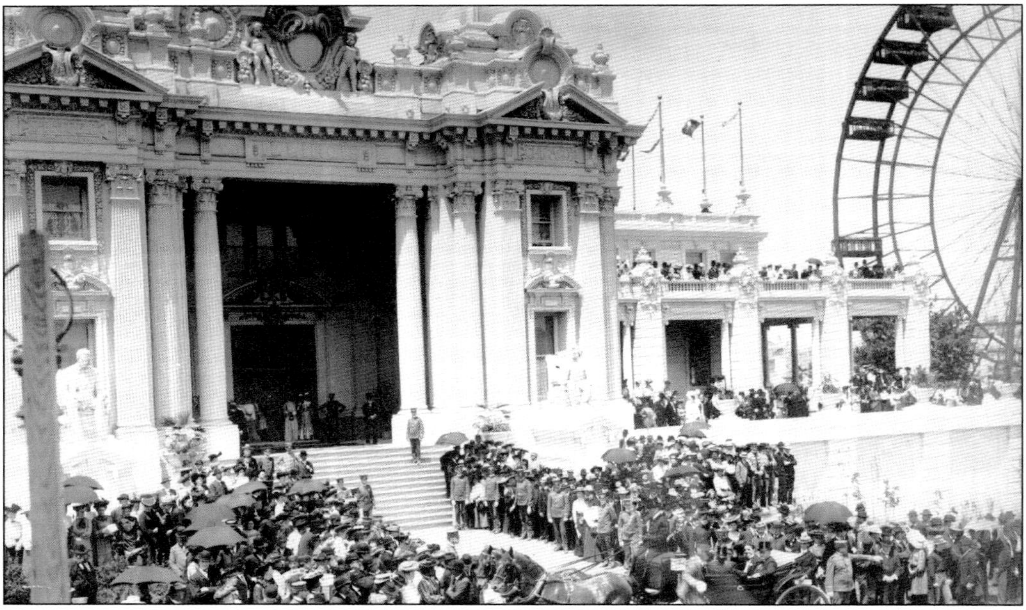

This is the dedication of the Illinois State building during the 1904 Louisiana Purchase Exposition in St. Louis. The photograph was taken by the Official Photographic Company in 1904. Foods rumored to be introduced to a mass market at the fair include hamburgers, hot dogs, peanut butter, and cotton candy. Doughnuts were already around for some time. (Missouri History Museum.)

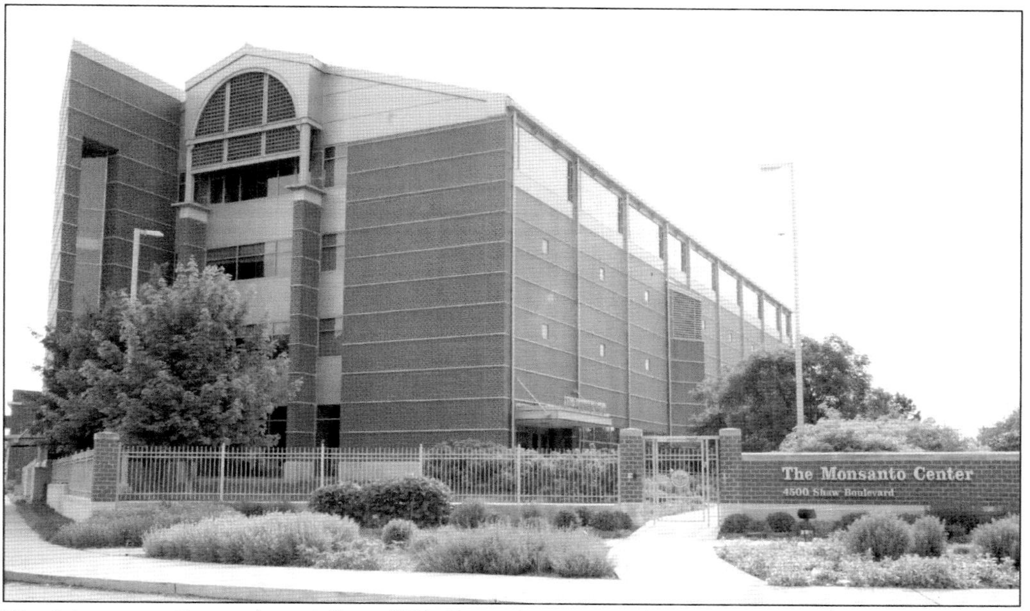


The Monsanto Center (site A5) at 4500 Shaw Avenue was built in 1997 for $19.4 million. The Polar Wave Ice and Fuel Company buildings were demolished in 1994 to make room for the center. Polar Wave was building at the location since 1909. In 1919, it built a one-story icehouse costing $20,000, followed by a one-story brick manufacturing plant for $110,000 in 1926. In 1918, the Missouri Pacific Railroad built a two-story brick stable. (Derek Cadzow Photography.)

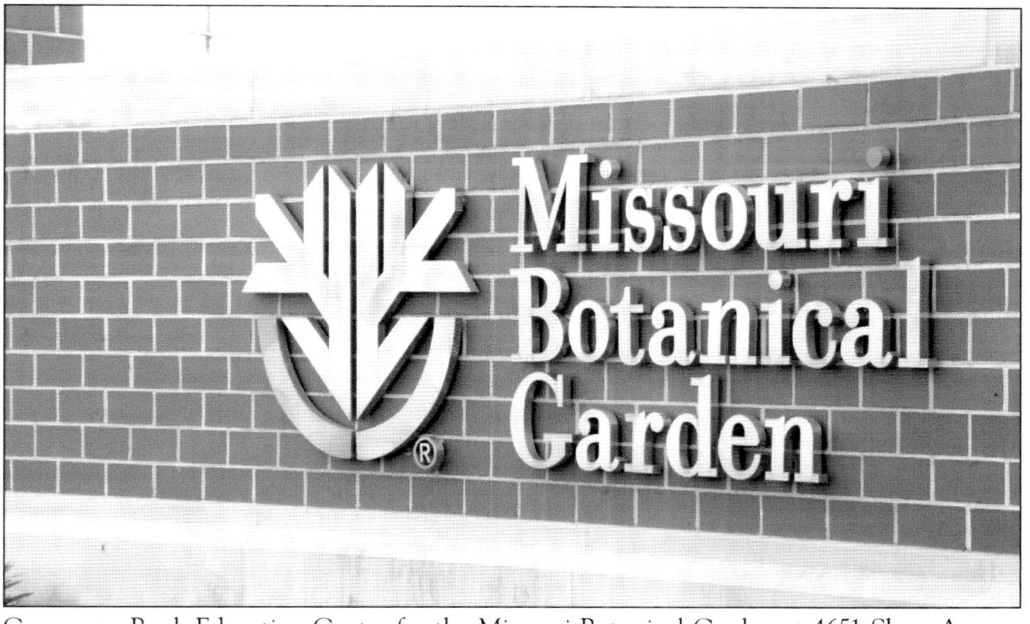


Commerce Bank Education Center for the Missouri Botanical Garden at 4651 Shaw Avenue was completed in 2003. In the early 1900s, this block was home to the lumber companies of A. M. Beckers and Eau Claire, horse stables, and a concrete-and-glass greenhouse for Bourden and Roehr. In 1914, Robinson Coal built an office, and in the early 1920s, Schroeder Coal built an office and a two-story brick stable. (Derek Cadzow Photography.)

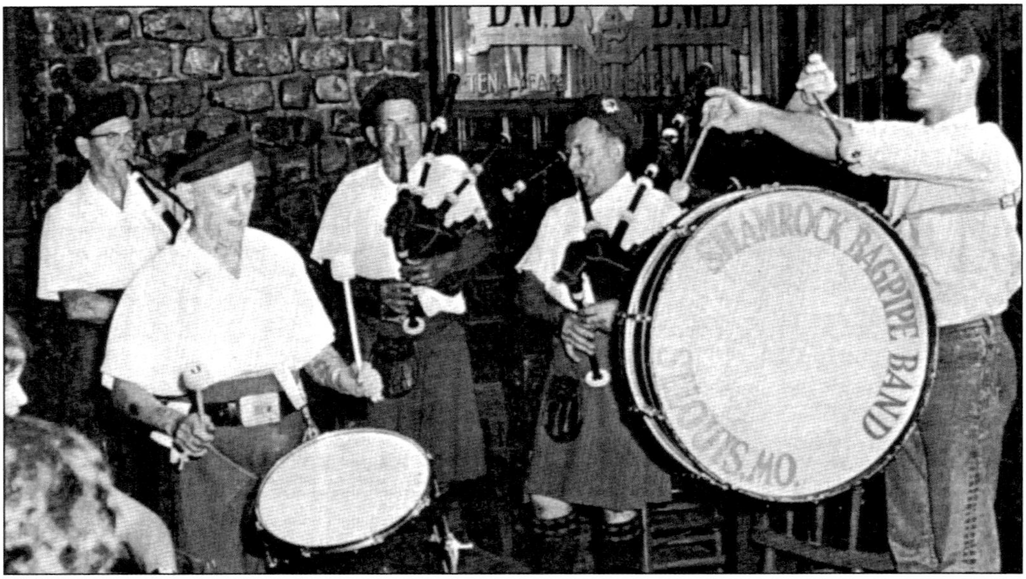


O'Connell's Pub (site A6) at 4652 Shaw Avenue was originally at 454 North Boyle Avenue in Gaslight Square. The square was an entertainment destination from the late 1950s to the late 1960s. Other businesses included the Gilded Cage, Frank Moskus' Gaslight, Gateway Theatre, La Margarita, Pepe's A Go Go, Peyton Place, Three Fountains, and Whisky A-Go-Go. Early in their careers, several celebrities entertained there, including Barbra Streisand, the Smothers Brothers, Woody Allen, George Carlin, Lenny Bruce, and others. (Jack Parker collection.)

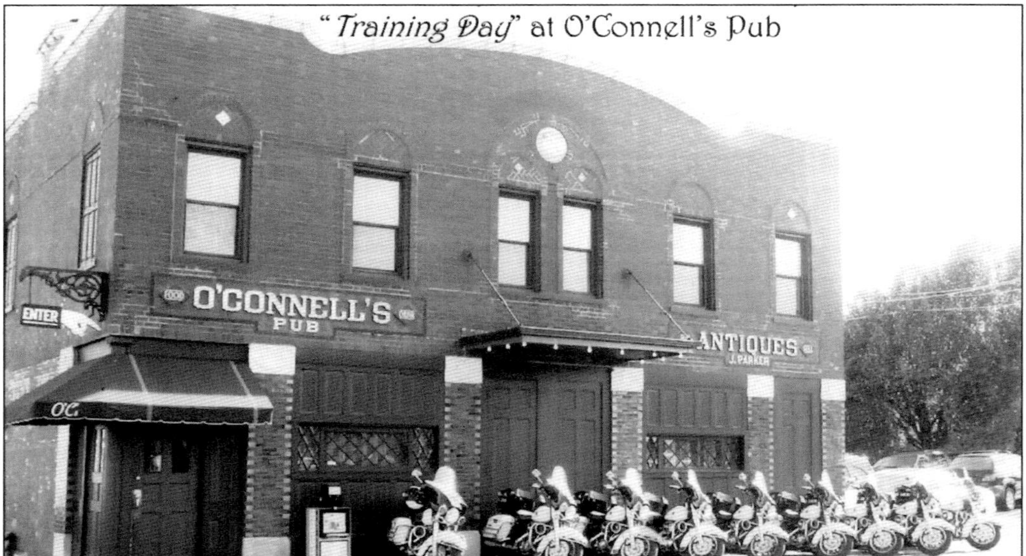


It is training day at the pub. The restaurant is downstairs; upstairs houses Jack Parker's Fine Arts and Antiques. This establishment across the street from the Italian neighborhood, the Hill, is a St. Louis destination. On St. Patrick's Day, everyone is Irish, and the crowd has the look of the early people from the neighborhood, including the Irish, Italians, Germans, and African Americans. These were the early residents who worked the surrounding clay and coal mines. (St. Louis Metropolitan Police Motor Squad.)

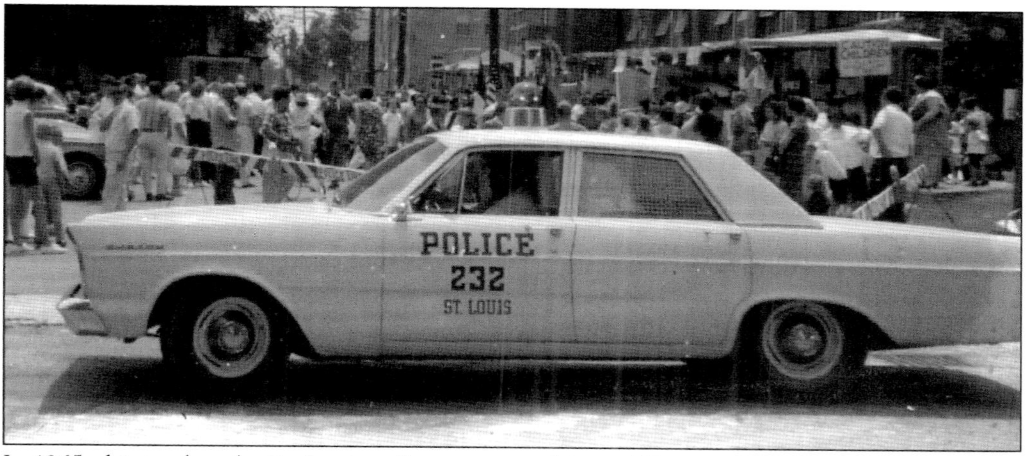


In 1965, this is what the St. Louis policemen were driving. The patrolman is cruising around at a festival at Holy Innocents Church, located at 4923 Odell Street. The South Patrol Division Districts 1, 2, and 3 are located at 3157 Sublette Avenue. The residents of the Southwest Garden are very appreciative of their police officers and firefighters. George and Sandy Grbac gather community volunteers and organize an annual appreciation barbecue to say thank you. (Grbac family collection.)

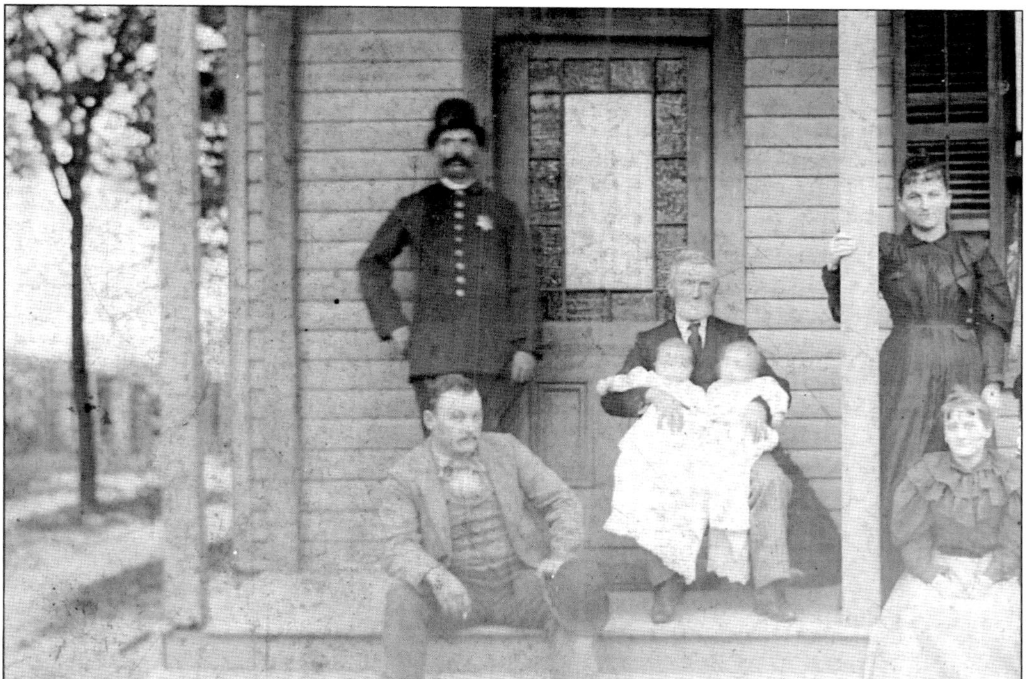

The English family was photographed at home. Pictured are, from left to right, John T. English (in uniform), John W. Fleming (sitting), an unidentified man holding Ed and John English, Annie English (standing), and Kate English (sitting) in front of their house in 1894. The English family lived at 5716 Southwest Avenue. John T. English was a mounted policeman and kept his horse, Prince, in the barn behind the house with the milk cows. (Mary Ann English Winkelmann and Marella Hardesty Baird collection.)

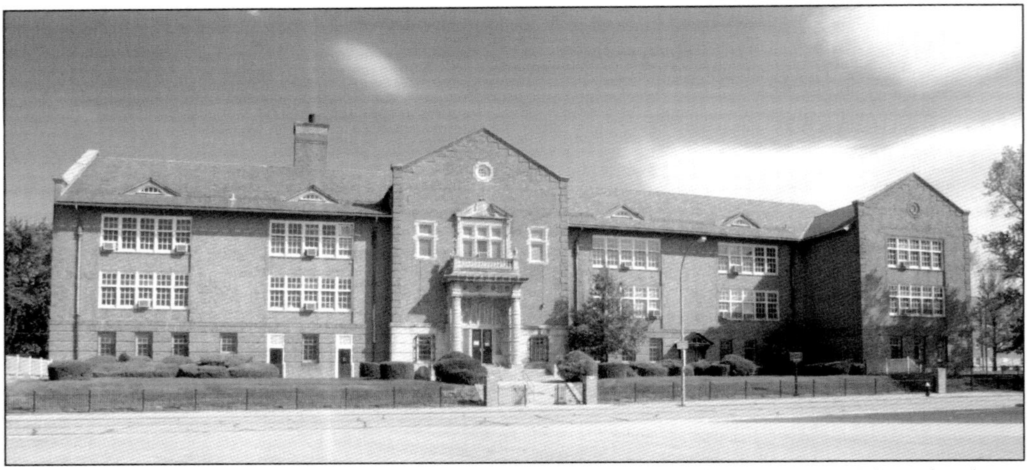

Festus Wade School (site A7) at 2030 Vandeventer Avenue was built in 1929. The school was designed by Robert M. Milligan and was named for a St. Louis banker and civic leader. According to the 1880 census records, Wade was born in Ireland to Thomas and Catherine Wade in 1859. He started his career as a clerk and in 1883 married Kate V. Kennedy in St. Louis. He died in 1927. (Derek Cadzow Photography.)

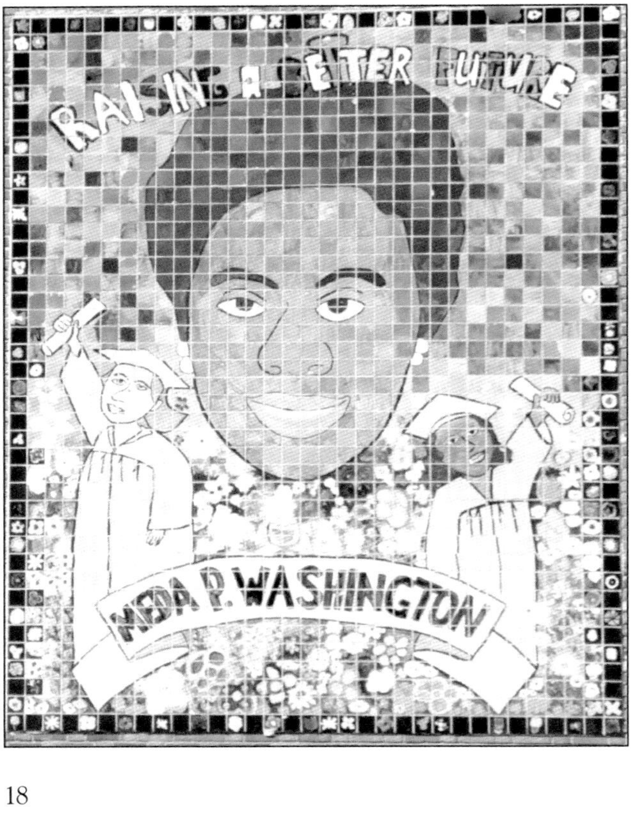


According to the archivist at the St. Louis Public Schools, this school opened for elementary students in February 1930 and closed in 1991. The school reopened as Meda P. Washington Alterative School in 1995 and closed again in February 2007. Currently the building is used as Meda P. Washington Early Childhood Center, which opened in August 2007. (Derek Cadzow Photography.)

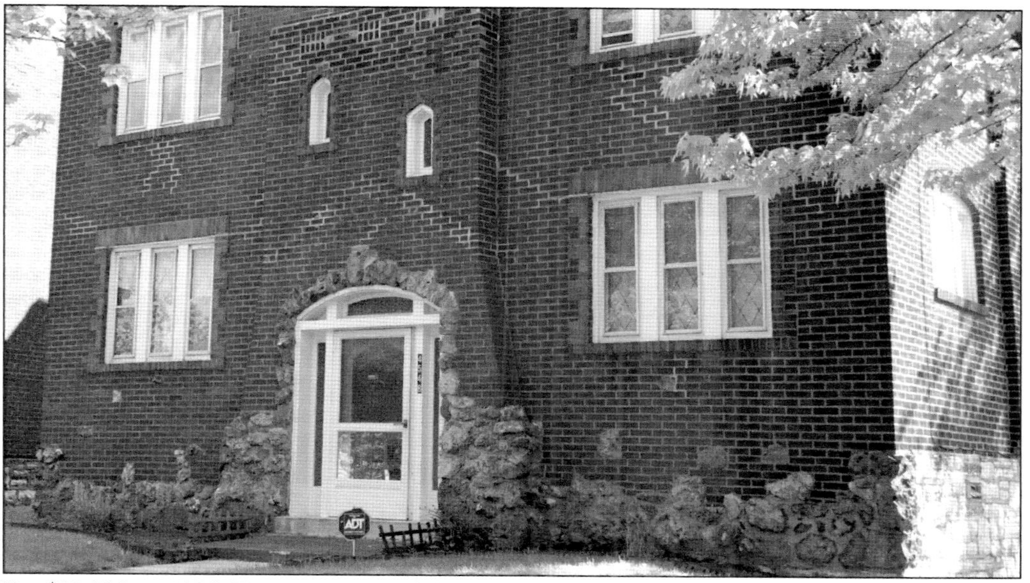

For $11,000 in 1925, Wagner-Newmark built this four-family structure (site A8) at 4548 Flora Avenue out of brick and stone, an unusual combination in St. Louis. The building permit was issued to owner A. A. Wagner and the contractor was listed as Wagner and Newmark. Similar designs were repeated at 4522 Shenandoah Avenue and 4539 and 4557 Flad Avenue, which were also built as three- and four-family dwellings. The current owner has been here since 1987. (Derek Cadzow Photography.)

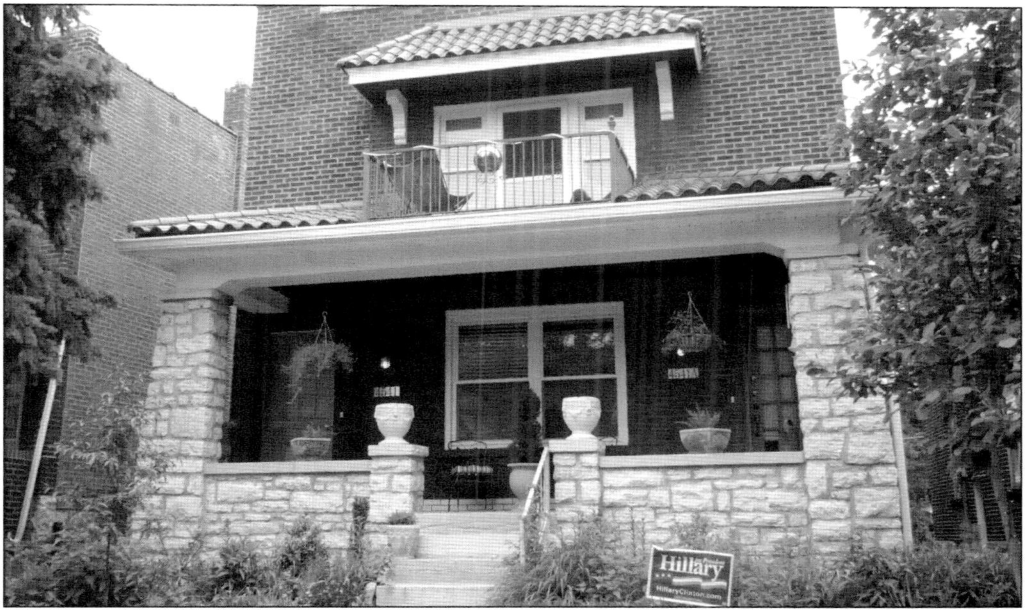


This home on Flora Avenue was built in 1925 and is the residence of Michel Krevenas and Chuck Fuhry, the block captains. In the 1930s census records, the address is listed as a two-family home. Charles Heisler, his wife, Mary, and Charles Jr. rented it for $60 a month. Heisler was a plumber. Fred Sunkel and his wife, Della, were the owners and lived there. Sunkel was a lumber salesman. The Sunkels were both born in Germany. (Photograph by Janice Markham.)

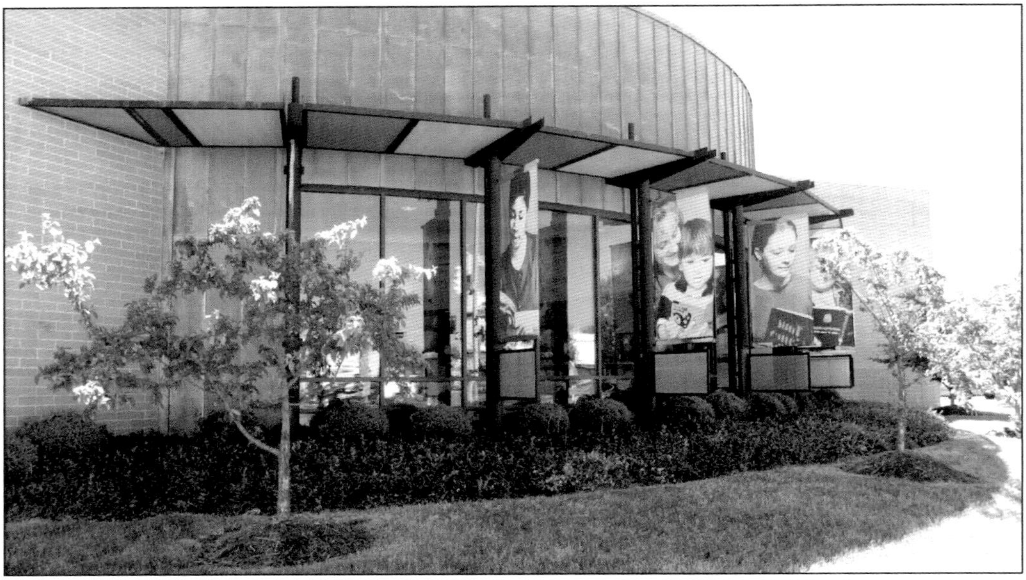

St. Louis Public Library Kingshighway branch (site A9) at 2260 South Vandeventer Avenue replaced the previous library that opened in 1962 at 4641 Shenandoah Avenue. The Shenandoah building was demolished in 2000 for this new library building, which opened in 2001. This branch replaced some small subbranch and station libraries in the area. The first library connection was at 5131 Shaw Avenue, where there was a book deposit collection in a store owned by Philip Rau. (Derek Cadzow Photography.)

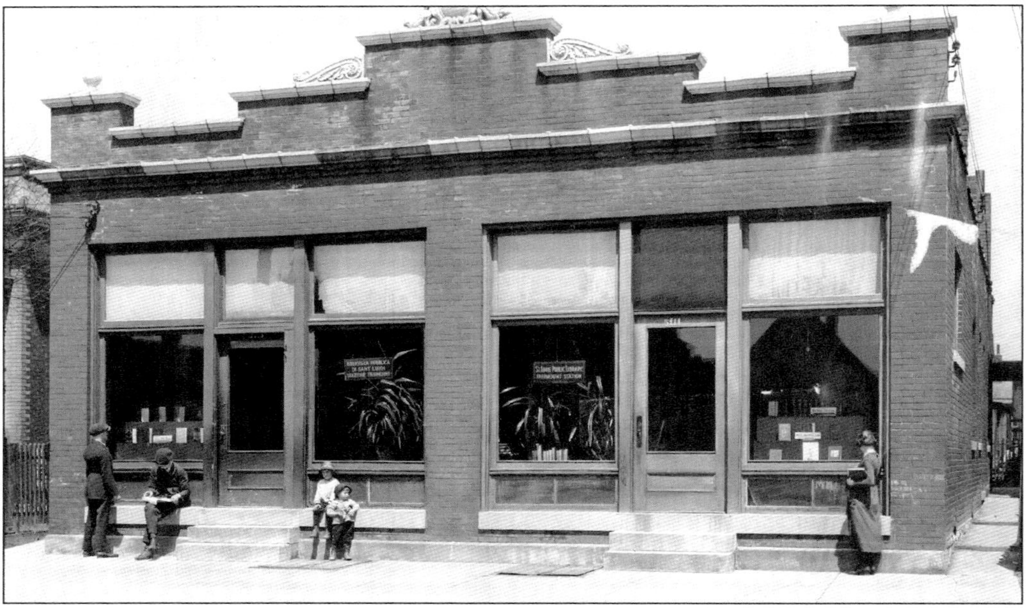

In 1920, the Fairmount subbranch library at 5113 Daggett Avenue served the Italian community. The sign in the left window reads, “Biblioteca Pubblica Di Sant Luigi Stazione Fairmount,” and the sign on the right reads, “St. Louis Public Library Fairmount Station.” The library substation opened in 1918. The first mention of the Fairmount Center location at 5139 Shaw Avenue was in the 1915–1916 St. Louis Public Libraries annual report. (St. Louis Public Library.)

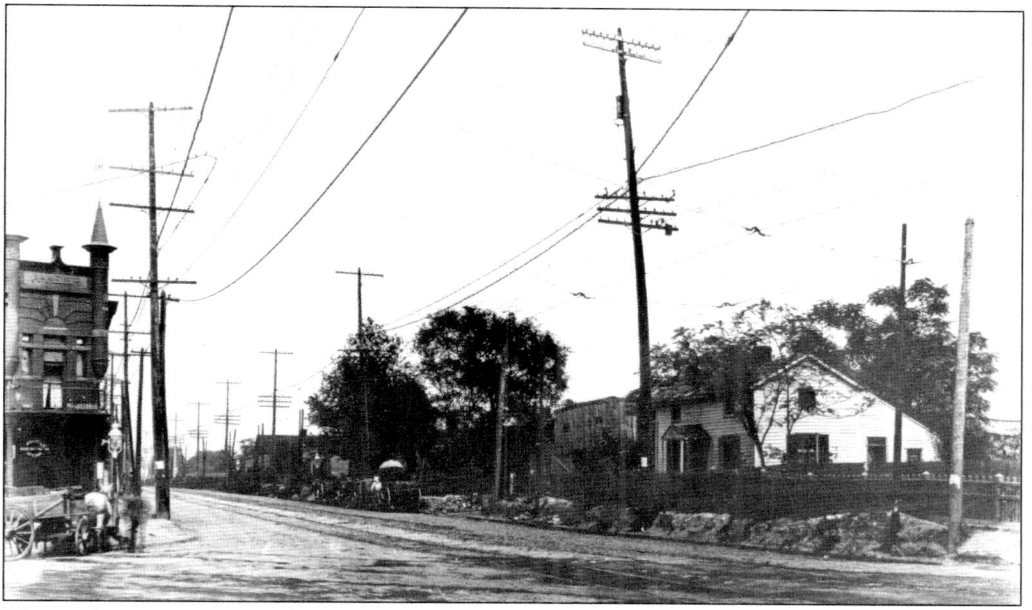

This early scene is at Vandeventer Avenue looking northeast from Kingshighway Boulevard in the direction of a heavy industrial area in the late 1800s and early 1900s. In 1891, the Oakhill Railroad had Tower Grove Brick Works build a two-story brick stable for $150. In 1890, Tower Grove Brick Works built four brick kilns for $4,000. In the 1890s, the Lohse Pat Door Company built a two-story brick-planing mill for $10,000. (Missouri Botanical Garden Archives.)

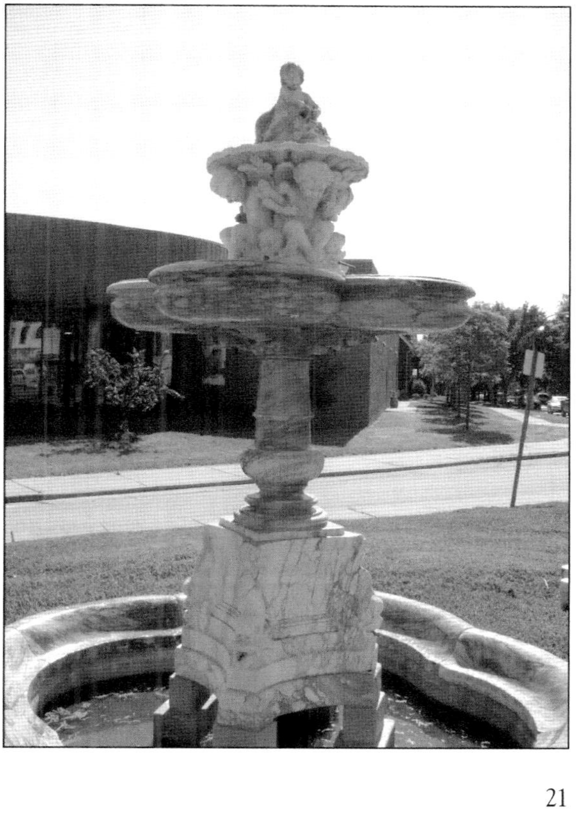

The Italianate fountain at the intersection of Kingshighway Boulevard, Shenandoah Avenue, and Vandeventer Avenue was created by the late A. B. M. Corrubia, a St. Louis architect and painter. The fountain was designed for and displayed at Garavelli's Restaurant at 300 DeBaliviere Avenue. The restaurant was built in 1926 and was demolished in 1987. The fountain was donated to the city and was moved to this location in the 1990s. Roger Giles researched the history of the fountain for the recent restoration. (Photograph by Janice Markham.)

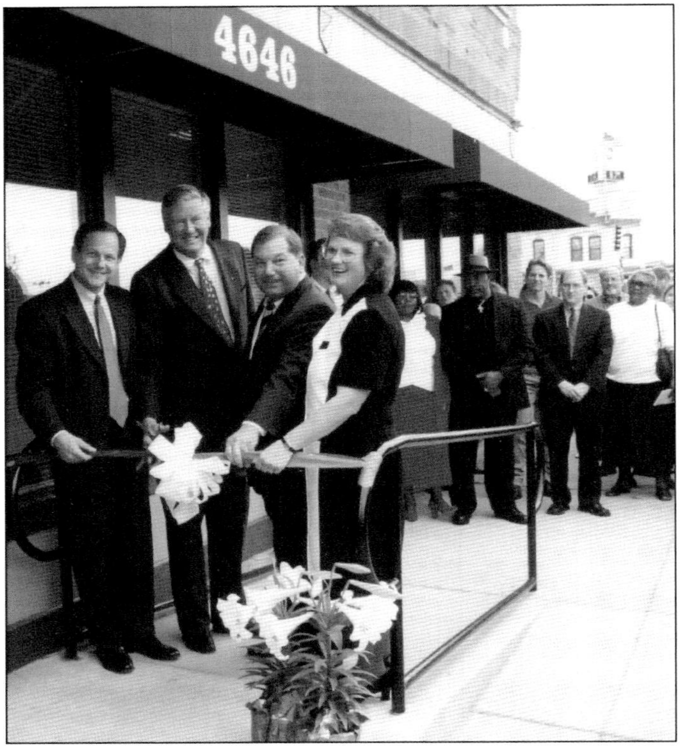


Operation Brightside at 4646 Shenandoah Avenue celebrates the opening of its new location by hosting a ribbon-cutting ceremony. Standing in back of the ribbon are, from left to right, Mayor Frances G. Slay; Andrew N. Baur, the former chairman of Southwest Bank; Paul J. Liberatore, the chairman of Operation Brightside Board of Directors; and Operation Brightside executive director Mary Lou Green. Also in attendance were founding chairman Robert R. Hermann and founding executive director Lucille Green. (Operation Brightside.)

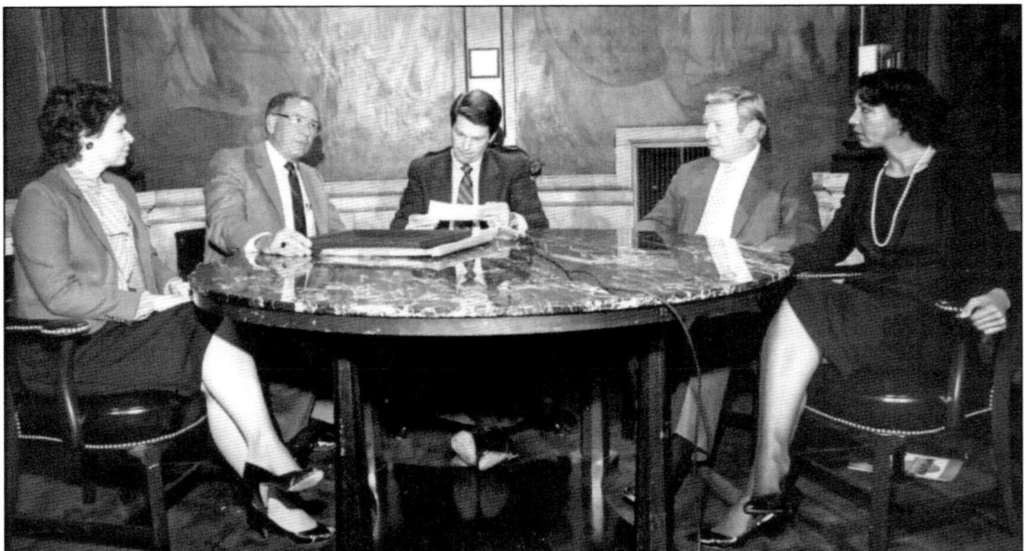

Seated in the center is former mayor Vincent C. Schoemehl Jr., who is credited with formulating the idea for Operation Brightside. Schoemehl served as mayor from 1981 to 1993; he was the 46th mayor of St. Louis. He was one of the city's youngest mayors, and his interests were in historic preservation and urban design. During his administration, more than 600 rehabilitation projects were completed. Schoemehl was a promoter of public-private partnerships. (Operation Brightside.)

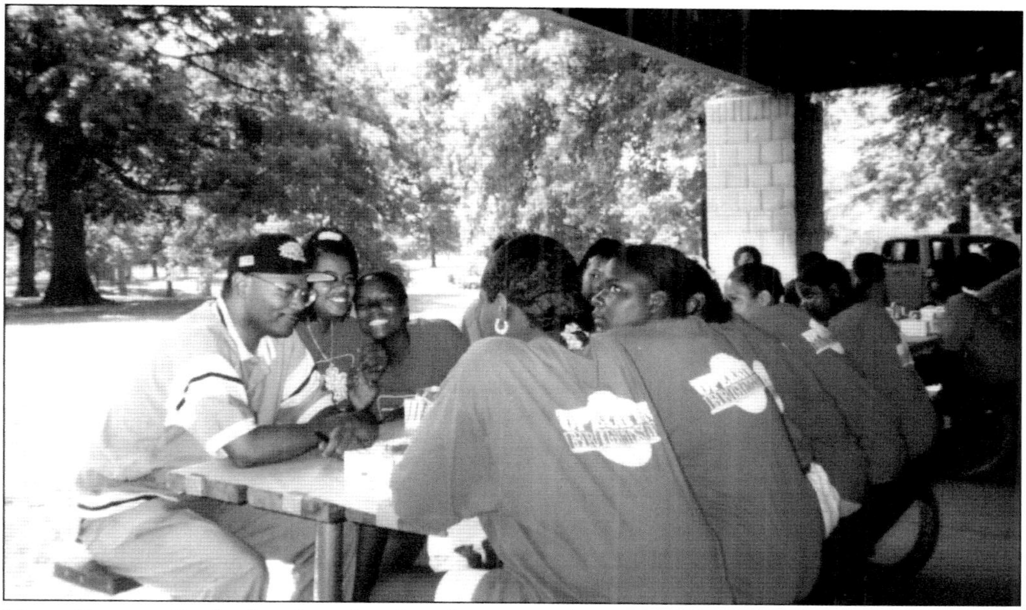

Mayor Freeman Bosley Jr. takes a break with young volunteers at Operation Brightside. He served as mayor from 1993 to 1997 and was a great role model for young people who stressed education as the key to success no matter where one comes from. His grandfather Preston Bosley was the son of a slave who came to St. Louis from Arkansas. His father, Freeman Bosley Sr., was a city alderman. Bosley Jr. was the first African American mayor of St. Louis. (Operation Brightside.)

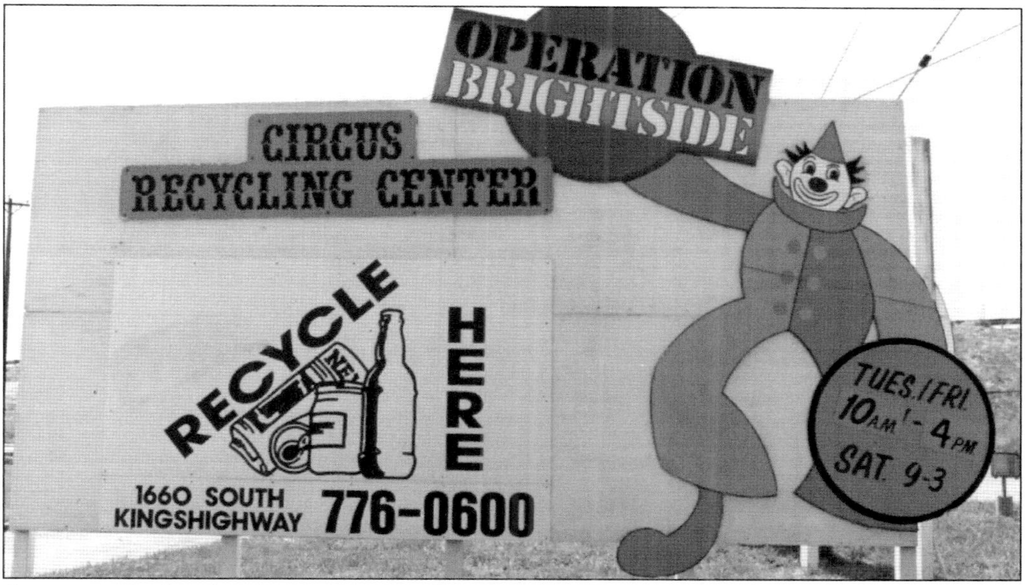


Operation Brightside, a private, nonprofit organization, celebrated 25 years of beautification in St. Louis in 2007. The organization runs the largest recycling center in the city of St. Louis at this location at Kingshighway Boulevard and Interstate 44 and works alongside the St. Louis Refuse Division. Operating on federal grants and donations with an annual budget of $500,000 to $600,000, Operation Brightside employs five full-time employees and oversees several volunteer programs. (Operation Brightside.)

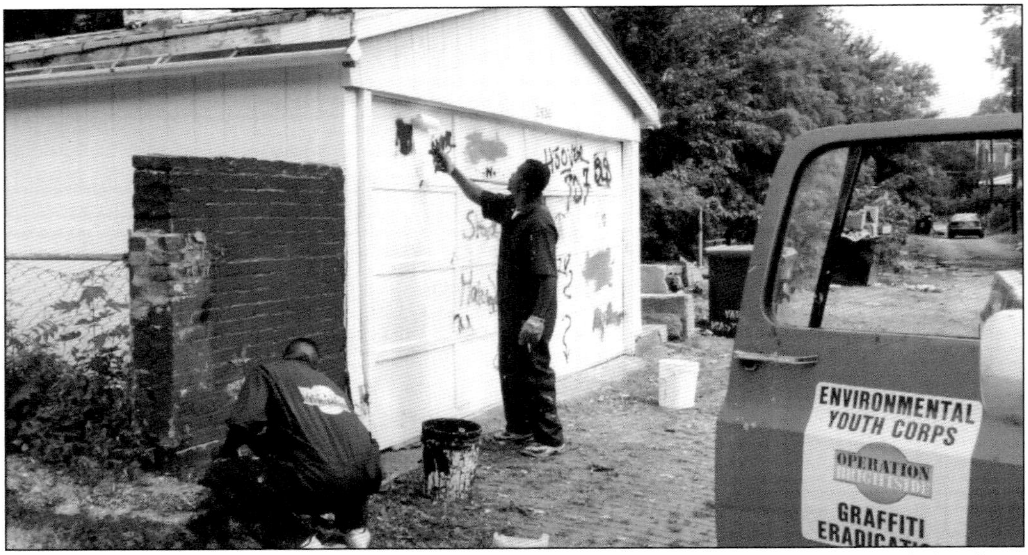


Operation Brightside's youth education includes removing graffiti. In a bulletin titled "About the Mayor," released on September 30, 1996, by the Web site usmayors.org, Mayor Freeman Bosley Jr. talks about firing the 30,000th cleaning blast to celebrate the success of the city and Operation Brightside's graffiti-removal program. The program engages youths through job training and community involvement. Crews paint over graffiti and use water blasting on concrete and brick surfaces. Graffiti removal is necessary in the rebuilding of city neighborhoods. (Operation Brightside.)

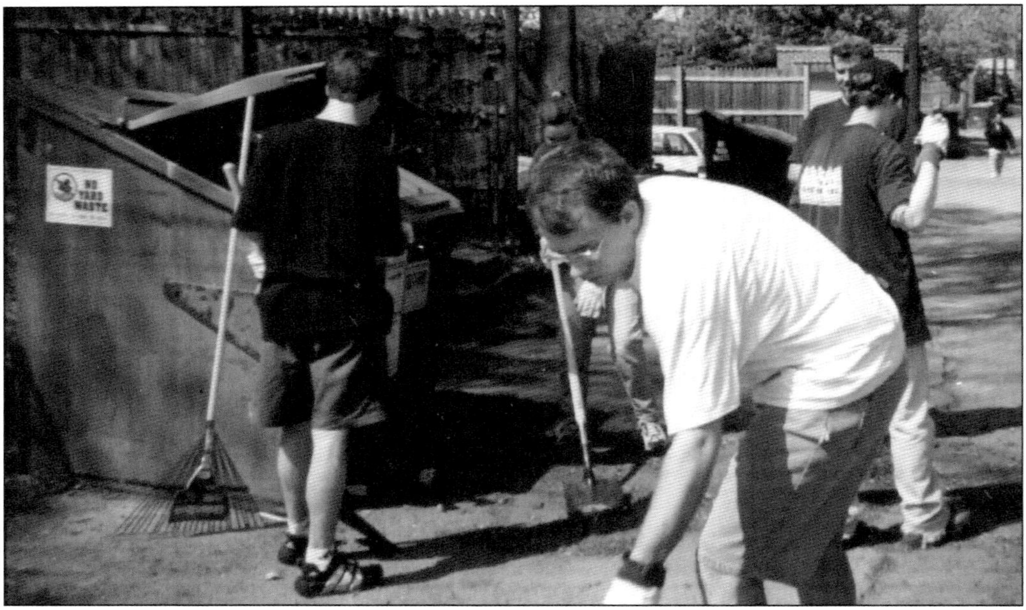


Volunteers from the neighborhood help Operation Brightside clean up the 3900 block of Botanical Avenue. Project Blitz is the organization's annual campaign to clean up city neighborhoods. It provides tools, trash bags, flowers, leadership, and education for volunteer block captains in an effort to clean and beautify the city. Volunteers clean and pick up trash in parks, alleys, and vacant lots. (Operation Brightside.)

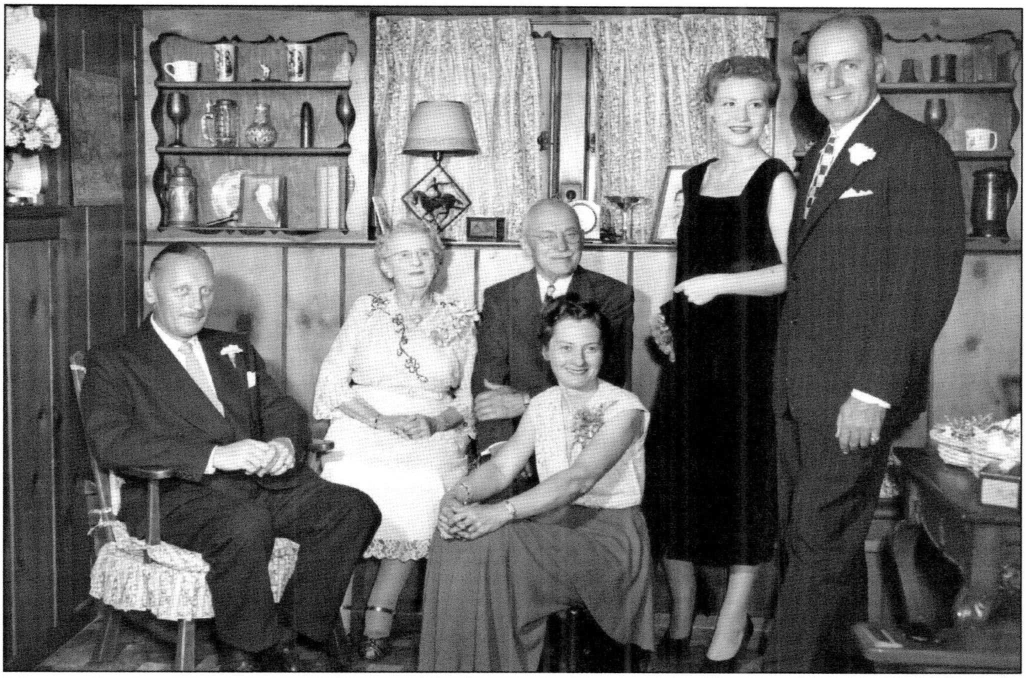

Here is the Imse home (site A10) at 4610 Shenandoah Avenue. The Imse-Kaiser family gathers in the basement in the late 1940s. Mrs. Robert Imse bought the house, originally built as a four-family home, in 1917. In 1929, her son Robert married Florence Kaiser. Jeff Wamhoff, a descendant of the Imses, lives with his family in the home that was converted to a two-family and is now a single-family residence. (Wamhoff family collection.)

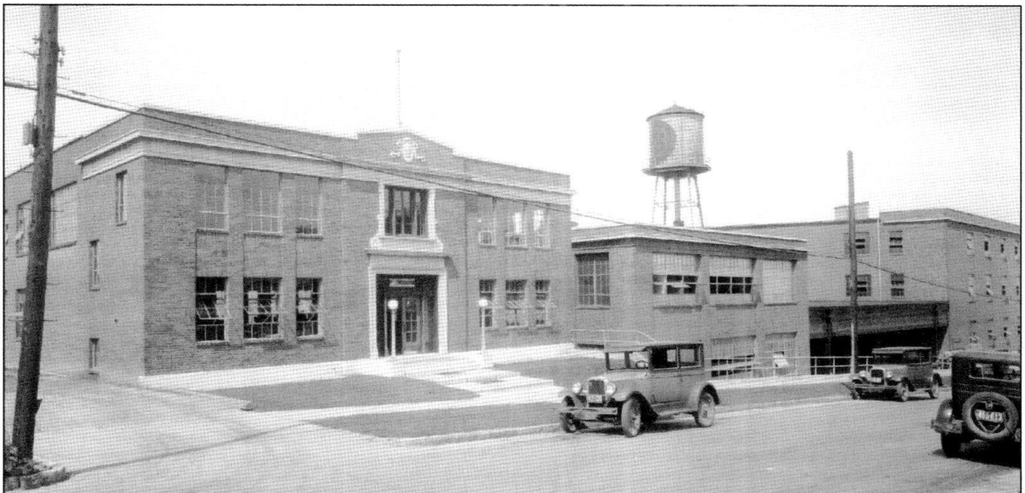

The Imse-Schilling Sash and Door Company, located at 4217 Beck Avenue, was in business until 1968. The 1920 city directory listed Robert C. Imse as president-treasurer, William Lothman as vice president, and Edward Schilling as secretary. At this time, the company was located at the southwest corner of Papin Street. In 1930, Robert C. was still president-treasurer, Charles K. Imse was vice president and secretary, and Lothman was second vice president. A 1930 advertisement stated the company dealt in millwork and hardware. (Wamhoff family collection.)

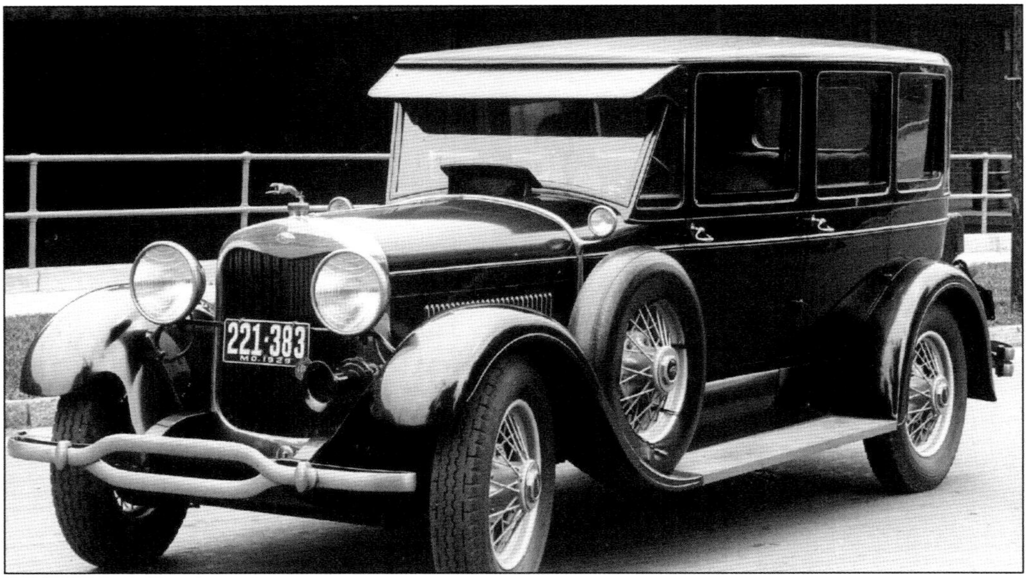


This was the Imse family car in 1929. Robert C. Imse, the president-treasurer of Imse-Schilling Sash and Door Company, was the son of German immigrants Charles and Margrette Imse. According to the 1880 census records, Charles was a carpenter from Prussia, Margrette was a housewife, and children Robert C. and Nellie were in school. Robert C. was a product of the American dream. The company was founded around 1905 and was one of the leading sash and door companies in St. Louis. (Wamhoff family collection.)

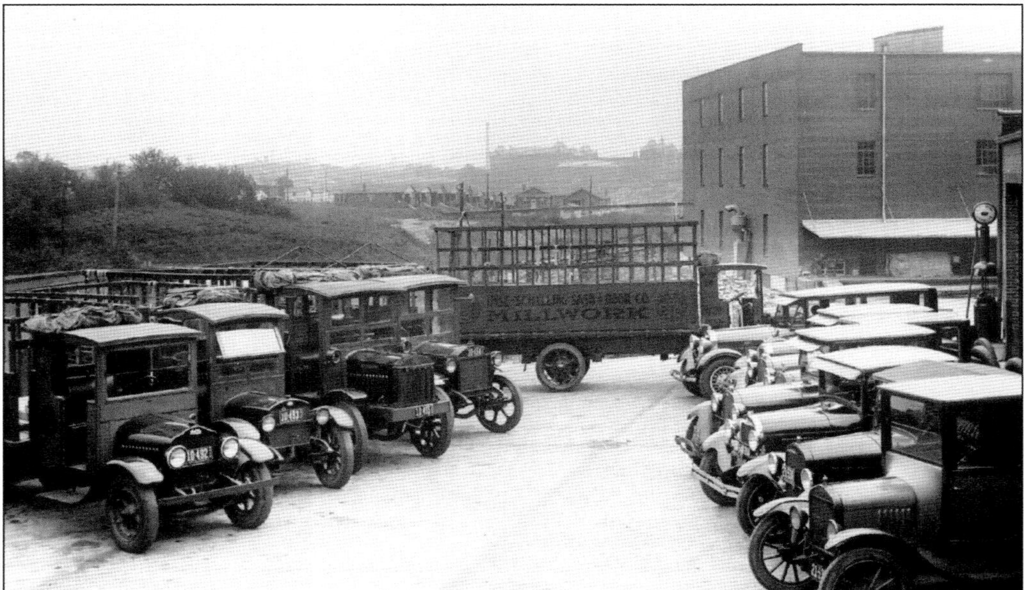


The Imse-Schilling fleet transported its products all over the city. In the 1920 city directory, the company advertised itself as "millwork of the better kind." It crafted quality building materials such as doors, windows, frames, moldings, columns, and interior finishing, and it specialized in wallboard. It also sold Majestic coal chute covers, which might explain why there are so many visible in the neighborhood today. (Wamhoff family collection.)

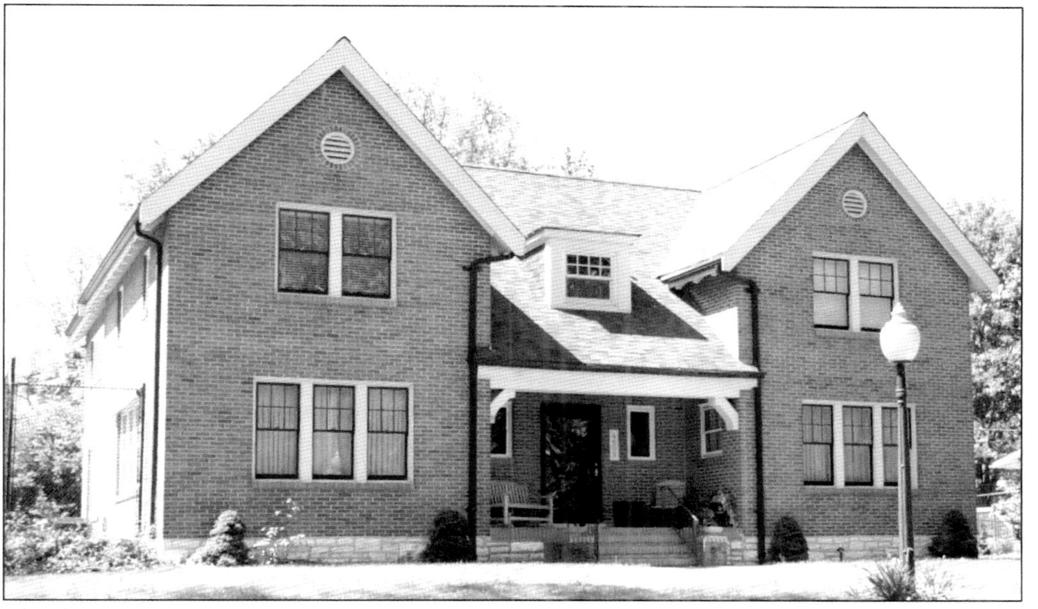

The former home of Thomas Eagleton, a U.S. senator from Missouri, was built in 1915 at 4608 Tower Grove Place (site A11) for Charon Realty Company for $4,500. In the 1918 city directory, Frank X. Hiemenz, a lawyer with an office at 706 Chestnut Street, is listed as the resident. By 1923, Mark D. Eagleton, a lawyer who later ran for mayor, lived in the house with wife Winifred. Thomas was born in 1929. (Derek Cadzow Photography.)

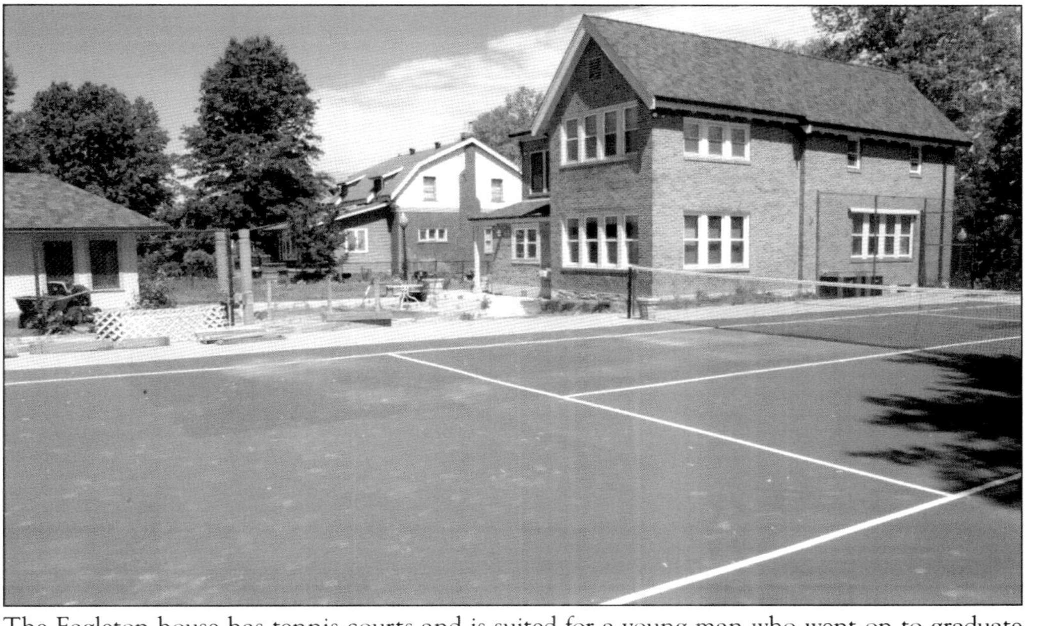

The Eagleton house has tennis courts and is suited for a young man who went on to graduate from Harvard Law School and grace the cover of *Time* magazine on August 7, 1972, after he withdrew from the Democratic ticket for vice president. He served as senator from 1968 to 1987. From 1987 until his death, he worked in St. Louis as an attorney and was a professor at Washington University. (Derek Cadzow Photography.)

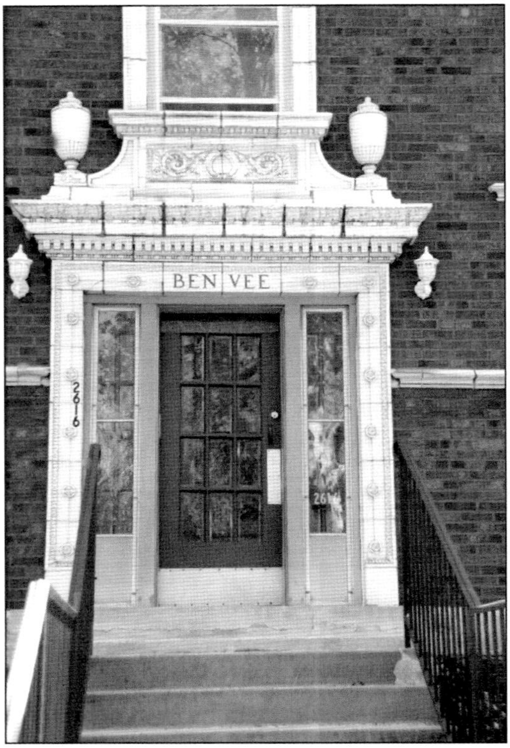


The former Benvee Apartments (site A12) at 2616 South Kingshighway Boulevard were converted into six condominiums with two units on each floor. They were built in 1924 for $51,000 by the Glen Eyrie Investment Company. One of the residents in 1930 was brick manufacturer Edward A. Garth. He and his wife rented their apartment for $75 a month. On the same floor lived Miles J. Beach and his wife, Bessie. Miles was a city salesman. (Derek Cadzow Photography.)

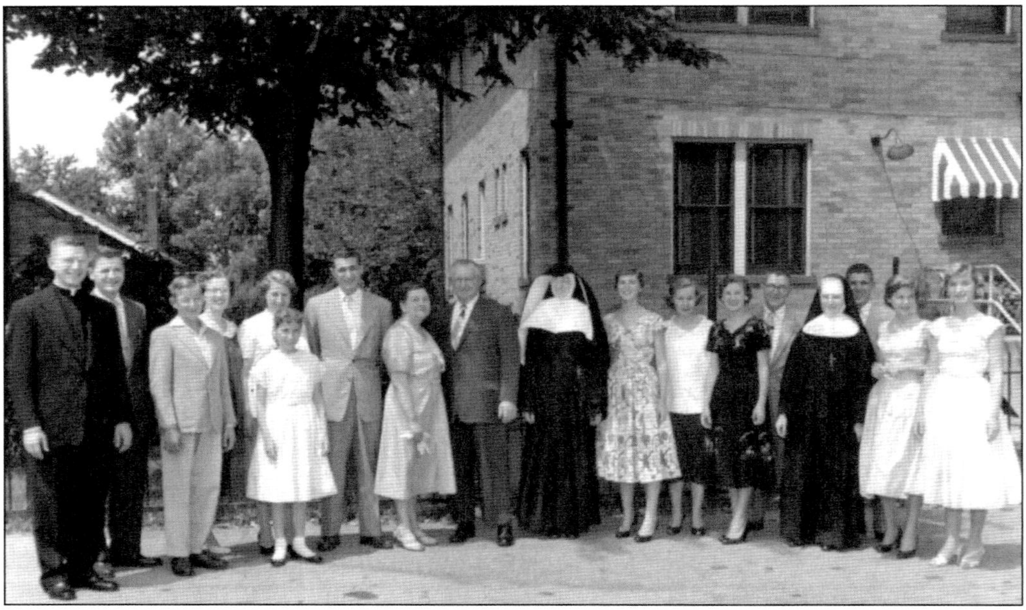

The residents of the Benvee Apartments were family people, just like the Wolf family in this photograph. In 1930 were Edward J. Hanzke and his wife, Frances. Edward was a contractor. On the same floor lived Benjamin Volz and his wife, Hatie, the owners of the building. On the third floor lived widow Antoinette Raterman, her son Alfred, and her sister Magdaline Welsch. Alfred was a general manager and Magdaline was a milliner. (Owens family collection.)

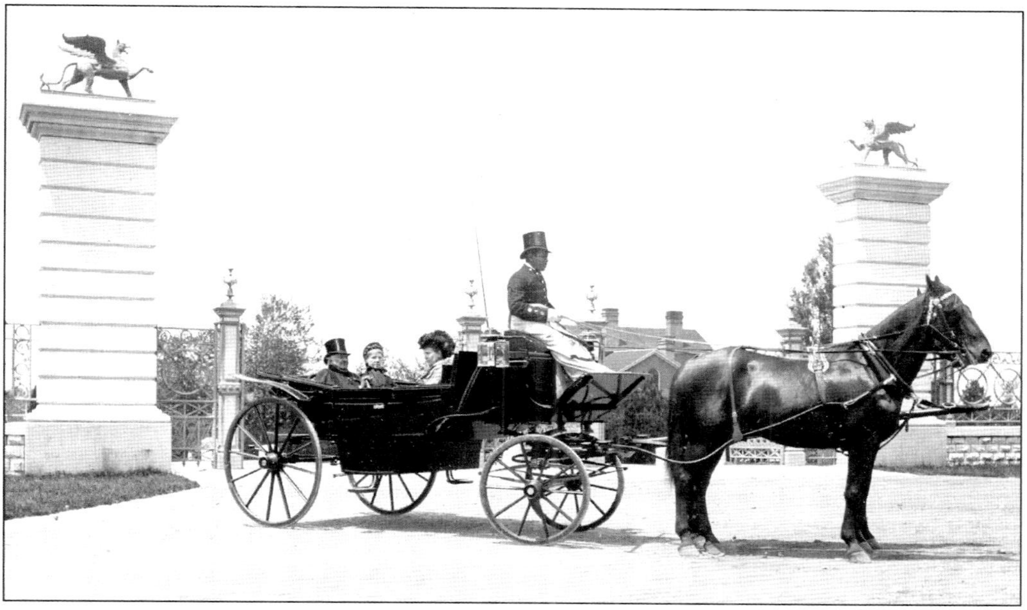

Tower Grove Park (site A13) is marked on the map on page 8 at the southeast corner of Kingshighway Boulevard and Magnolia Avenue. There are several entrances to the park. In the photograph, Henry Shaw and two unidentified ladies in the carriage are at the main entrance on South Grand Boulevard. Shaw established the park in 1868 and gave it to the city of St. Louis. Today the park takes up 289 acres. (Missouri Botanical Garden Archives.)

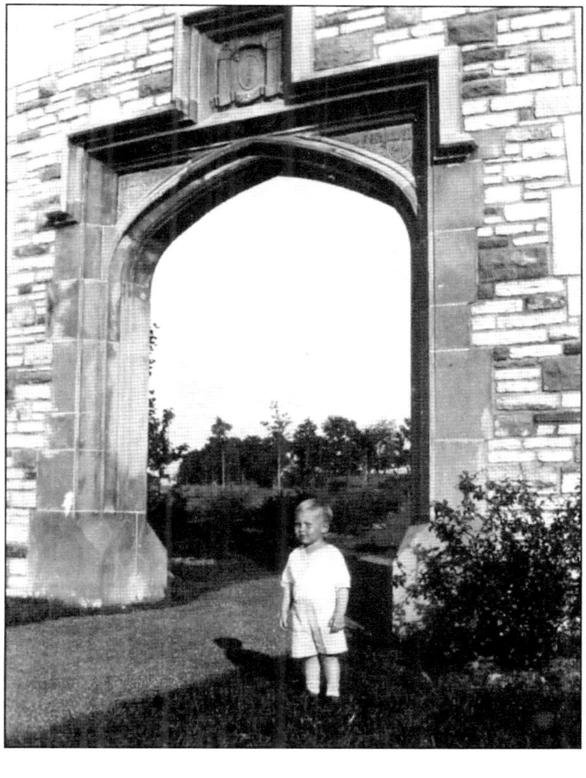

Leo Thierry is pictured at the Tower Grove Park southeast entrance in 1931. Leo and Dorothy Thierry have lived on Gurney Court across from the park since 1968. Long-standing block captains for the court, the Thierrys have organized block parties in this tight-knit community for more than 30 years. (Thierry family collection.)

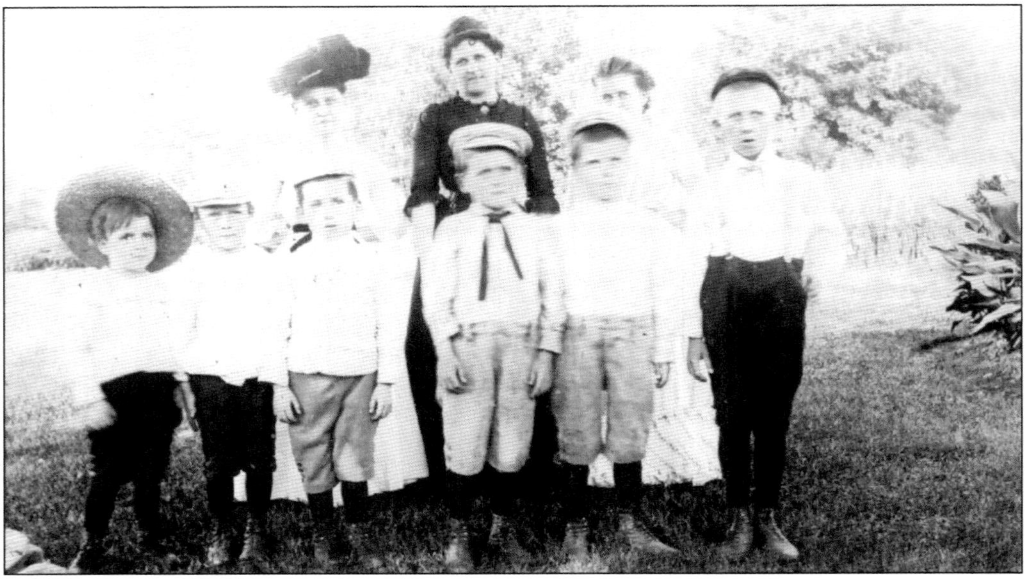

Neighborhood residents enjoy a picnic in Tower Grove Park in 1901. Pictured are, from left to right, (first row) Francis English, Henry English, Arthur English, John English, Edward English, and Fred Hardesty; (second row) Kate Fleming, Ellie Fleming Hardesty, and Alice Fleming Steinman. Today the park is still enjoyed by picnickers drawn to the Victorian pavilions and other spots with views of the sculptures throughout the park. (Mary Ann English Winkelmann and Marella Hardesty Baird collection.)

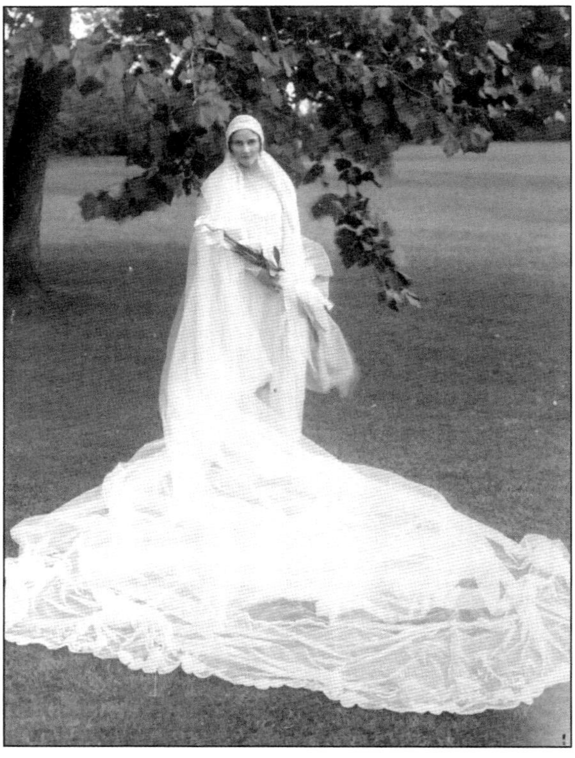

This photograph of a bride in a courtyard in the 1920s could have been taken at Tower Grove Park. The Imses lived at 4610 Shenandoah Avenue, a few blocks from the park. The park has been a favorite location for portraits of brides in their wedding gowns for over a century. The most popular backdrop is the pond fountain with the ruins in the background. (Wamhoff family collection.)

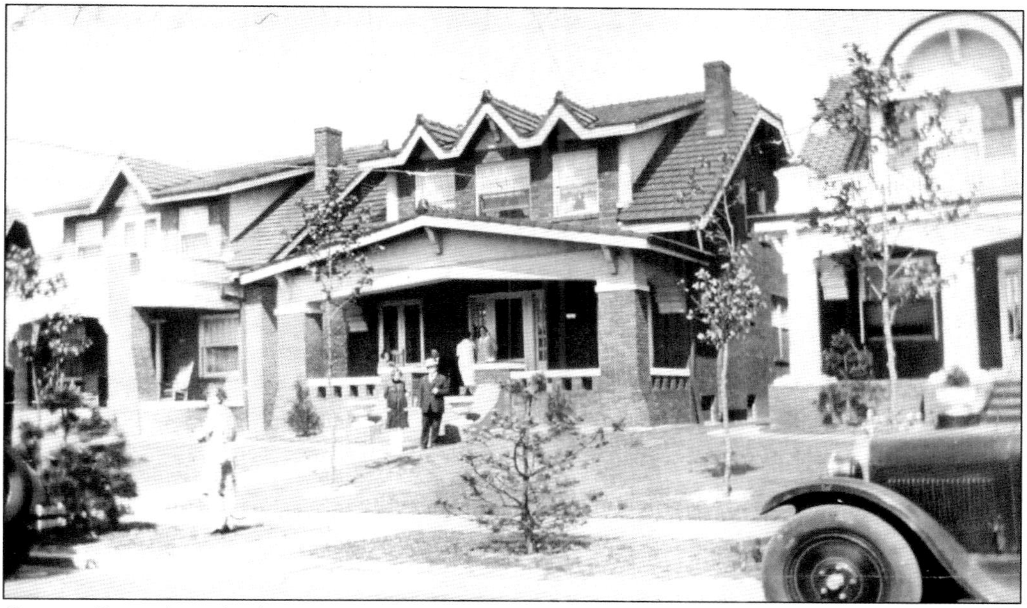

Gurney Court (site A14) is a private street dating back to 1922. Dolores Hitch and her mother, Dolores Lipic, were the last of the original property owners to move out of the court in 1991. Before Hitch left, she put together a booklet of Gurney Court history from notes her family had kept dating back to 1923. She gave the booklet to her neighbors as a going away gift. (Thierry family collection.)

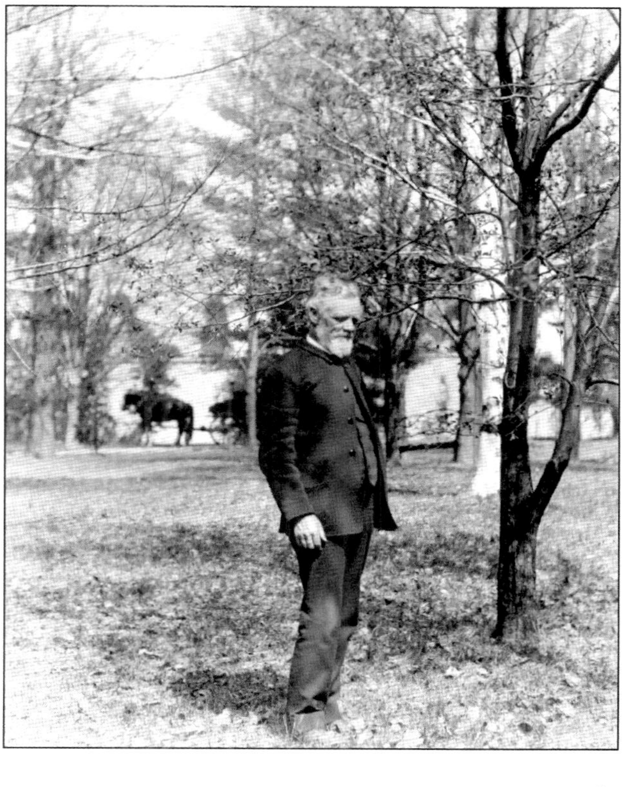

Gurney Court was named after James Gurney, who was born in 1831 and died in 1920. He was the head gardener under Henry Shaw. Gurney is pictured standing in the arboretum. Shaw recruited Gurney to come to St. Louis in 1868 from England to work at Tower Grove Park. Gurney started out working as a florist and arboriculturist, and after Shaw's death in 1889, he became the first superintendent of the park and resided at 4274 Magnolia Avenue. (Missouri Botanical Garden Archives.)

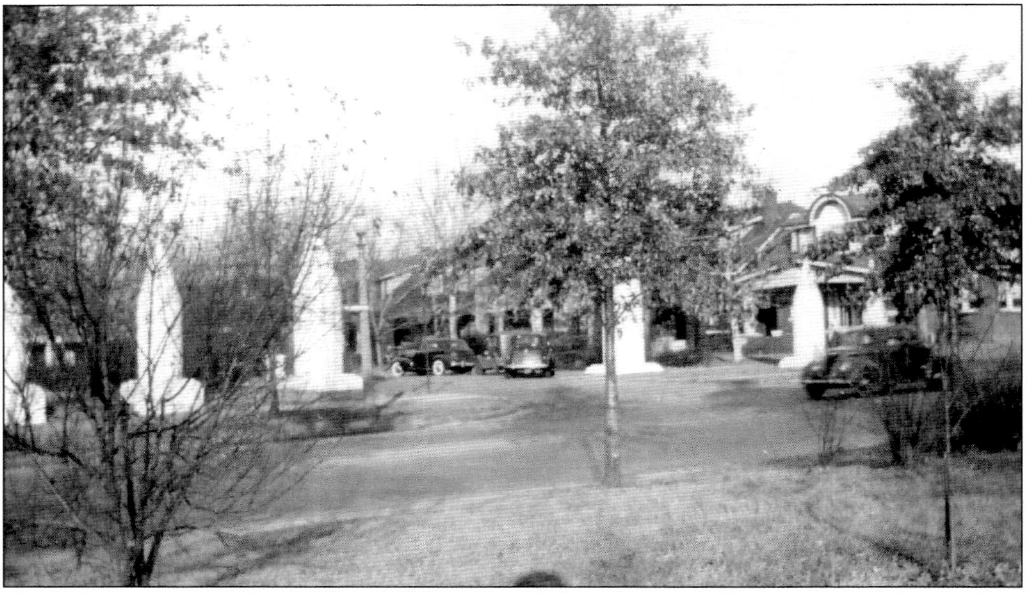

The old-timers referred to Gurney Court as "Milk Bottle Court," because of the shape of the white plaster markers or columns in the court. In this 1930s photograph, they resemble giant missiles, but no one can say for sure why they were built. Dolores Hitch's research through the association's records did not turn up anything. She does state, "I know they were there in the 30s and were gone by the time we moved in, in 1942." (Thierry family collection.)

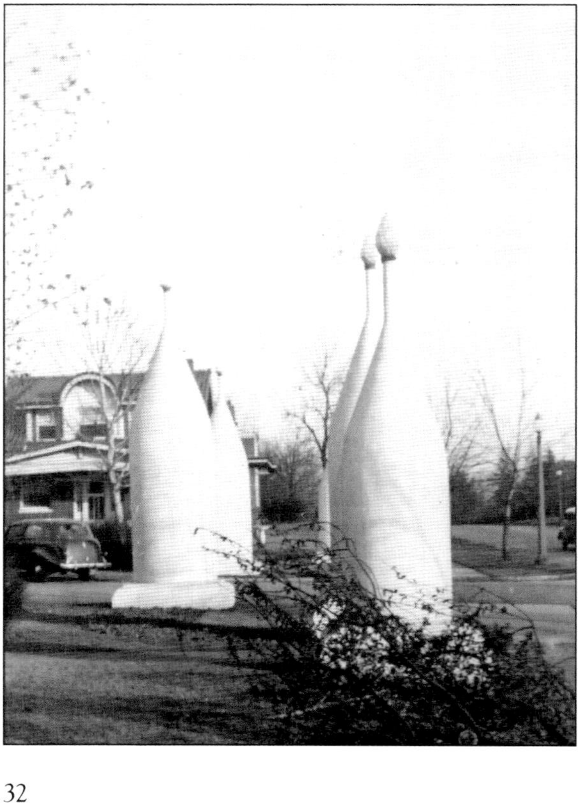

A closer look at the plaster bottles explains why the old-timers also referred to Gurney Court as "Bootlegger's Row." Hitch does tell the story of her Croatian grandfather making wine in the Gurney Court cellars, but she doubts there was any bootlegging going on. Hitch's family lived here from 1923, when her grandfather Joseph Lipic bought the house at 2614 Gurney Court, to 1991, when she and her mother moved on, leaving their history with the neighbors. (Thierry family collection.)

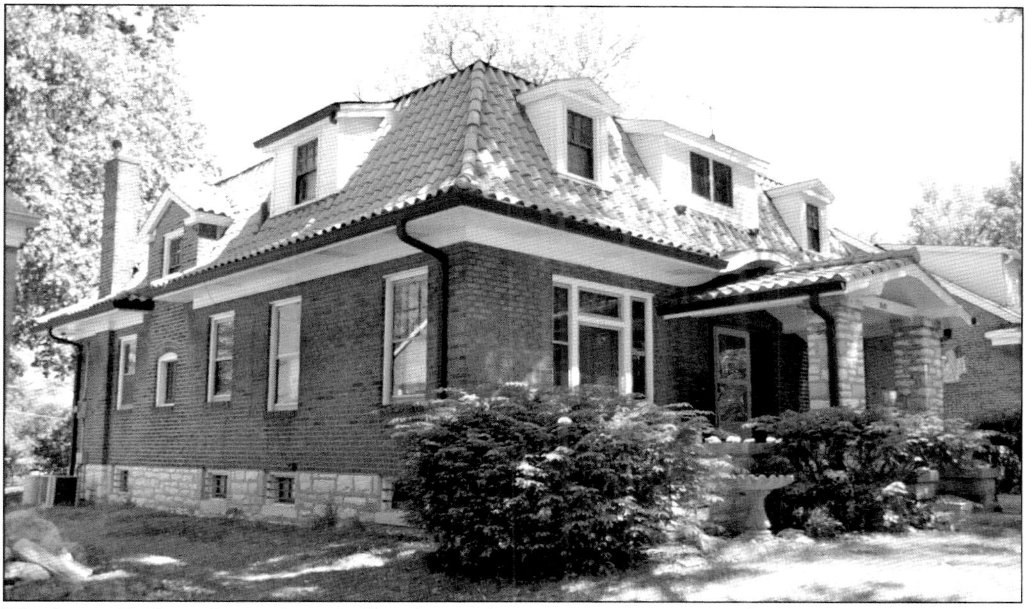

The Louis F. Heger home (site A15) is located at 2620 Heger Court. The Hegers resided here for more than 60 years. According to his obituary in the *St. Louis Post-Dispatch* on February 2, 1986, Heger was born in 1895. He was in the wholesale poultry and egg business from 1920 to 1973 with Fred Heger and Son Poultry Firm. The firm was founded by his father, Louis F. Heger Sr., who built Heger Court. (Derek Cadzow Photography.)

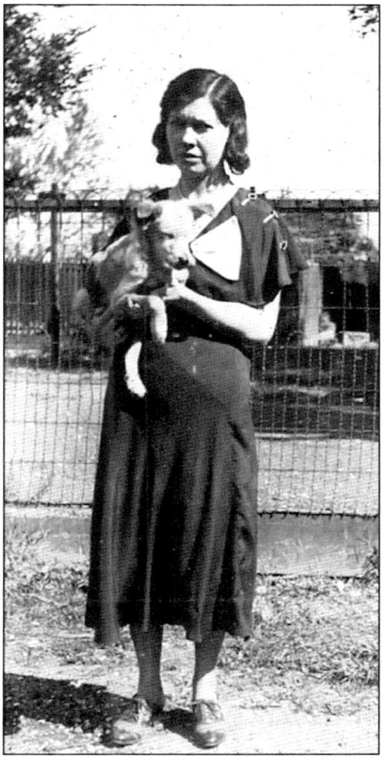

This unidentified woman may have been photographed on Heger Court, listed as a private street in 1930. Residents included Fred Heger, president of Mount Olive Building and Loan Association; Edward Heger, president of Hy Grade Laundry (located at 2745 Park Avenue), and his wife, Corrine; and Louis F. Heger, secretary-treasurer of Hy Grade Laundry, and his wife, Beatrice. The Heger family, whose great-grandparents Louis and Rosa Heger were German immigrants, achieved the American dream. (Butler's Pantry.)

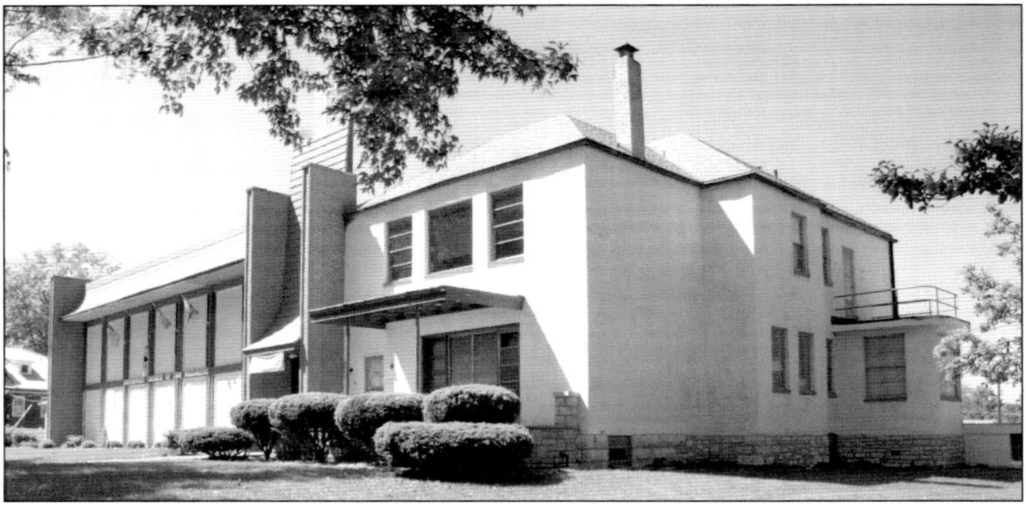

The Southwest Church of the Nazarene, located at 4543 Magnolia Avenue, was the former Lafayette Park Church of the Nazarene, organized in 1924. The church started in a tent at 1320 Dolman Street, led by Rev. C. I. Deboard. The first official pastor was Rev. A. L. Roach, who served from 1928 to 1952. In 1929, it moved to 2800 St. Vincent Avenue, and in 1969, the church bought this building, the former Compton Heights Christian Church. (Derek Cadzow Photography.)

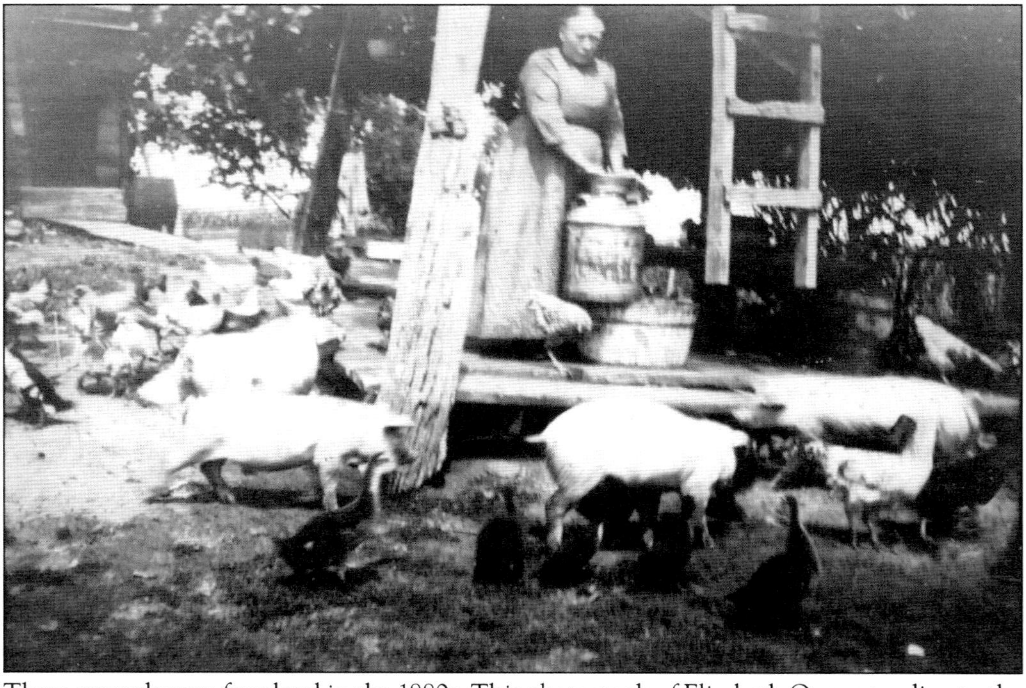

These grounds were farmland in the 1880s. This photograph of Elizabeth Owens tending to the animals would have been a familiar sight in the area before 1900. By the early 1900s, houses were built where livestock had roamed. Louis Helm, a German carpenter, built his house on this site, and by 1930, the house was occupied by Gustav and Lydia Schoenberg. Gustav was the president of the F. E. Schoenberg Company, manufacturers of wire screens. (Owens family collection.)

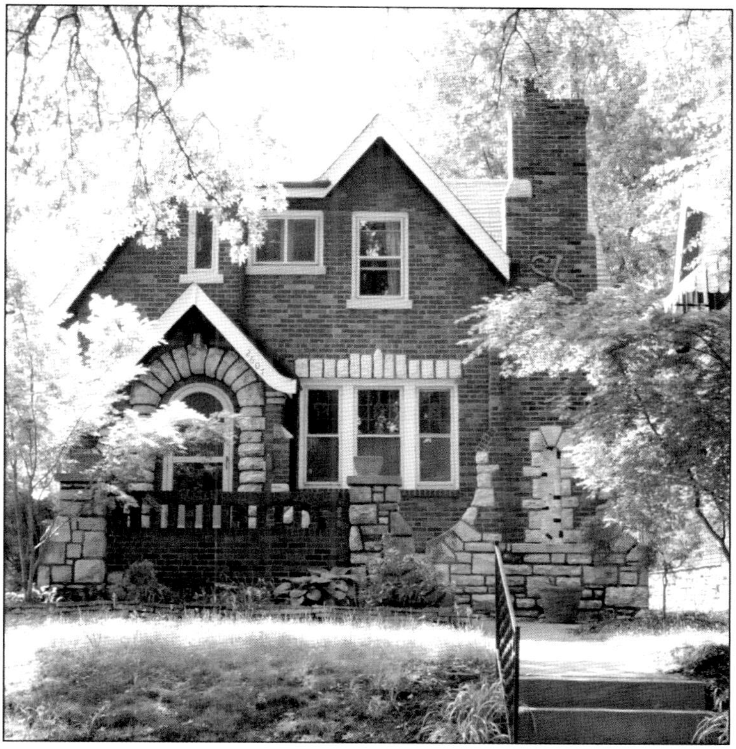

This eclectic Tudor house (site A17) at 2607 Alfred Avenue was built by Sol Abrahms for the University Building Company. On December 4, 1923, the city issued a building permit to build the houses at No. 2607, No. 2613, and No. 2614 for $36,000. On November 30, 1923, the city also issued a building permit to Abrahms to build a house at 2603 Alfred Avenue for $12,000. In 1940, Albert E. Frantz and his wife, Alma, lived at the 2607 property. Albert was a salesman. (Derek Cadzow Photography.)

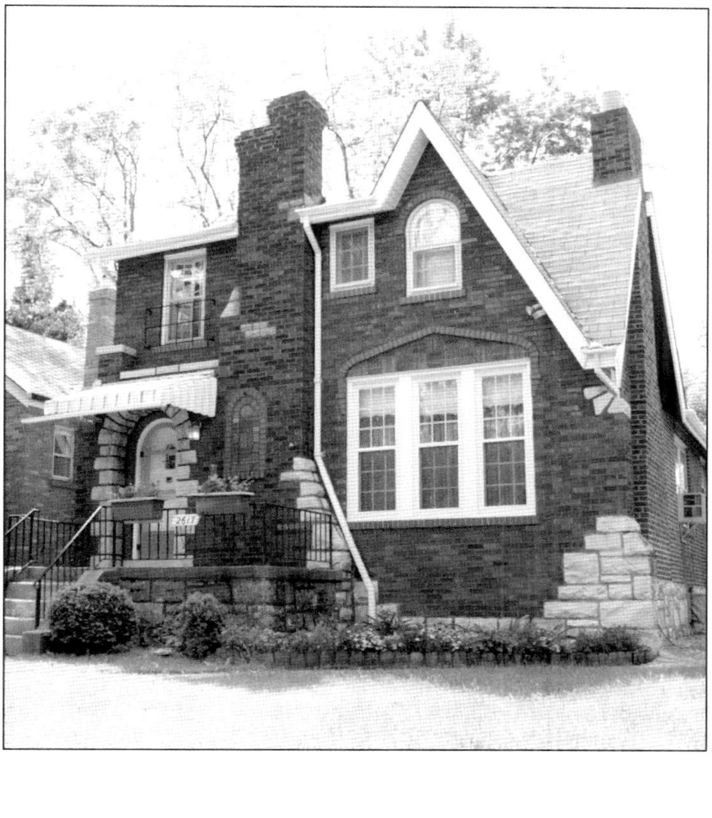

Chimney pots crown the chimneys at 2617 Alfred Avenue, a classic example of Tudor architecture. The 1940 city directory lists Jack J. Dowling and his wife, Bertha, as the residents. Jack was the owner of Dowling Motor Company at 3418 South Kingshighway Boulevard. He dealt in used cars. In 1930, the residents at 2621 Alfred Avenue were George and Theresa Lutz. George worked as a laborer for a planing mill. They came from Hungary and became American citizens in the early 1890s. (Derek Cadzow Photography.)

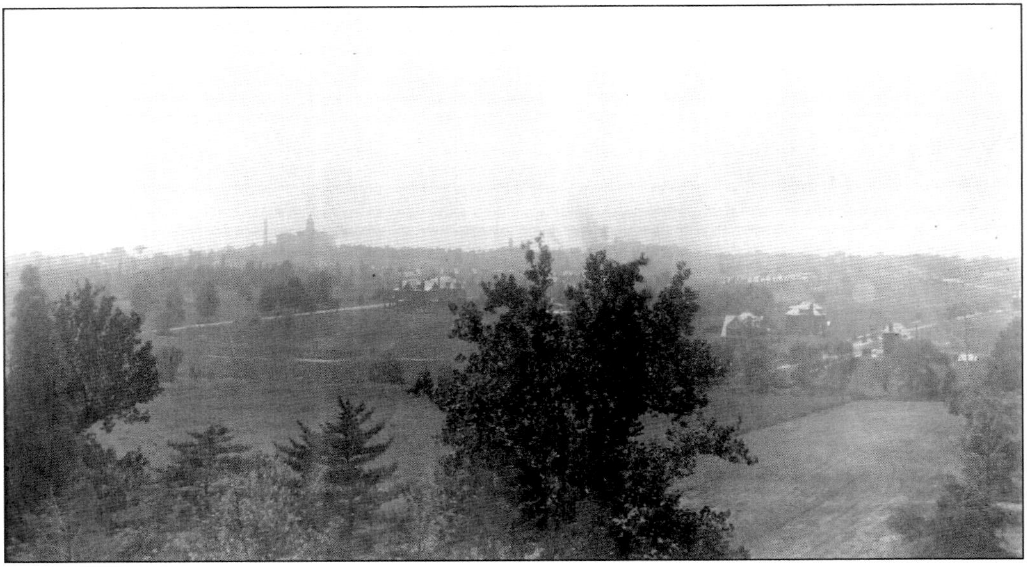

An aerial view from Tower Grove House around 1890 shows the Guidici house (site A18) at 4518 Tower Grove Place, at right. Charles and Jennifer Guidici have deep roots in the neighborhood. Jennifer's family owned the Haenni's market at 5424 Magnolia Avenue. Cosmo and Charles Guidici owned a restaurant at 4549 Shaw Avenue in the 1920s and 1930s. Other relatives live at Tower Grove Place. (Missouri Botanical Garden Archives.)

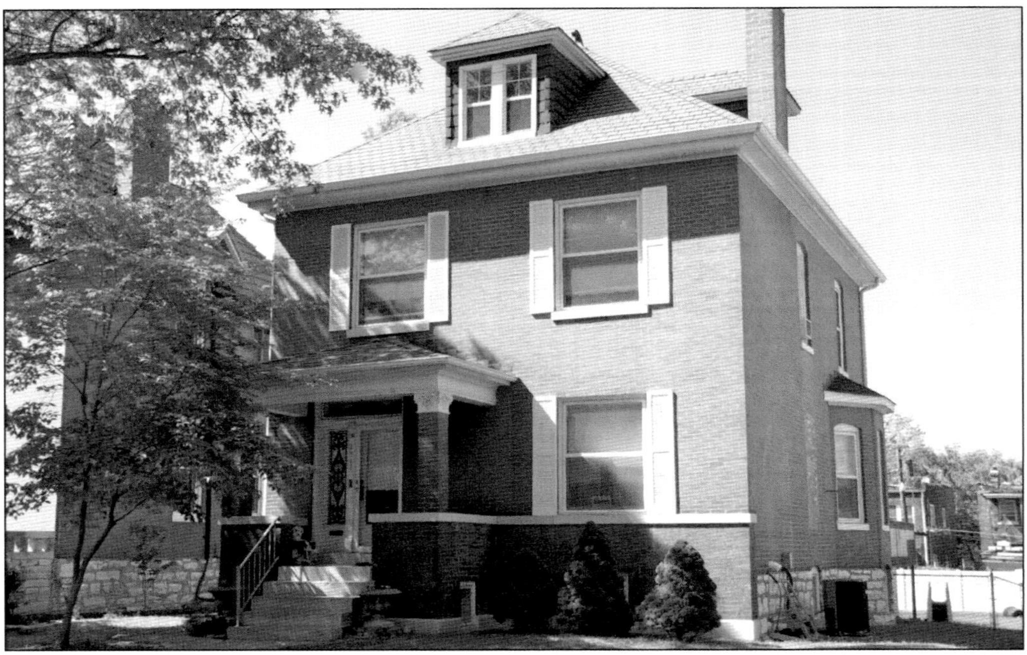

On April 21, 1911, the city issued a building permit to construct a house at 4517 Tower Grove Place for $3,000 for C. W. Buehler. In 1930, William Ewart and his wife, Orpha, rented the house for $100 a month. The Ewarts were Canadians and obtained their American citizenship in 1910. In 1940, Peter J. and Emily McAliney lived in the house. In 1952, James H. Durham, an attorney with an office at the Railway Exchange Building, lived there. (Derek Cadzow Photography.)

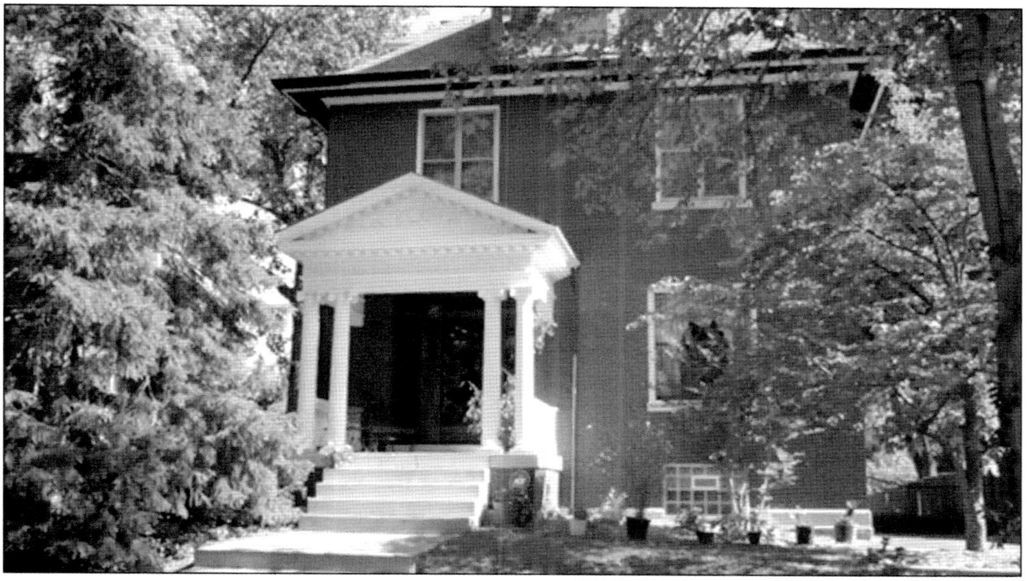

The Lecoutour house at 4533 Tower Grove Place was built for Emil Lecoutour in 1910. In 1900, Emil and his brother Charles lived at 1945 Arsenal Street. They were the owners of the Lecoutour Brothers Stair Manufacturing Company; Emil was secretary and Charles was president. The company's first building was located at 3015 Salena Street in the Benton Park neighborhood. In 2004, the building was sold to Killeen and Killeen Development, and today the offices for Killeen Studio Architects are located here. (Photograph by Janice Markham.)

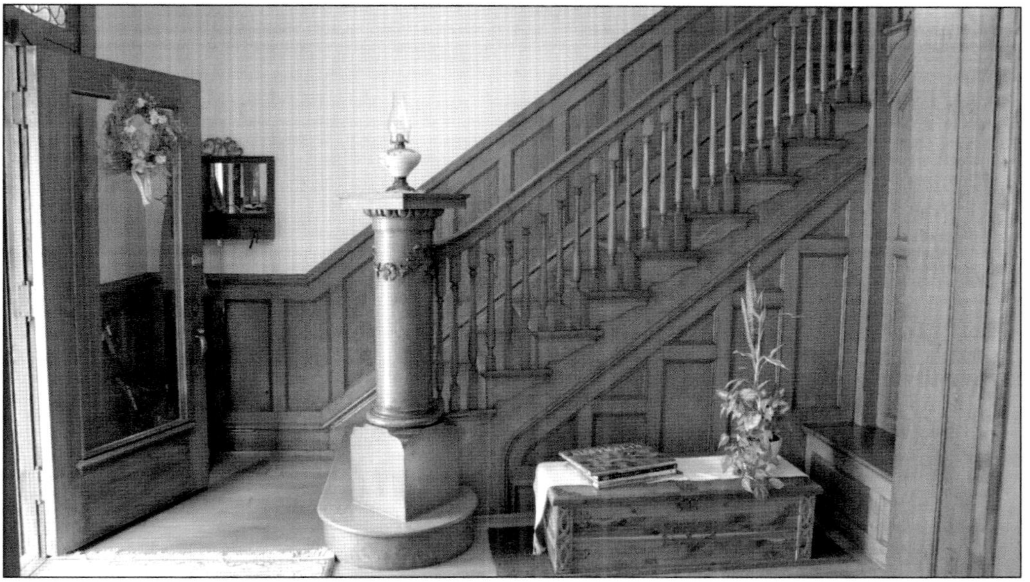

In 1906, the city issued Charles Lecoutour a building permit to construct a two-story brick manufacturing plant for $7,500 at 4521–4523 Shaw Avenue. In 1912, the Lecoutour family added a one-story brick factory at 4515–4519 Shaw Avenue for $10,000. The next building permit for work at 4523 Shaw Avenue was issued in 1920 to the Lecoutour Brothers Stair Manufacturing Company. By this time, Emil was president and treasurer. By 1930, the company moved to 3176 Brannon Avenue. (Derek Cadzow Photography.)

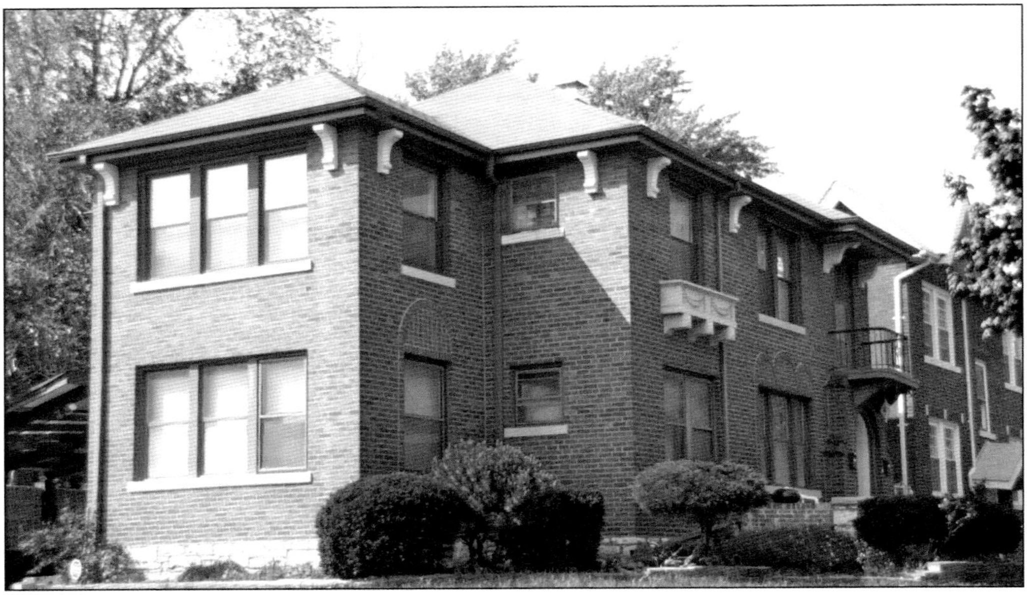

The Charles Peterman house (site A19) at 2123 Portis Avenue was built as a two-family unit, and it remains that way today. In 1930, Peterman and his wife, Grace, lived on the first floor, and Paul and Viola King rented the second floor for $62.50 a month. Peterman was an accountant for a railroad, and Paul was in the dry goods business. There is a coal chute cover marked "Manufactured by Manchester Iron Works" in the garage. (Derek Cadzow Photography.)

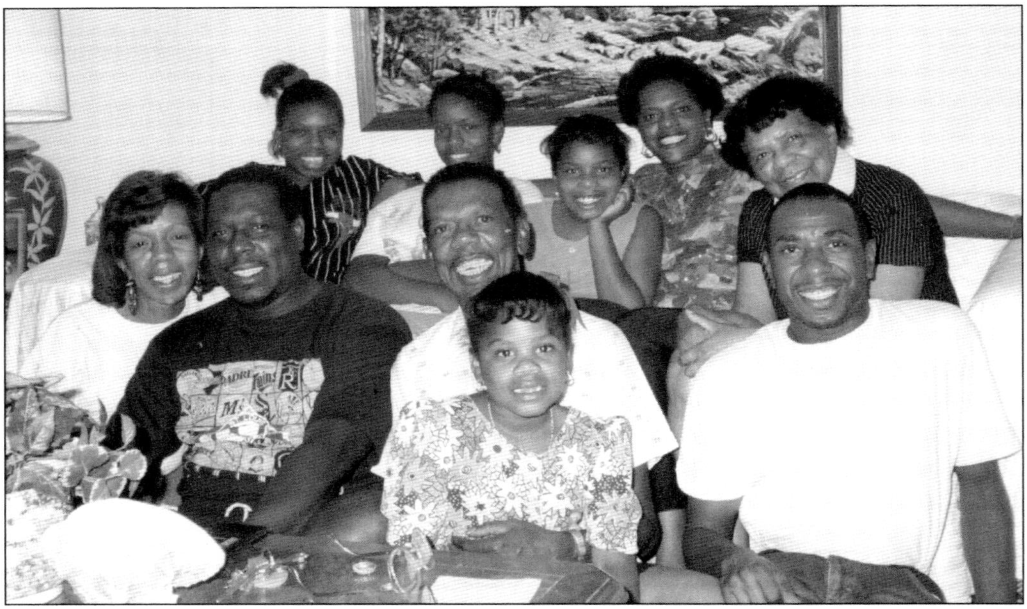

Keith Brookens, pictured on the far right in this Brookens family portrait, is the current owner of the former residence of Bernard W. and Lucy Nordmann. Bernard W. was the secretary of the family business, Nordmann Printing. Bernard H. and Katherine Nordmann lived at 3641 Flora Avenue. Bernard H. was the president of the family business. The printing company went out of business in 1989. (Brookens family collection.)

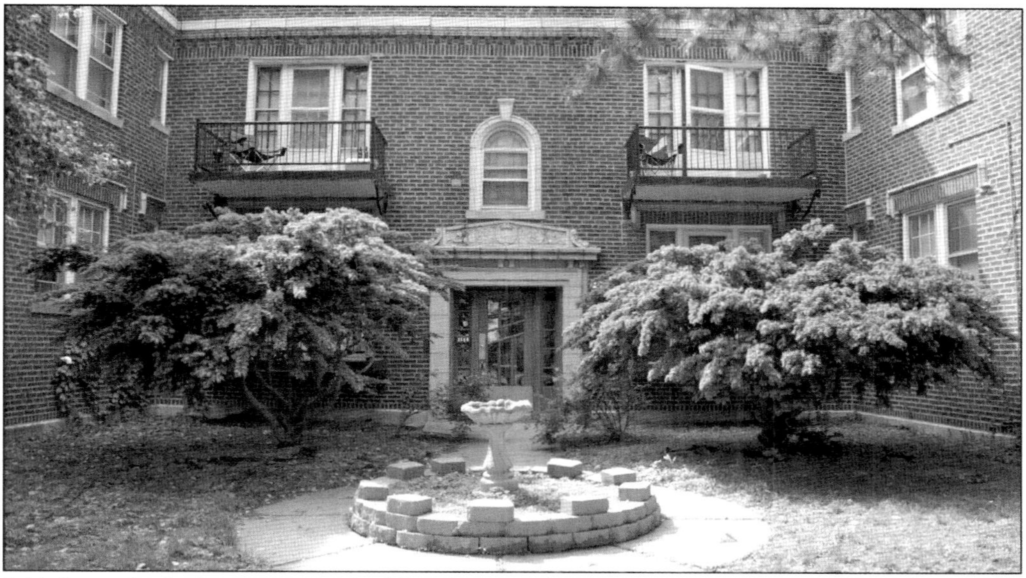

J. T. Cairns built this apartment building (site A20) at 1925–1933 Alfred Avenue for $40,000 in 1926. The apartment building across the street is one of several properties owned and developed by John Nash. Nash is a cofounder of the Special Security Taxing District, which helped to stabilize and revitalize the area. Tom Kelling is credited as a leader in the beautification of the neighborhood. (Derek Cadzow Photography.)

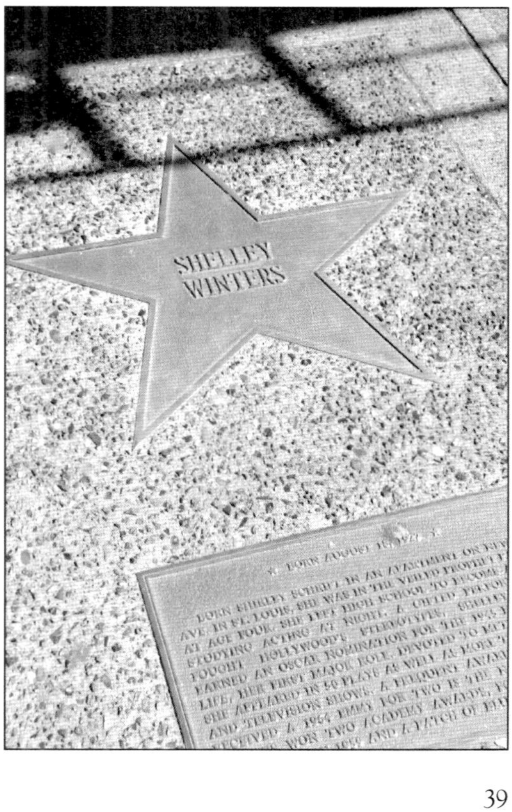


Actress Shelley Winters's star of fame at the St. Louis Delmar Loop is pictured. As a child, Winters lived with her parents just outside the neighborhood boundary at 4114 DeTonty Street. The house was demolished recently; the vacant lot is owned by Millennium Restoration and Development. Winters was born in St. Louis on August 18, 1920, to Jonas and Rose Schrift. Winters attended Mullanphy School. (Derek Cadzow Photography.)

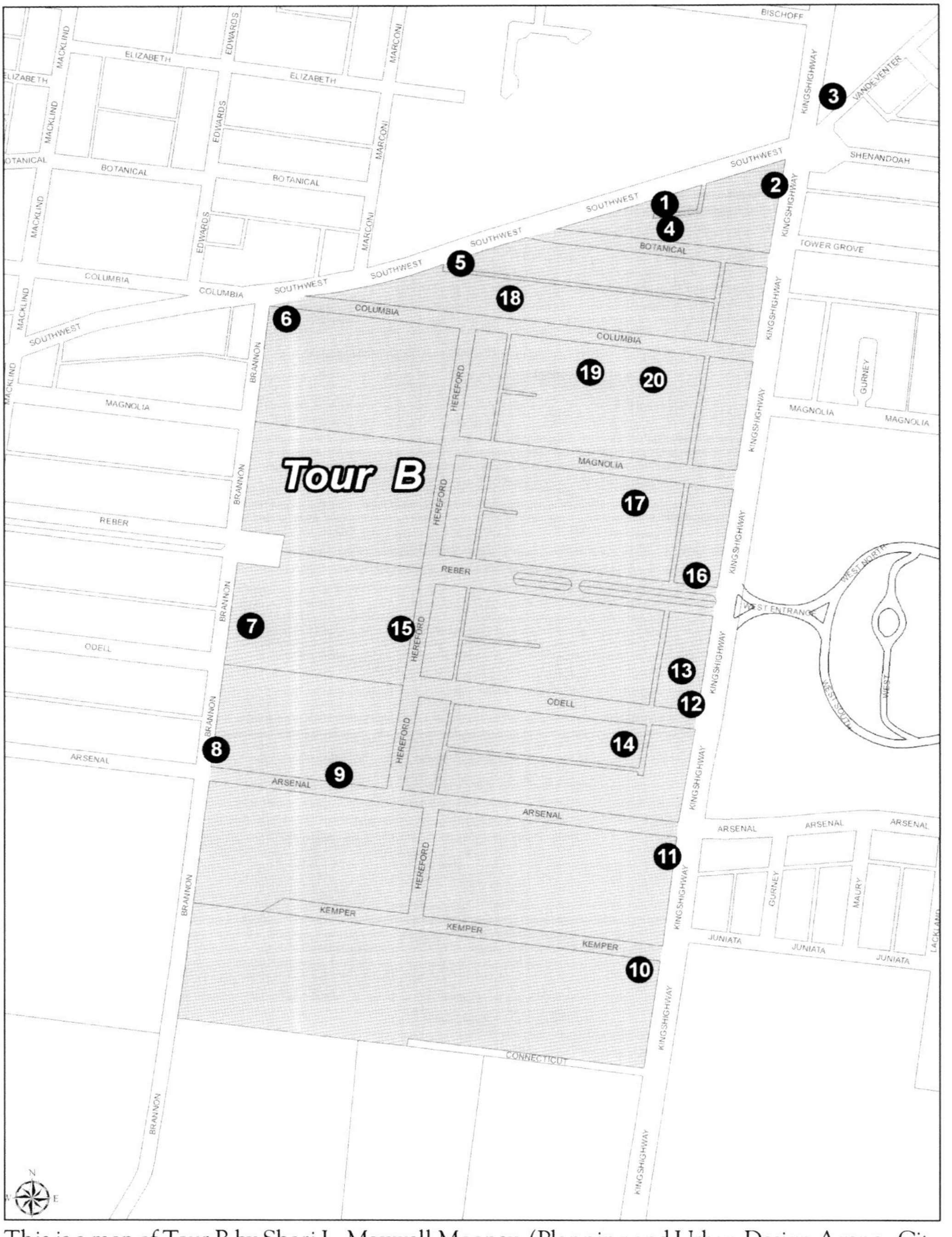


This is a map of Tour B by Shari L. Maxwell-Mooney. (Planning and Urban Design Agency City of St. Louis.)

# *Two*

# Tour B

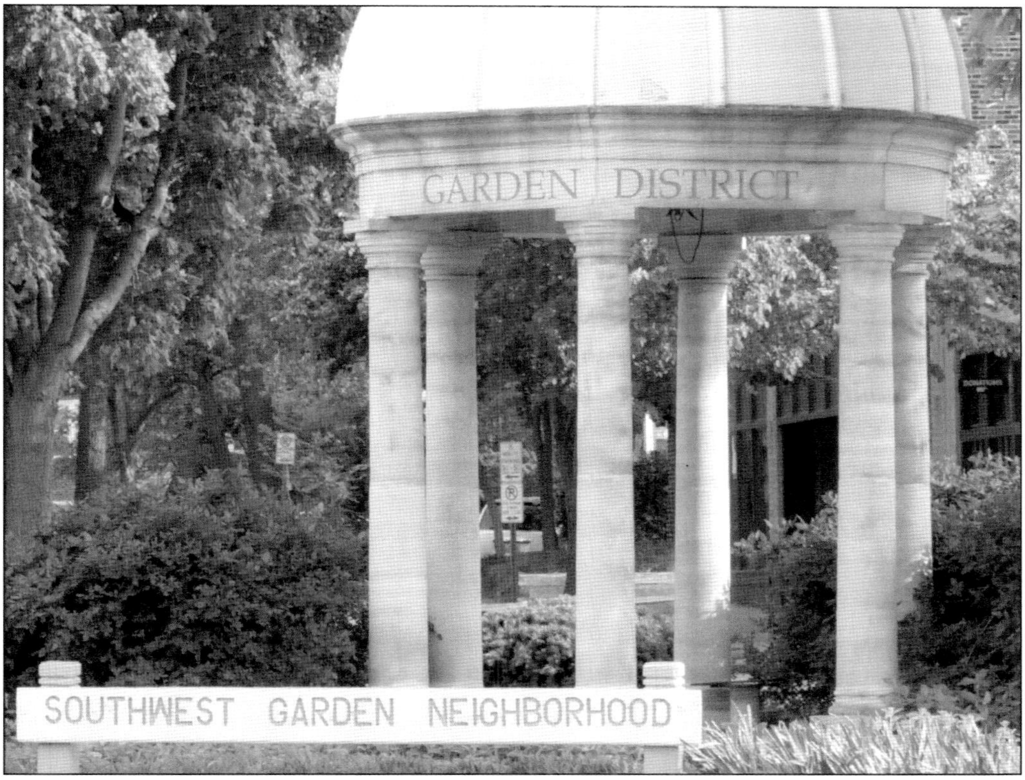


The Southwest Garden neighborhood is part of the Garden District. Each neighborhood has its own association to help with the revitalization and stabilization of these historic communities. The Southwest Garden Board of Directors consists of Floyd Wright, president; Chuck Fuhry, first vice president; Ron Matejka, second vice president; Danny Daniele, third vice president; Barbara Beck, treasurer; Barbara Anderson, recording secretary; Peter Hovey, corresponding secretary; Judy Lewin; Virgil Moore; and Dana Gray, executive director. (Derek Cadzow Photography.)

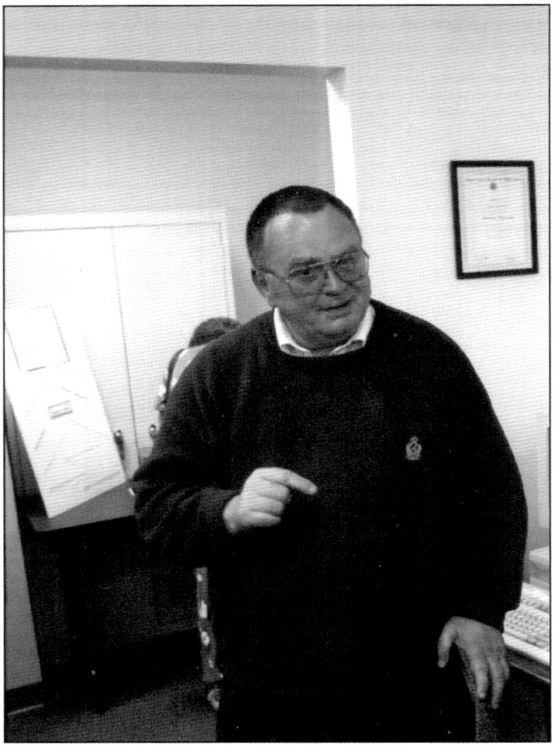

The office of the Southwest Garden Neighborhood Association (site B1) is located at 4950 Southwest Avenue. Floyd Wright, the current president, is pictured at an event for Operation Brightside. A building permit was issued to owner George E. Brenner for construction at this location on June 1, 1915. At that time, Southwest Avenue was known as Old Manchester Road. The association office is manned by executive director Dana Gray. The association was organized in 1978. (Operation Brightside.)

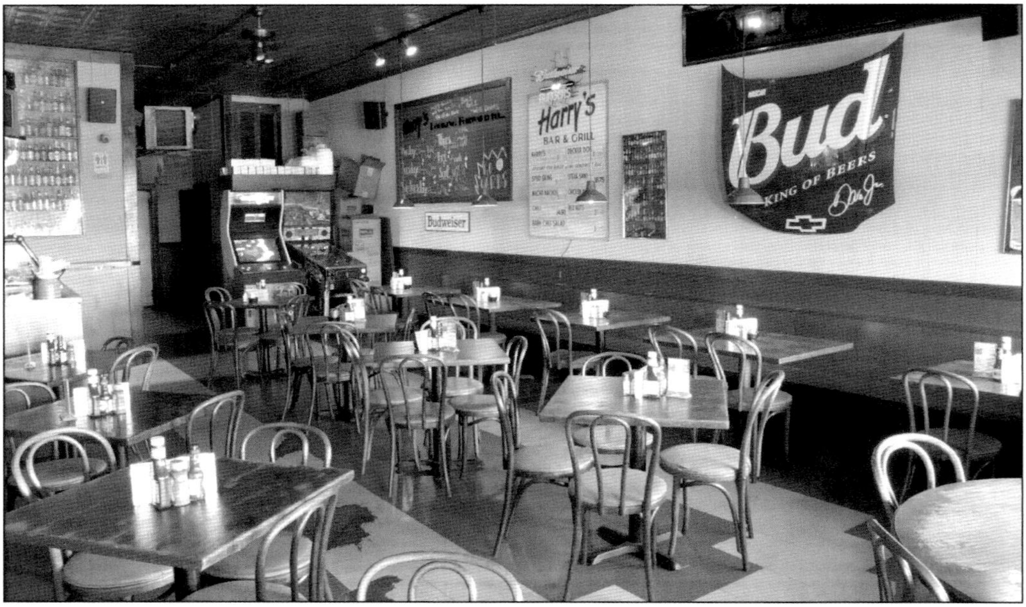


Just a few doors down, Harry's Bar and Grill is located at 4940 Southwest Avenue. This neighborhood establishment opened in 1989. The building dates back to 1925. A building permit was issued to build between 4940 and 4948 Southwest Avenue for a row of stores at a cost of $9,000. The structures were built by the Southwest Investment Company. According to the 1930 city directory, Steve Gounis had a restaurant at this location. (Derek Cadzow Photography.)

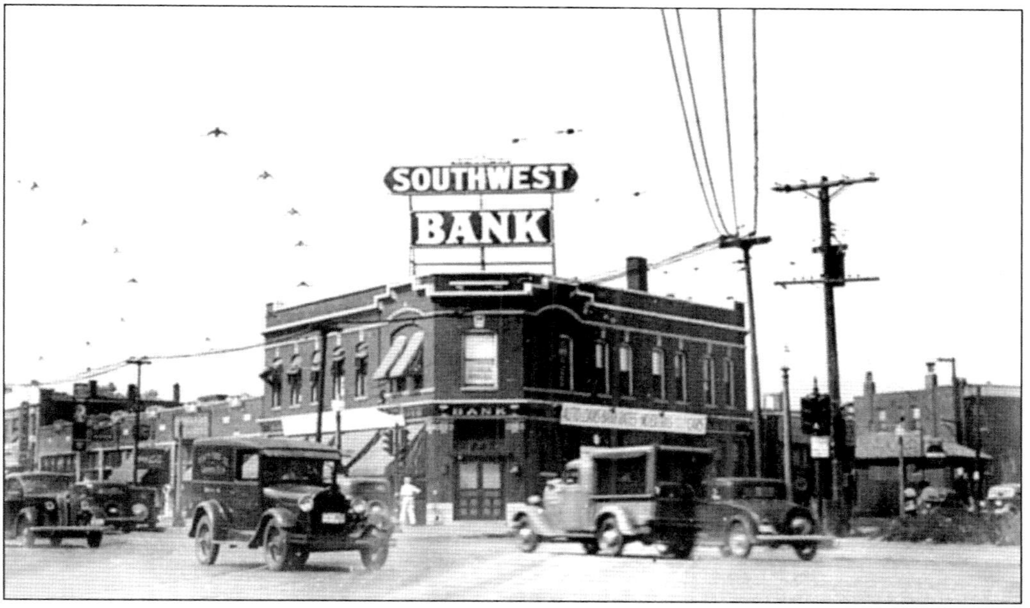


Southwest Bank (site B2) at 2301 South Kingshighway Boulevard was established in the 1920s. The first building permit found listing the bank was in 1923. The structure was built in 1905 for D. F. McCausland by A. F. Drischiler at a cost of $8,000. The address listed was 2301–2303 South Kingshighway for a store and flats. In 1925, a sign was erected for Southwest Bank. In 1937, an alteration was made to the building for the Southwest Trust Company. (Southwest Bank.)

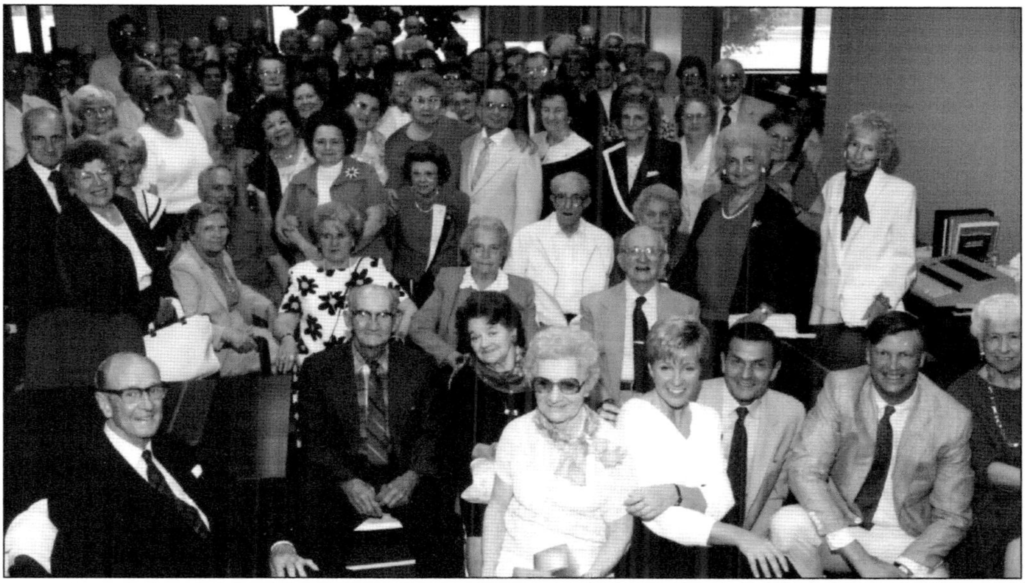

The people in this photograph are very special to the bank—they have been customers for 50 or more years. On May 19, 1991, the officers and directors of the bank hosted an afternoon cocktail party for their loyal clients. The bank has serviced residents from the Southwest Garden and the Hill since the 1920s. The Hill neighborhood, known as "Little Italy," still has many residents who speak Italian. The newspaper *Il Pensiero*, meaning "the thought," is available at the bank's entrance. (Southwest Bank.)

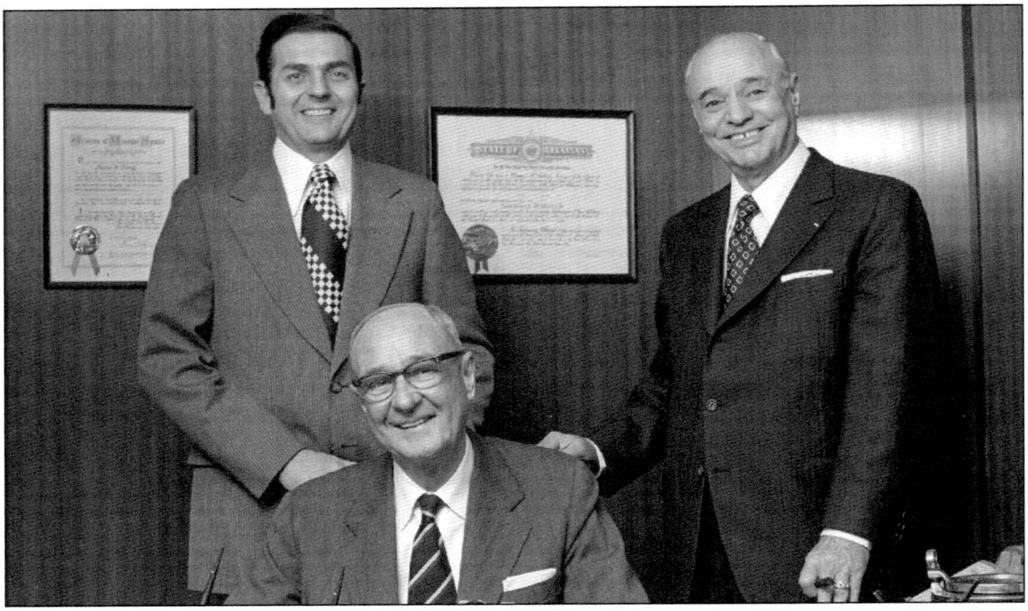

Southwest Bank executives in the mid-1970s are, from left to right, Ed Berra, president; I. A. Long, chief executive officer; and F. A. Giacoma, vice chairman of the board. In 1984, control of Southwest Bank was purchased by Andrew N. Baur, Linn H. Bealke, and associates. In 2002, the bank was bought by Marshall and Ilsley Corporation, headquartered in Milwaukee, Wisconsin. (Southwest Bank.)

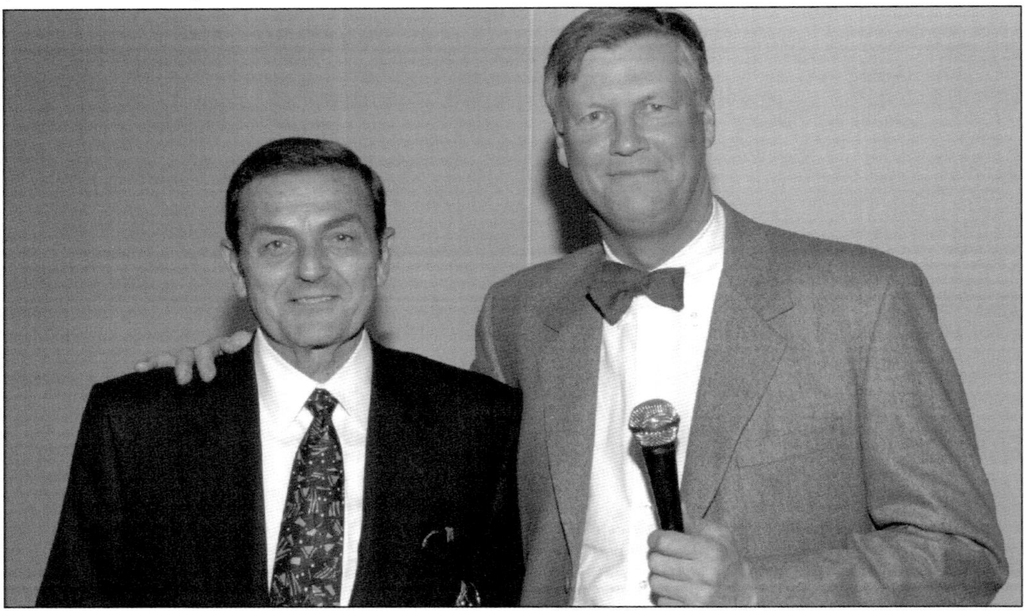

Ed Berra (left) receives an award presented by Drew Baur, the bank's chairman and chief executive officer in the early 1980s. Currently Andrew N. Baur is chairman of the board, Linn H. Bealke and Ed Berra are advisory members of the board, Andrew S. Baur and Robert Witterschein are bank presidents, and Michelle L. Beerman is manager of the branch in the Southwest Garden neighborhood. (Southwest Bank.)

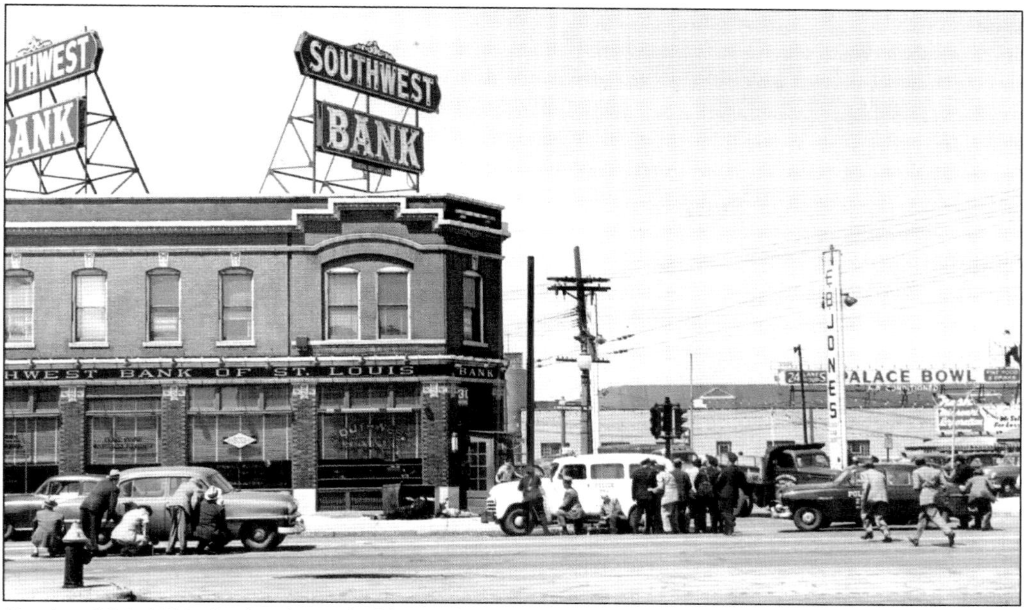


On April 24, 1953, the bank was held up. This photograph gives an idea of the crowd the robbery attracted. After an officer and a robber were wounded and two robbers were killed, the police recovered about $140,000 in stolen money. In 1959, the movie based on this robbery, *The Great St. Louis Bank Robbery*, was released by United Artists. Steve McQueen, a new star, acted in the movie. (Photograph by Jack January; St. Louis Post-Dispatch.)

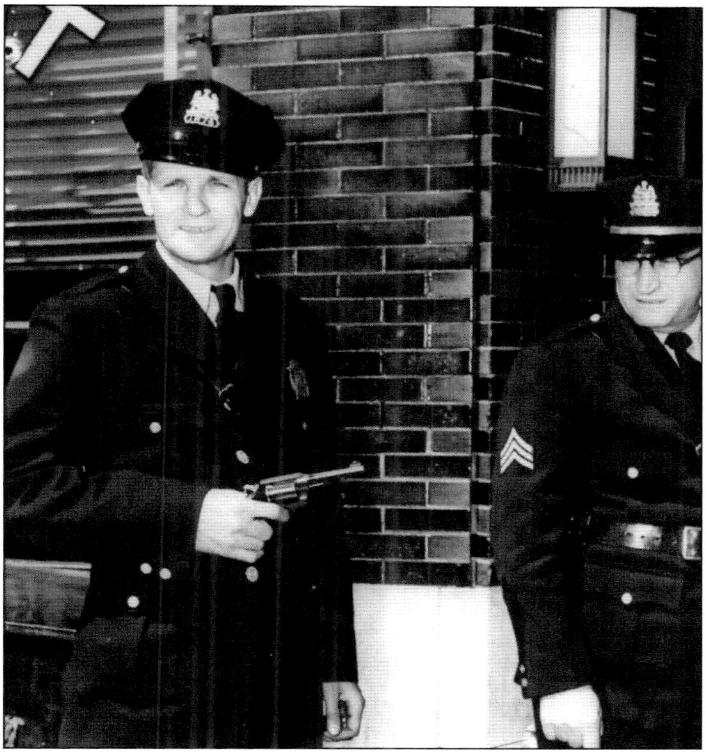

Officer Melburn F. Stein (left) and Sgt. Frank Stubis Sr. are photographed at the scene of the robbery. A bullet hole is visible at the top left of the window. During the robbery, a hostage was taken, and it was Stein who shot and killed the criminal. In the movie, Stein played his own role. Former city police officer Stein completed 31 years of service and retired in 1973. (St. Louis police sergeant John T. Vollman collection.)

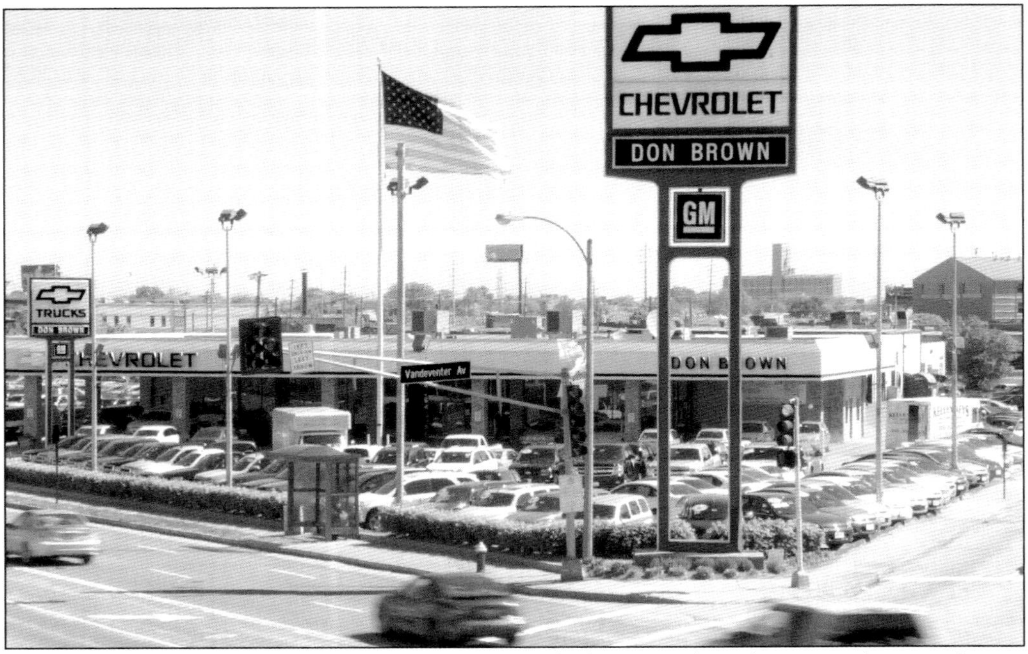


Don Brown Chevrolet (site B3) at 2244 South Kingshighway Boulevard sits very close to a former Chevrolet dealer location from the 1930s. In the 1930 city directory, Hilmer-Robert Chevrolet Company is listed at 2300 South Kingshighway. Brown's other location is at 3300 South Kingshighway. The business that was started in 1984 is a dealer for Chevrolet, Dodge, and Chrysler Jeep. The company advertises this address as at the entrance of the Hill. (Derek Cadzow Photography.)

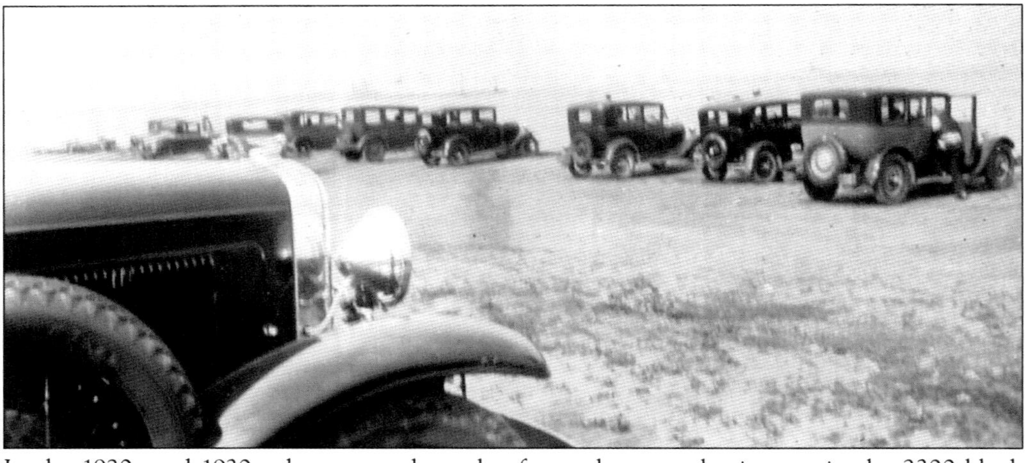

In the 1920s and 1930s, these were the style of cars that were buying gas in the 2300 block of South Kingshighway Boulevard. In the 1918, 1925, and 1930 city directories, the Pierce Petroleum Company is listed as having a filling station at 2300 South Kingshighway. There was another Pierce station located nearby in the 1800 block of Tower Grove Avenue, owned by E. H. Wendel. (Butler's Pantry.)

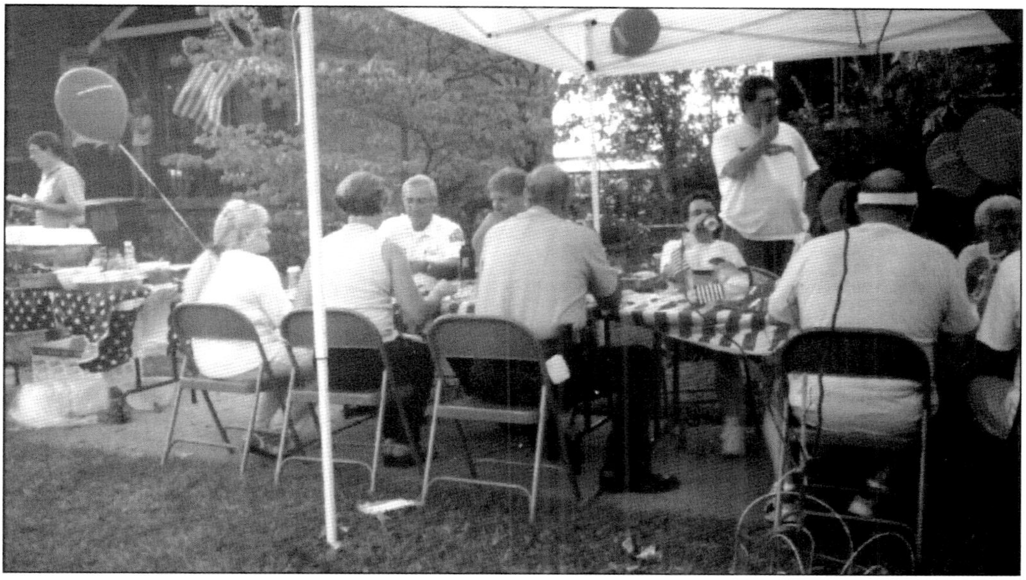

The Grbac house (site B4) on Botanical Avenue was built in 1910. The city issued a building permit to Albert B. Finch to construct three two-story tenements at No. 4937, No. 4941, and No. 4943 Botanical Avenue for $9,000. The Grbacs are well known in the community for their volunteer work. In 2002, they hosted a block party in front of their house to honor the neighborhood heroes. The honored guests included persons from the police, fire, and paramedic departments. (Grbac family collection.)

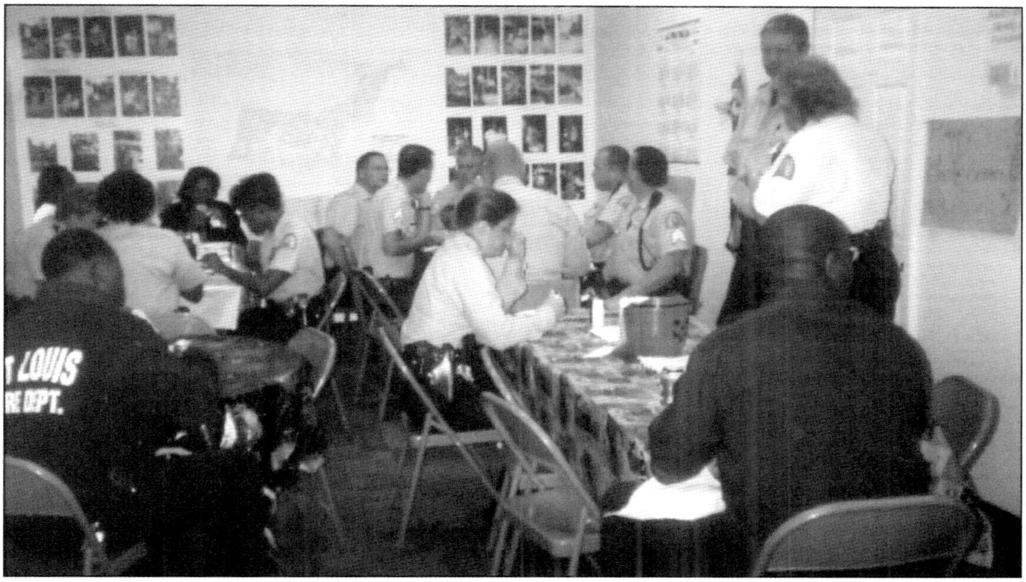


George and Sandy Grbac know the neighborhood and its residents well. Sandy grew up on South Kingshighway Boulevard, and in 1954, George moved to Botanical Avenue with his parents, George and Cecilia. The Grbacs appreciate living in a safe and friendly community. Every year, they organize an appreciation barbecue to thank area policemen, firefighters, and paramedics. In 2007, this event took place at the Southwest Garden Neighborhood Association offices. (Grbac family collection.)

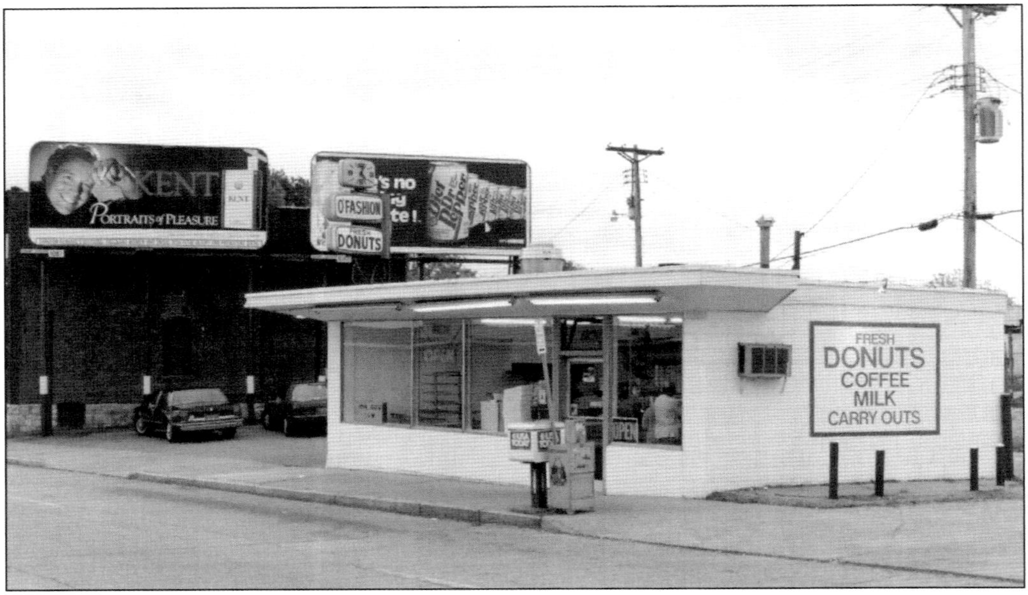


O'Fashion Donuts (site B5) is located at 5120 Southwest Avenue. The shop, photographed in 1991, was built in 1926 as a garage and service station at a cost of $18,000. In the 1940s, it was still a station, and later it was used as an insurance and real estate office. Gene and Colleen Hiens opened the doughnut shop in 1980, and in 1987, they bought the building. The Hiens family has been making doughnuts since 1977. (Photograph by Arteaga Photos, Hiens family collection.)

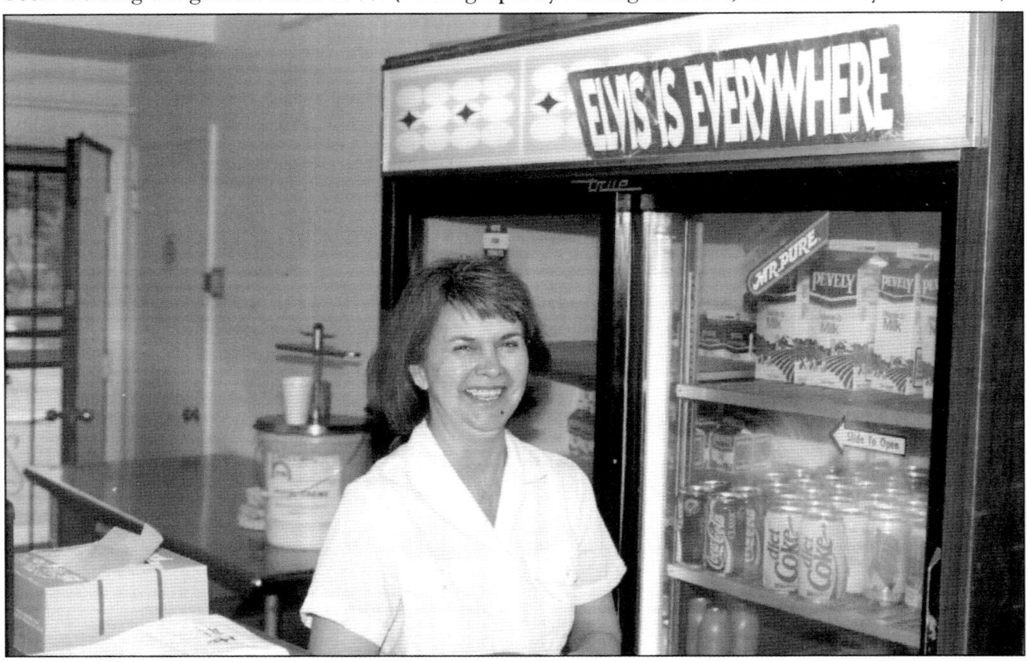


Colleen Hiens serves Pevely milk to go with her doughnuts. In 1989, Pevely, the oldest independent dairy in St. Louis, was bought by Prairie Farms Dairy, whose headquarters are in Carlinville, Illinois. Pevely made its mark when it won a contract to supply milk to the world's fair in 1904. (Photograph by Arteaga Photos, Hiens family collection.)

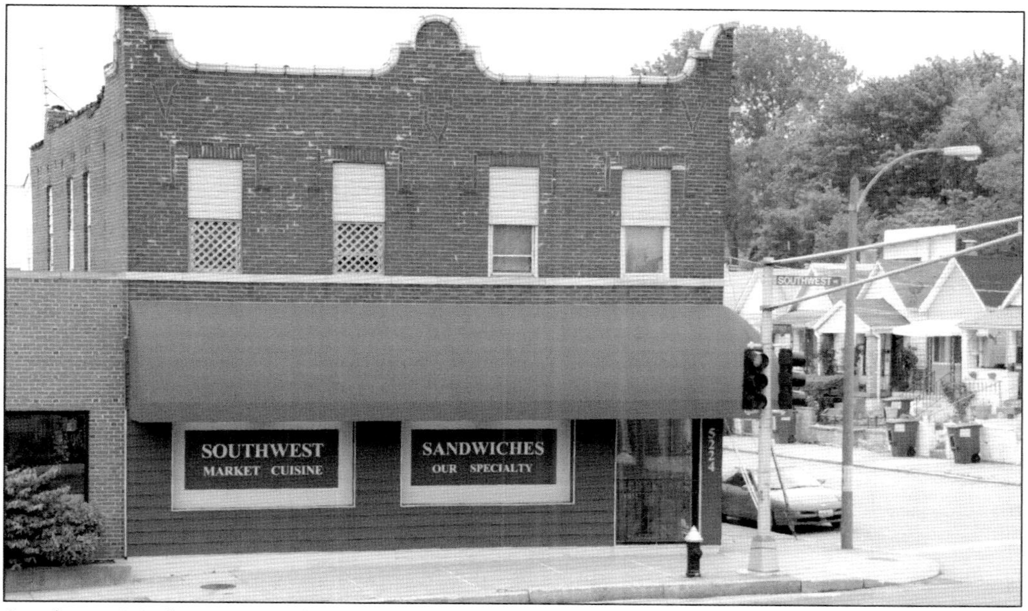


Southwest Market Cuisine (site B6) at 5224 Columbia Avenue was originally Oldani's Market. In 1913, the city issued a building permit to owner A. Oldani and contractor P. Ceresa to build a store and dwelling for $5,200. In the 1918 city directory, Anton Oldani is listed as a grocer. In 1924, there was an alteration made to the store and dwelling for $400, and the contractor was A. Casagrande. In 1925, Antoinette Oldani is listed as the grocer. (Photograph by Renée Crane.)

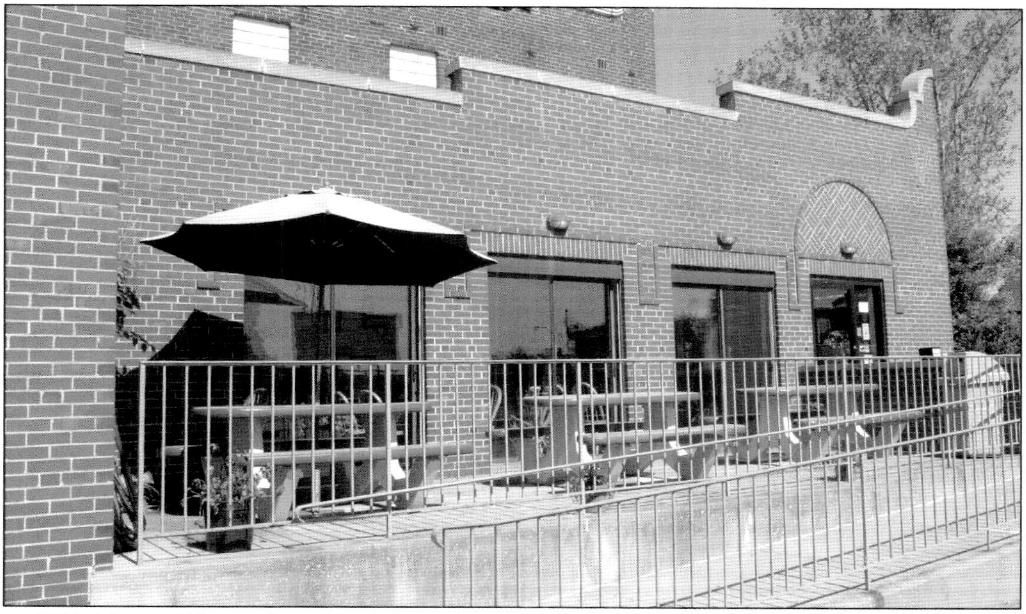

In 1930, Mario Oldani is listed as the grocer with Antoinette listed as a resident. In 1942, Mario was still running the family grocery, but by 1955, Mary Oldani had taken over the business. In 1965, the address is listed as Oldani Market, and by 1975, the Oldani name was gone, replaced by the A. G. Market. Today the market is owned and operated by the Burr family. (Photograph by Janice Markham.)

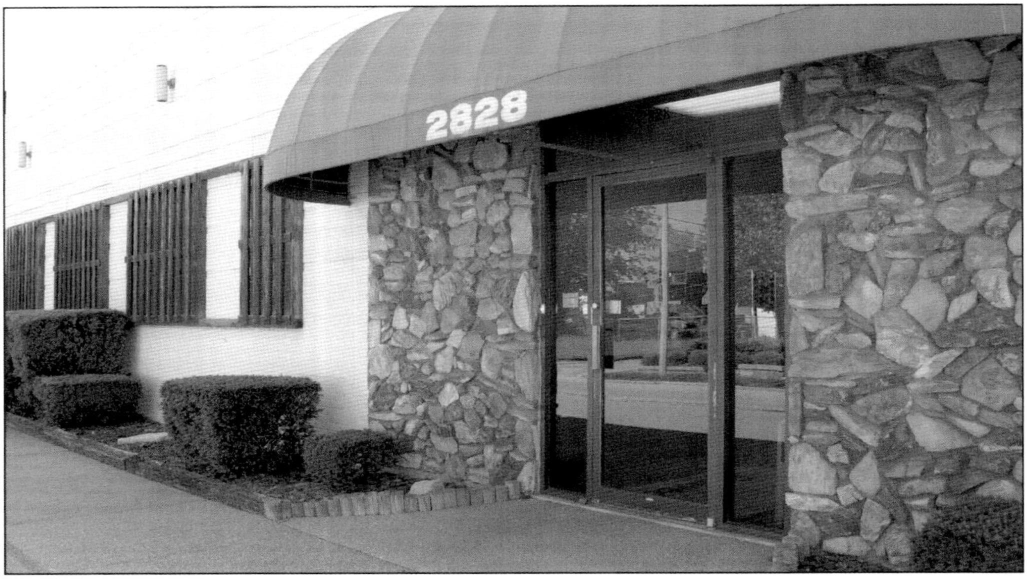


Cenveo (site B7), located at 2828 Brannon Avenue, is the printer of the Southwest Garden Neighborhood Association newsletter. Its business offices are located at 10300 Watson Road. Cenveo does commercial printing and has other locations in Arizona, California, Georgia, Indiana, Maryland, Minnesota, North Carolina, Ohio, Oregon, Pennsylvania, Tennessee, Texas, Washington, and Ontario, Canada. This building has been in use since the 1950s. In 1955, H. N. Saylor, a corporation dealing in paper, was located at this address. (Derek Cadzow Photography.)

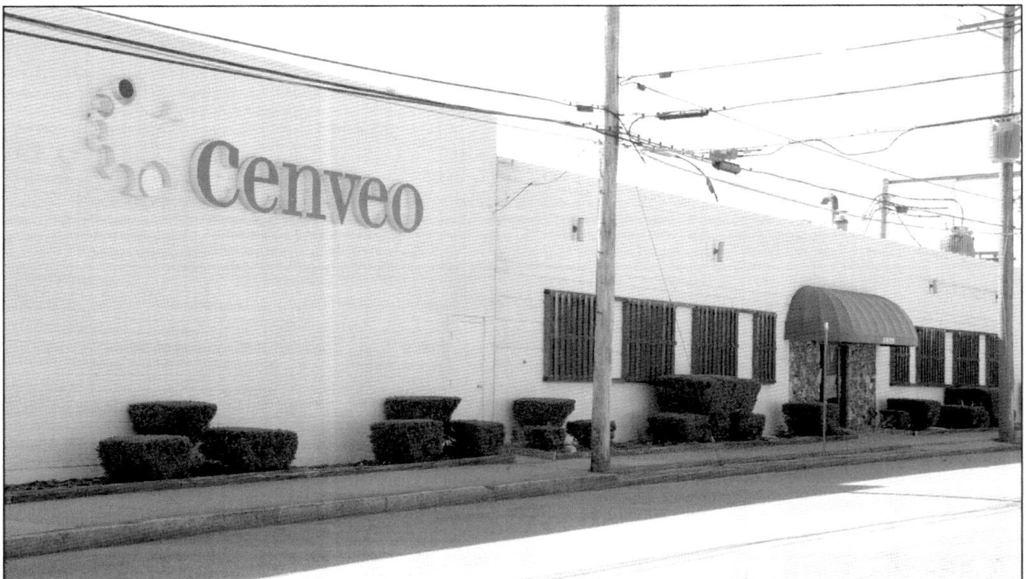


The 1965 city directory lists the Saylor corporation as a printer housed in this building. In 1975, Pan American Industries—also printers—occupied this commercial building surrounded by residential properties. Down the street toward Southwest Avenue, the houses at 2631 through 2641 Brannon Avenue were all built in 1903 for A. B. Finch. (Derek Cadzow Photography.)

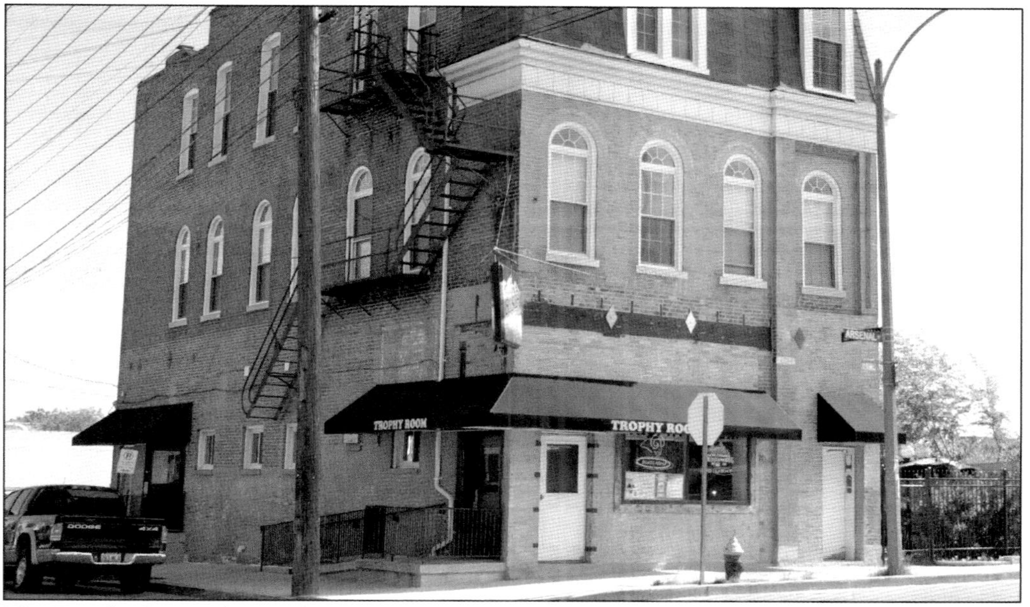


The Trophy Room (site B8) at 5099 Arsenal Street was built in 1893 for use as a store and dwelling for Josephine Lenfle. In 1923, the new owner, A. Minnick, hired H. Leish and Son to make some alterations. In 1939, more alterations were done for H. Izard, the owner. This location, which had served as a grocery in the early years, is now a neighborhood bar with a game room and beer garden. (Derek Cadzow Photography.)

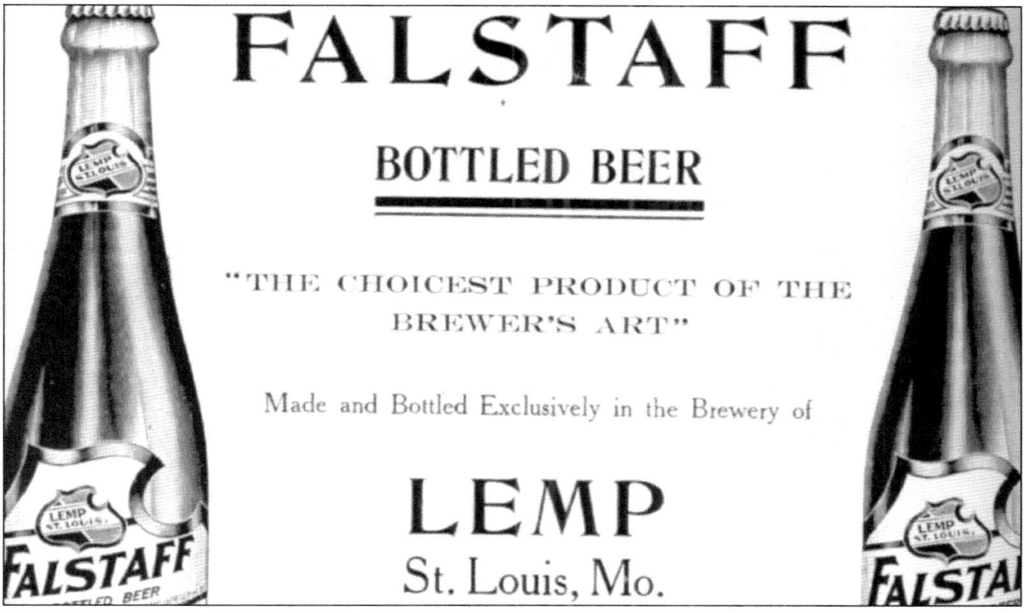


The Lemp Brewery was as important in the city as Anheuser-Busch. While the Anheuser-Busch brewery waited for Prohibition to end, it produced nonalcoholic products, such as a baker's yeast and Bevo drinks. The Lemp family decided to wait it out. Prohibition began on January 16, 1920, and was overturned in 1933. In 1922, the Lemp Brewery complex was bought at an auction by the International Shoe Company. (Diane Rademacher collection.)

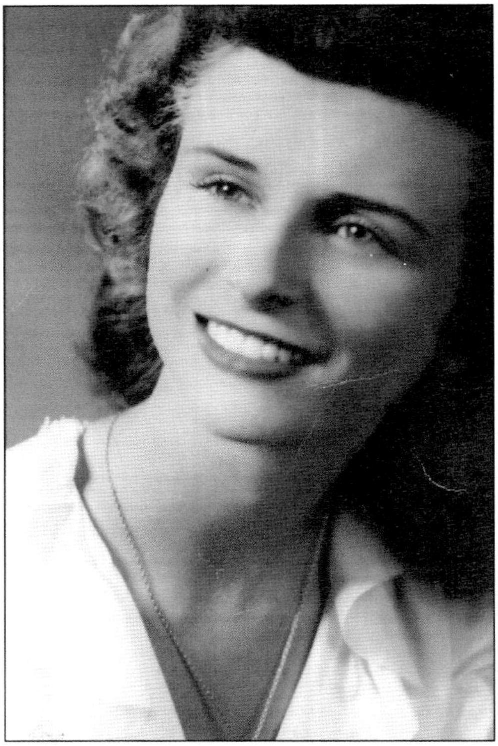

Sandrina's at 5098 Arsenal Street is listed as Cesar Re Saloon in 1918. In 1925, his business is listed as "drinks," and there were two apartments upstairs. Peter Oldani lived there in 1930 with no occupation listed. In the photograph is Angeleen Purcelli; Sandrina was her mother's name. Frank and Angeleen Purcelli owned Sandrina's from 1974 until 2007. The new owners are Sandra and Larry Erwin. Along with their daughter Tricia Erwin, they have a partner, Al Trice. (Purcelli family collection.)

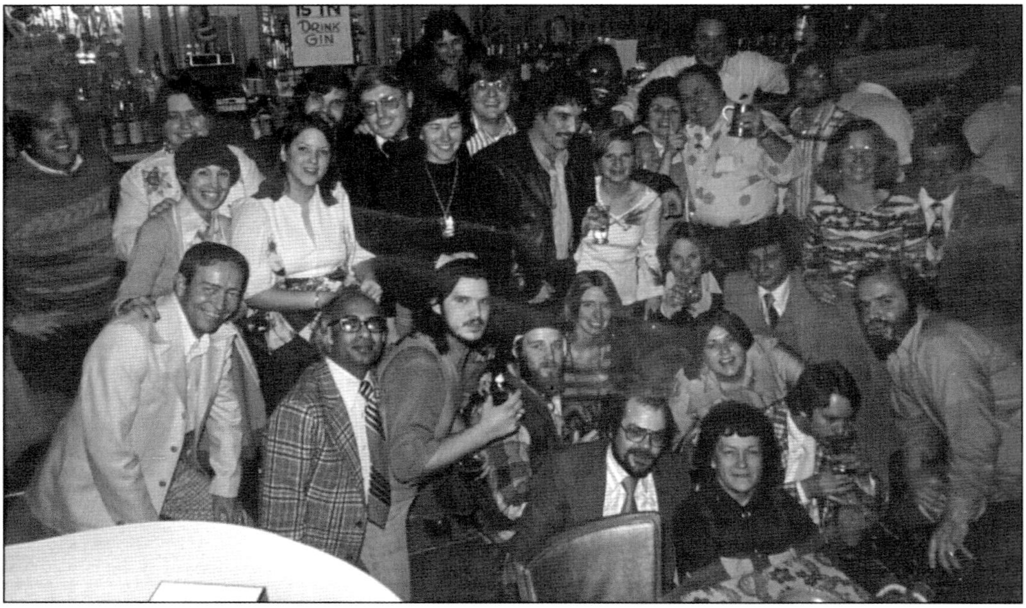

This photograph of Sandrina's from the 1970s was found when the current owners were renovating. Part of this building, originally built for use as a stable, dates to the 1870s. It has been renovated to include the restaurant and bar downstairs with a game room and a banquet room for special events upstairs. The new owners opened the doors on December 14, 2007. (Purcelli family collection.)

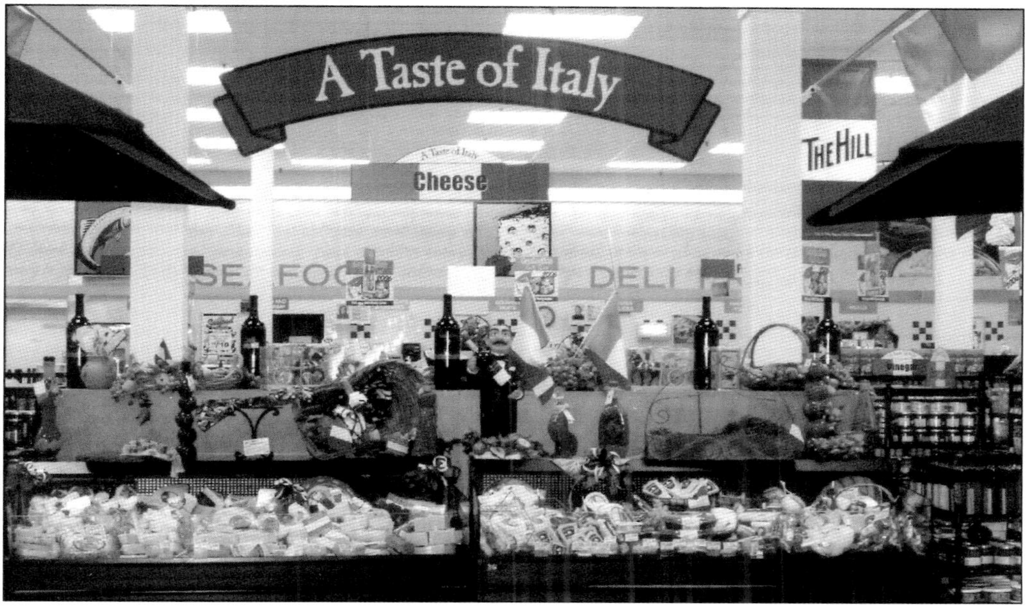


Schnucks (site B9) at 5055 Arsenal Street caters to the Hill, a neighborhood settled by Italian immigrants in the late 1800s. The shop within a store, A Taste of Italy, is a destination for residents in the neighborhood as well as visitors from around the country. This shop is a place to sit or pick up authentic Italian foods to take home. Its specialty is a sandwich appropriately named King of the Hill. (Photograph by Kevin Fitzpatrick, Schnucks Markets.)

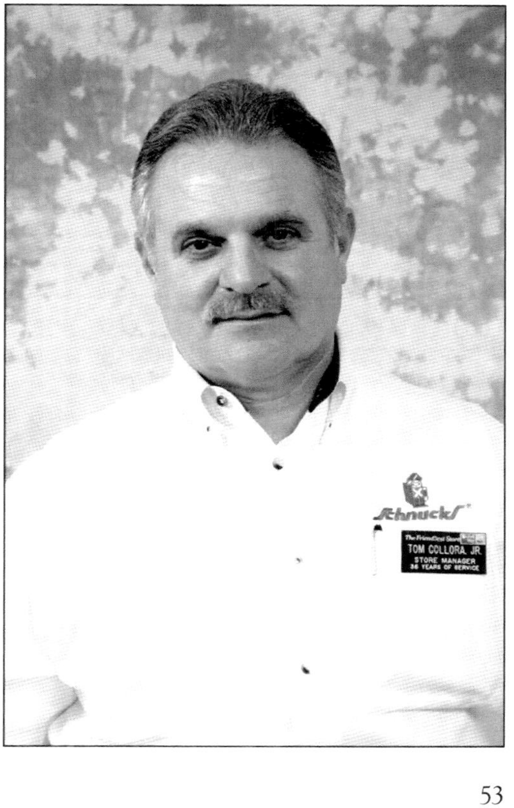


Thomas Collora has been Schnucks store manager since 1985. He has been with the company since 1969. Collora can trace his roots back to Palermo, Italy. His family came to the United States through Ellis Island in 1911 and settled in St. Louis's Italian community. He has this to say about his neighbors: "We respect our elders who brought us here from the old country." (Schnucks Markets.)

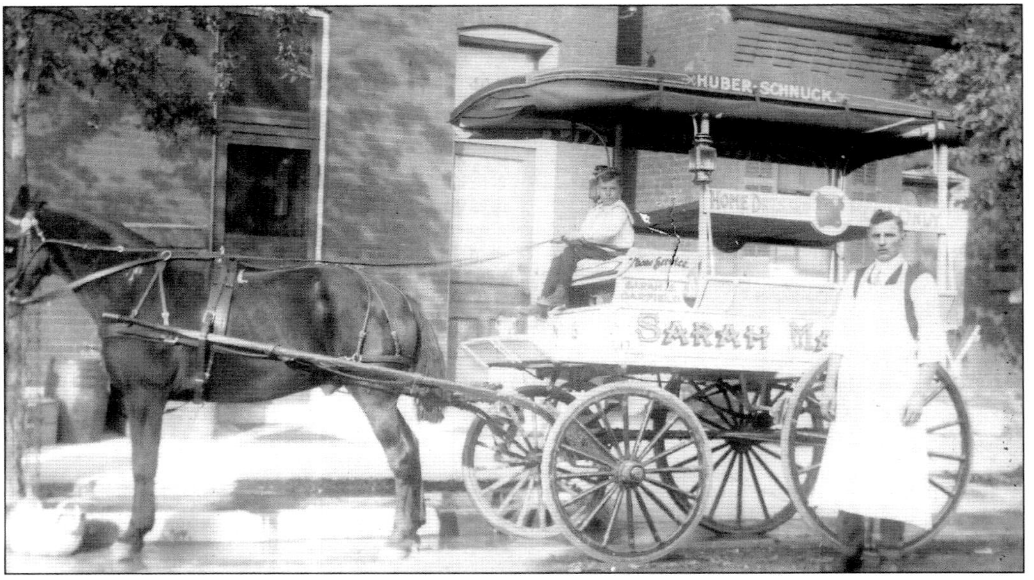


The Huber-Schnuck delivery wagon was probably photographed around 1903 at Herman Huber's residence at 4039 Garfield Avenue. In 1903, the city directory lists Huber, a butcher, at 225 Market Street, and Harry H. Schnuck is listed as his bookkeeper. Schnuck lived at 4042 North Market Street. The only year a connection could be found between Huber and Schnuck was 1903. The following year, Huber is still listed as a butcher, but Schnuck is listed as a partner in Schnuck and Banks. (Schnucks Markets.)

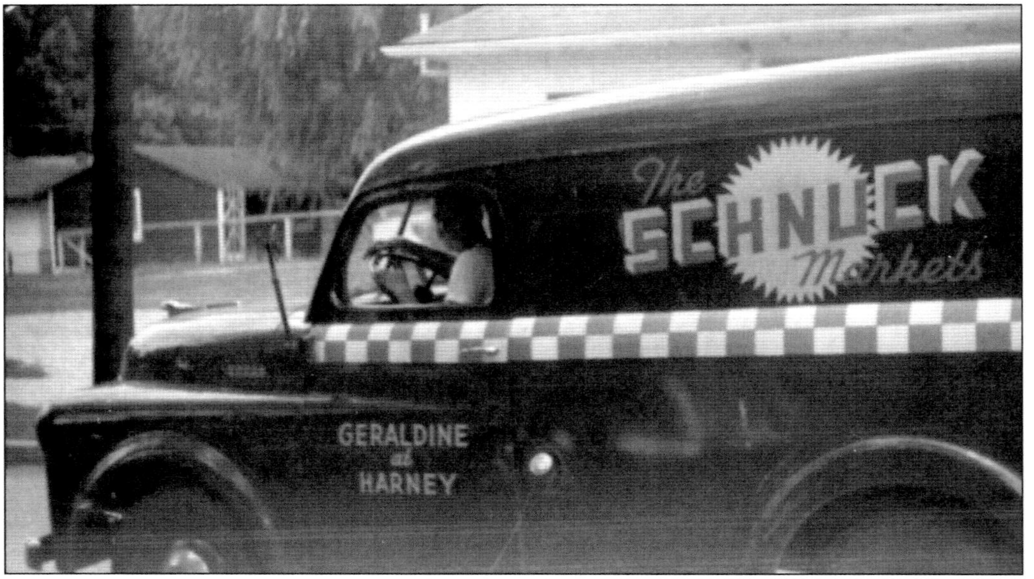


Donald O. Schnuck, Schnucks cofounder, is pictured at the wheel of the delivery truck. The truck was purchased in 1945 and was used for the store at Geraldine and Harney Avenues. Schnuck practiced the golden rule, treating others as he wanted to be treated. Schnucks offered its customers free grocery deliveries. The goodwill practice continued at the Schnucks store at 4356 Manchester Avenue until 1963. Donald O. Schnuck died of a heart attack on June 17, 1991. (Schnucks Markets.)

Anna and Edwin Schnuck were known as Mom and Pop Schnuck. They are photographed at the Dellwood store opening in 1955. Schnucks started in 1939 as a confectionery in North St. Louis. The confectionery was up front, and the wholesale meat business was in the back. Anna made potato salad and coleslaw to add a personal touch to the store. The whole family helped out; the confectionery was open every day from 8:00 a.m. to 9:00 p.m. (Schnucks Markets.)

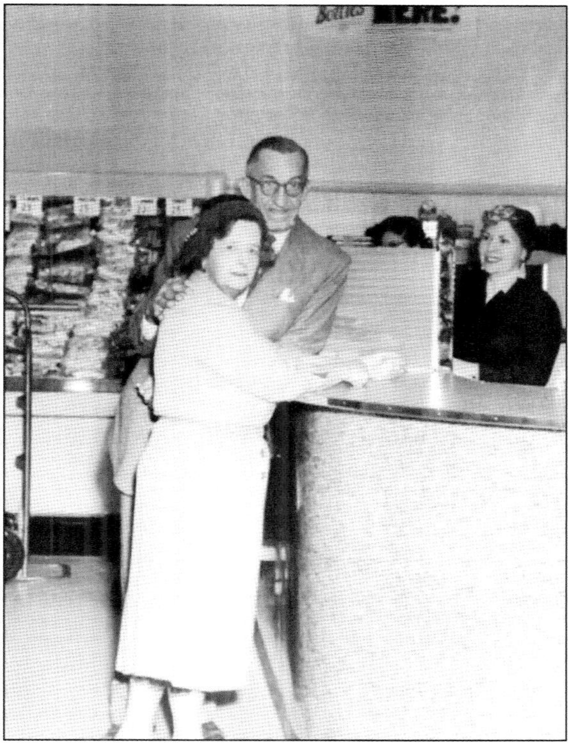

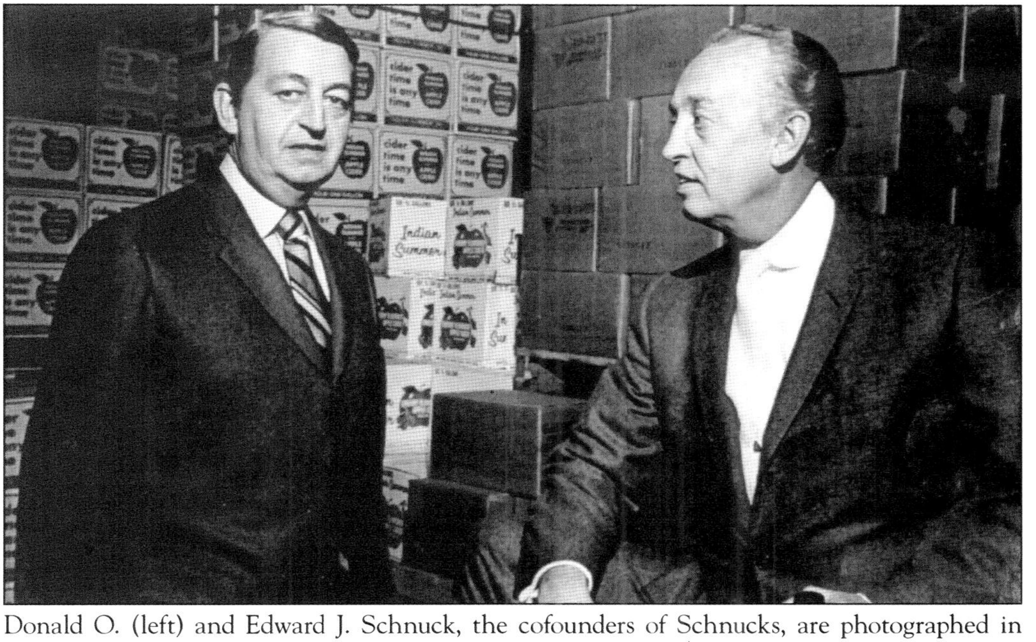

Donald O. (left) and Edward J. Schnuck, the cofounders of Schnucks, are photographed in the early 1970s. In 1970, the year ended with a sales volume of $68 million. In 1971, sales went up to $111 million, and by 1972, they were at $168 million. Today the company that started as a family confectionery has stores in Missouri, Illinois, and Indiana and employs more than 17,000 associates. (Schnucks Markets.)

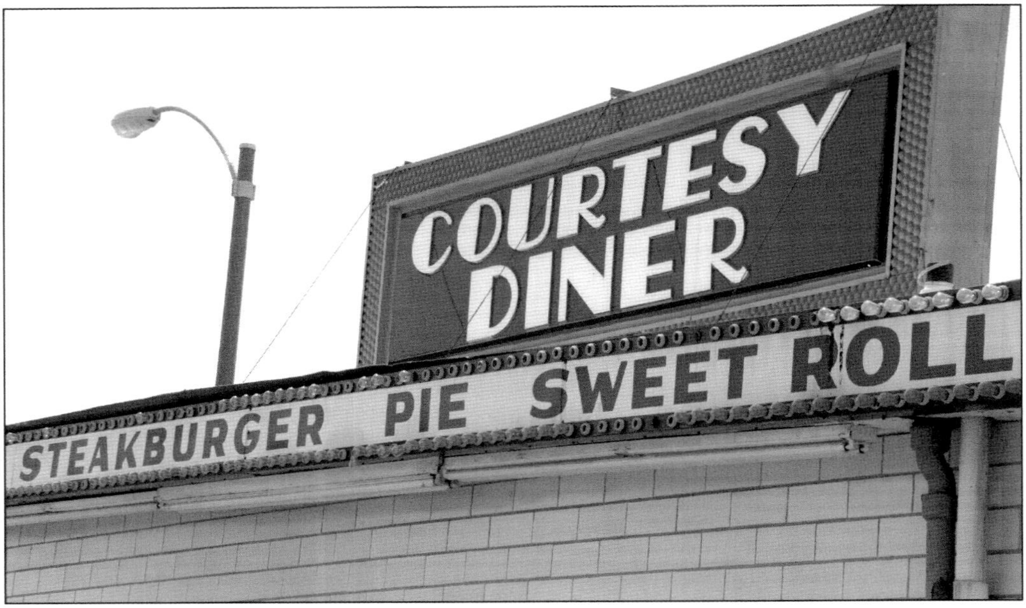


The Courtesy Diner (site B10) at 3155 South Kingshighway Boulevard was originally the Kingshighway Sandwich Shop in the 1950s and 1960s. Since it was right across the street from Southwest High School, it was a popular teen hangout. In the 1920s and 1930s, this was the site of Valley Electric Company plants No. 1, 2, and 3. The diner has a second location at 1121 Hampton Avenue. They are currently owned by Unlimited Restaurants of Chesterfield. (Derek Cadzow Photography.)

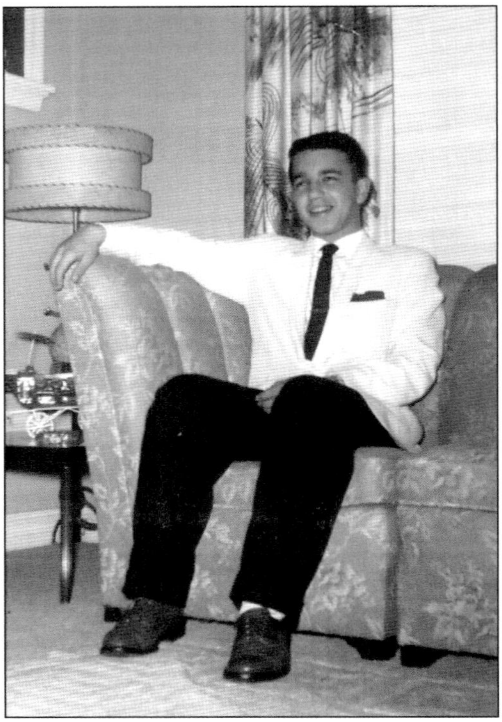

Southwest High School teen idol John Catalano was the drummer for the rock-and-roll band the Teen Tones. The bandleader was Jules Blattner, and the other members were Bob Caldwell and Harold Simons. The school had a Teen Tones Fan Club, and in 1959, Rosalie Venezia was the president. In April 1959, the band's song "Rock and Roll Blues" was in the top 30 on St. Louis radio stations WIL 1430 and KWK 1380. (Rosalie Venezia Koch collection.)

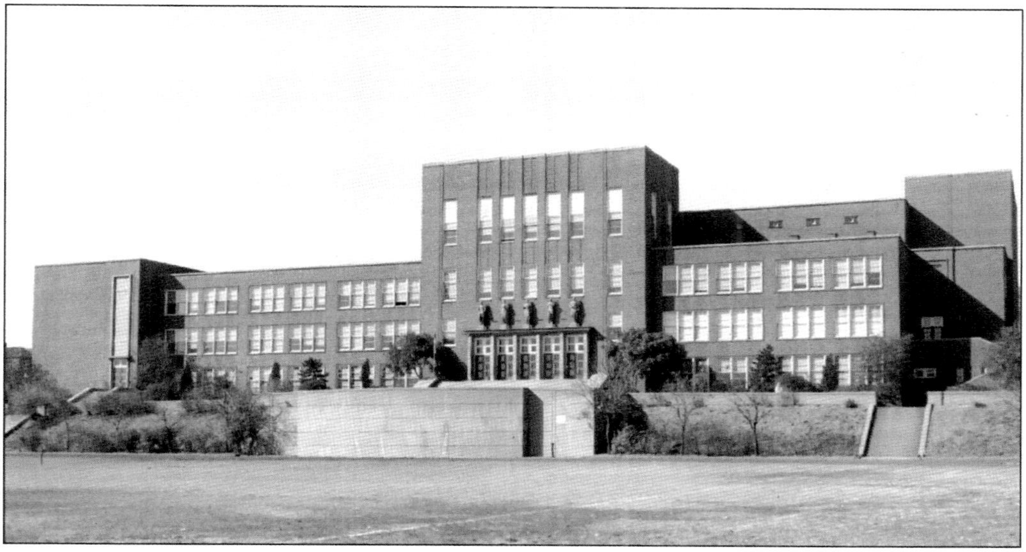

The former Southwest High School (site B11) at 3125 South Kingshighway Boulevard is now Central Visual and Performing Arts High School. The building, shown here in 1952, was erected in 1936 and built for $800,000. It was designed by George W. Sanger. Fred Morie, a 26-year-old St. Louis artist, was commissioned to design the figures over the entrance. (St. Louis Public Schools Records Center/Archives.)

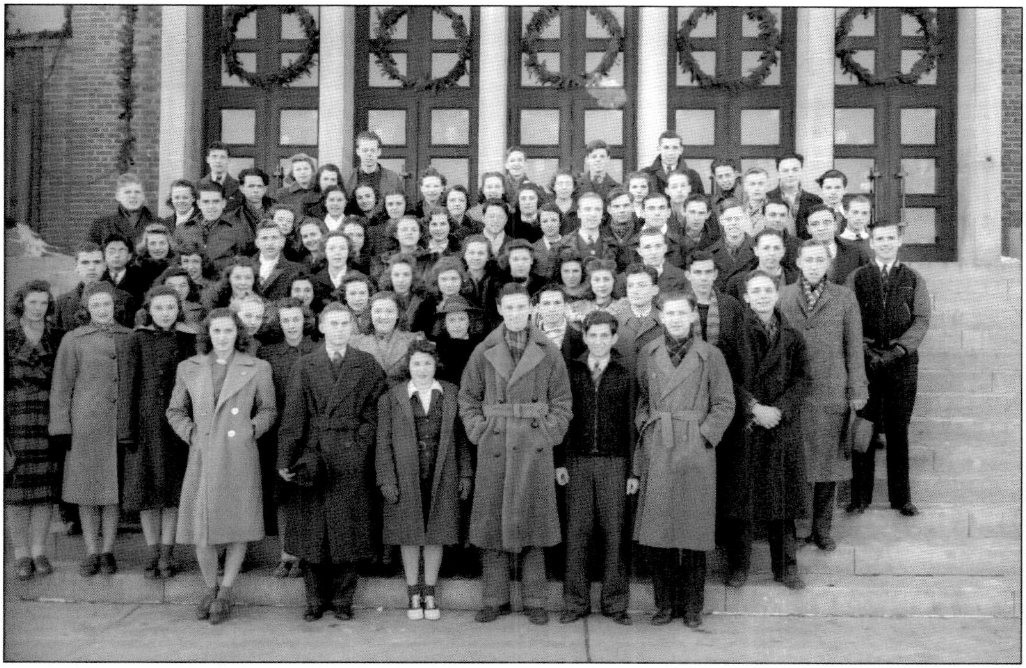

Some of the young men in the class of 1940 probably signed up to serve their country in World War II instead of signing up for college. In this time of radio, not only did Americans hear news about the war, but they also listened to the big band sounds of Glenn Miller, Tommy Dorsey, Duke Ellington, and Benny Goodman. The popular dance was the jitterbug, and zoot suits were the vogue. (St. Louis Public Schools Records Center/Archives.)

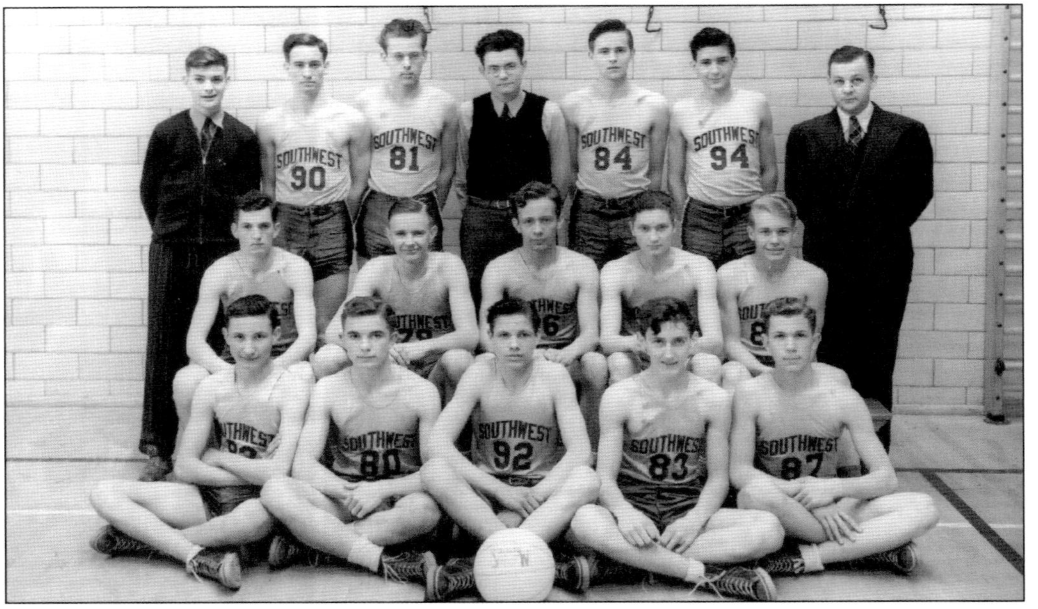


The 1939 basketball team and the teams that followed could practice in the school gymnasium, but in the 1950s and 1960s, the students on the bowling teams had to go across the street to Arway Bowling Alley, where Walgreens is today. The boys practiced on Tuesdays after school, and the girls practiced on Wednesdays and Thursdays. There were not many sports for the girls to choose from, so bowling was popular. (St. Louis Public Schools Records Center/Archives.)

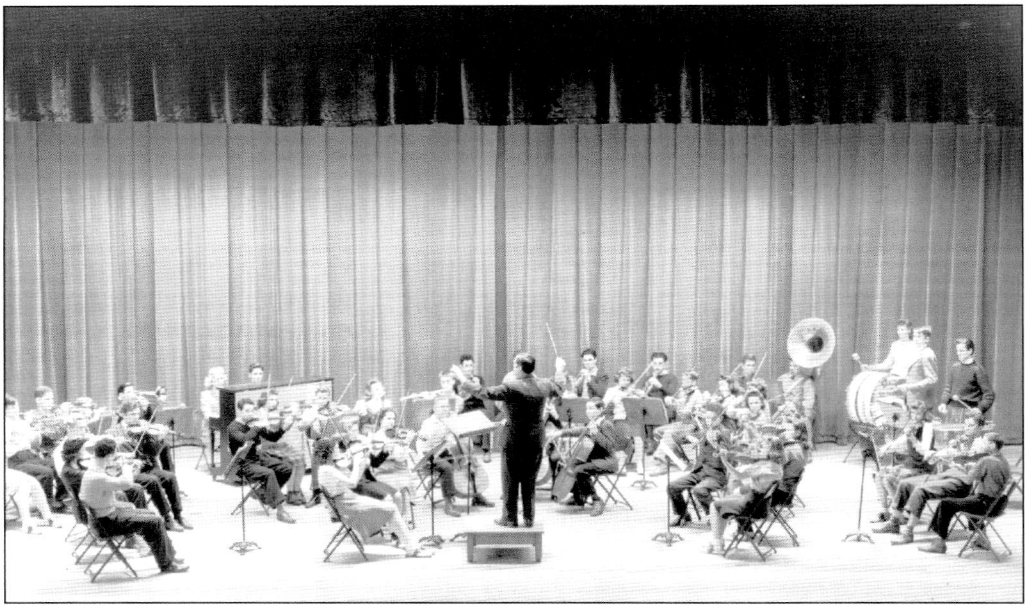

The students in the school's orchestra in 1941 were listening to the big band sounds like Glenn Miller and Duke Ellington on the radio. Jazz was popular along with swing dancing and the jitterbug. The place to listen to big bands in South St. Louis was the Casa Loma Ballroom on Cherokee Street. Today, as a visual and performing arts magnet school, students study guitar, brass, and woodwinds. (St. Louis Public Schools Records Center/Archives.)

Richard Gephardt, class of 1958, went on to receive a bachelor's degree from Northwestern University in 1962. In 1965, he graduated from the University of Michigan School of Law. From 1968 to 1971, he served as a Democratic committeeman for the City of St. Louis, and from 1971 to 1976, he served as a city alderman. He served in the U.S. House of Representatives from 1977 to January 2005. (St. Louis Public Schools Records Center/Archives and John Tanurchis.)

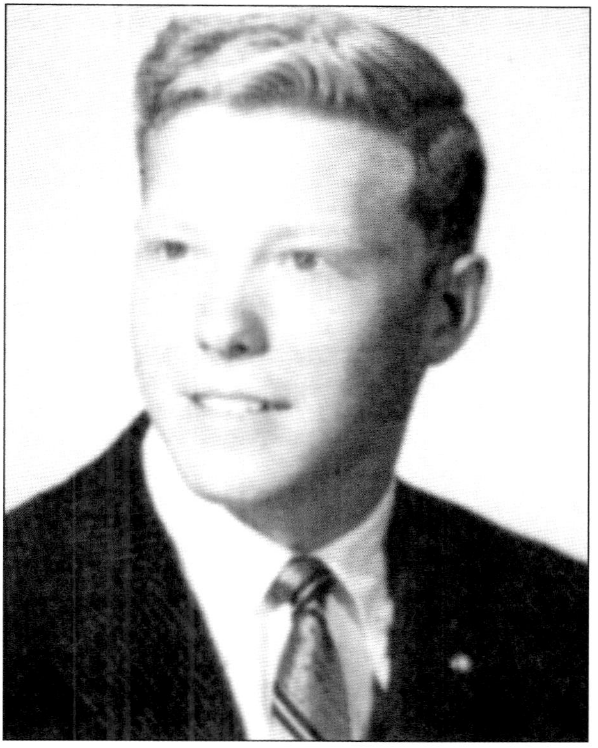

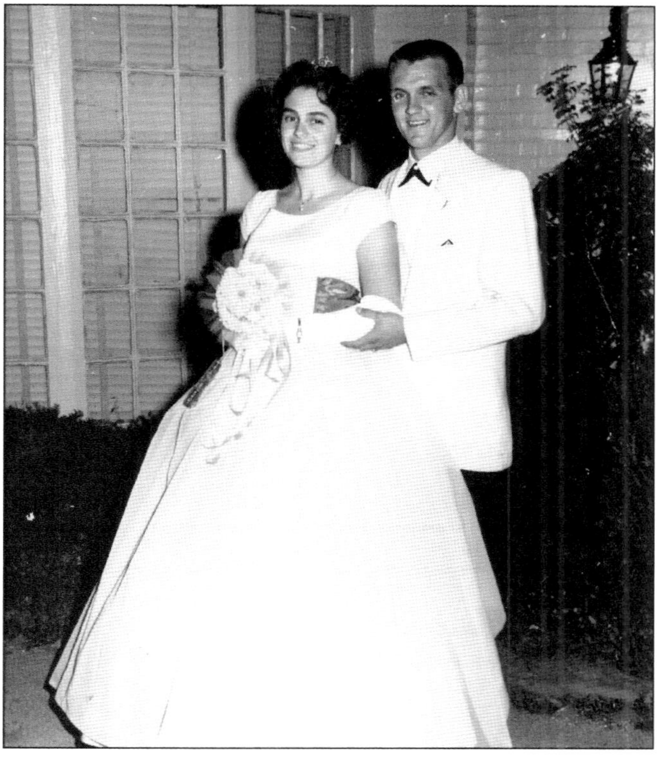

James Gahn and Rosalie Venezia attended the prom for the class of June 1961. The green and gold senior prom took place on May 26, 1961. Billy Bay provided the music. A ballot for queen and king was included in the invitation. The candidates for queen were Marylee Smith, Donna Due, Kathy Pinckert, Karen Mikes, and Janet Heitman. The candidates for king were John Stumpf, Don Flacke, Joe Hunt, Denny O'Brien, and Bob Ude. (Rosalie Venezia Koch collection.)

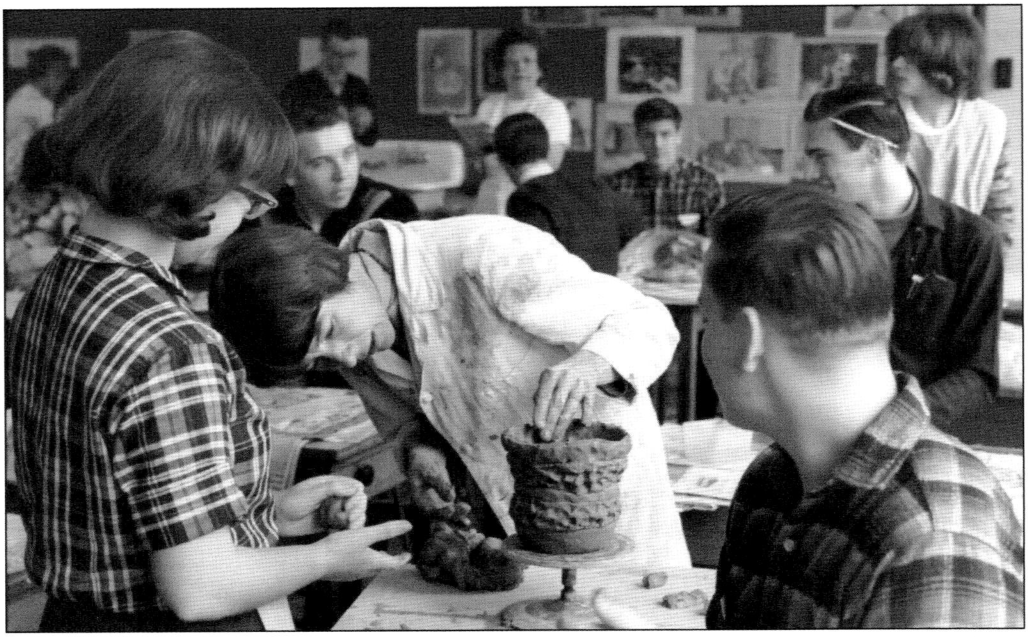

As evidenced in this art class in 1965, St. Louis schools were still segregated at this time. Even after the 1954 *Brown v. Board of Education of Topeka* decision, segregated schools were the norm for quite a few years. Most whites lived on the south side, while blacks lived in the north part of the city. (St. Louis Public Schools Records Center/Archives.)

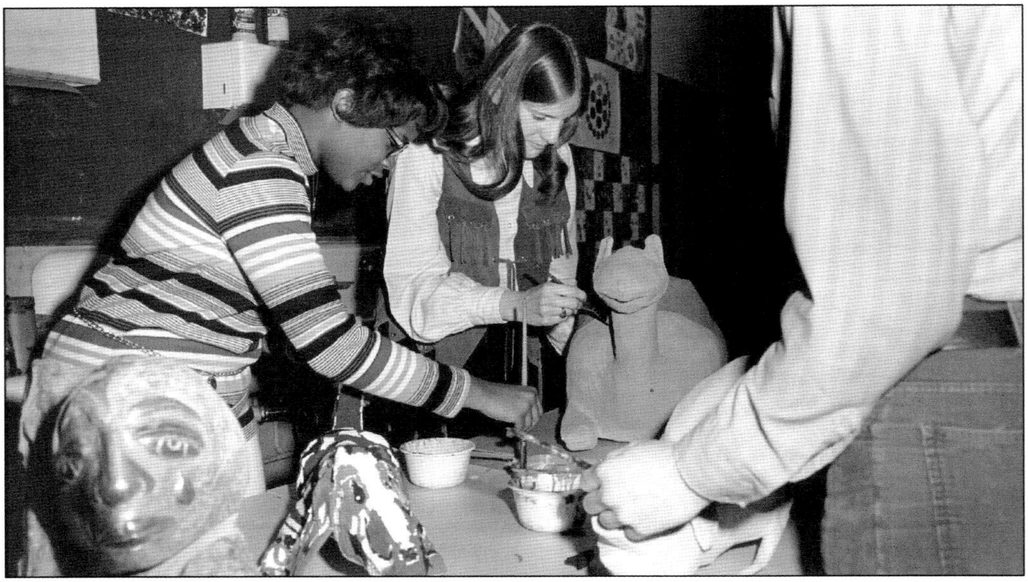

By 1974, things had changed in the classroom; whites and African Americans attended the same schools. In 1980, white students began to attend county schools. In the city schools, three students out of every four were African American. To integrate public schools, court-ordered desegregation began. African American students from the city were bused to county schools, and white county students were bused to city schools, in an effort to achieve racial balance. (St. Louis Public Schools Records Center/Archives.)

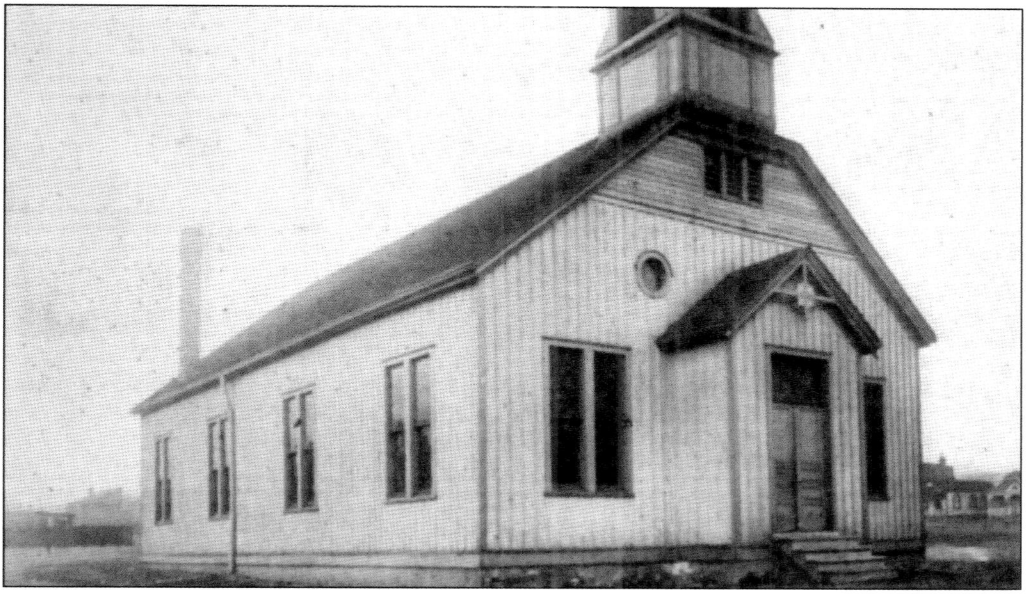

Holy Innocents Church (site B12) was the original church at 4923 Odell Street—now the Journey Church. The original church was this structure built in 1893 at Brannon Avenue and Reber Place. In 1922, the city issued a building permit to J. Smithers to set up a tent for religious services at 2801 South Kingshighway Boulevard, on the corner of Odell Street, at a cost of $100. On June 26, 2005, Holy Innocents celebrated its last mass in this structure built in 1957. (Diane Rademacher collection.)

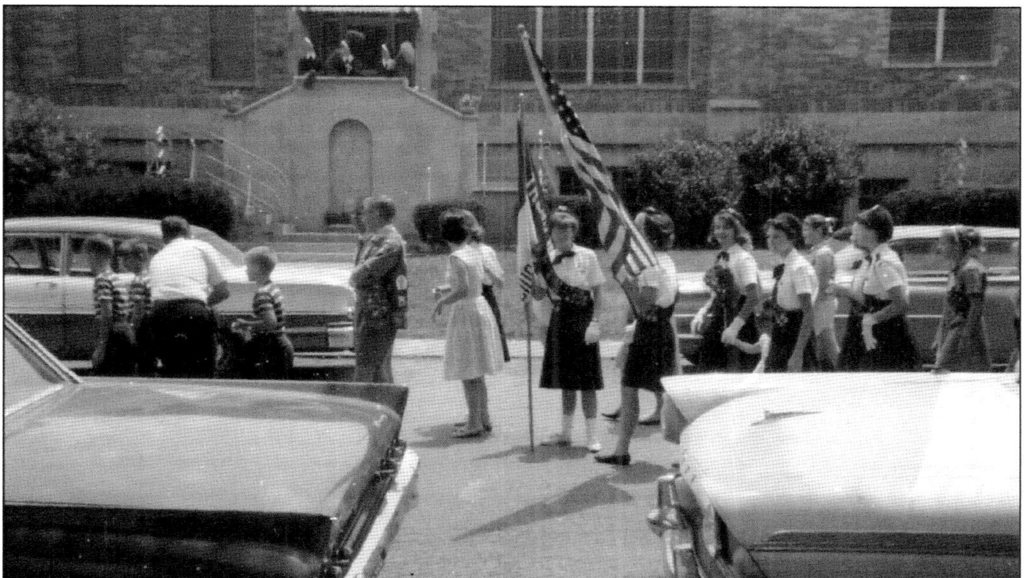

The former Holy Innocents Convent at 4900 Reber Place is now the Luminary Center for the Arts. The Girl Scouts take part in a parade in 1965 and are photographed in front of the convent. Today the people milling around the convent are artists. The Luminary Center is a not-for-profit organization that provides studio space and materials to artists at no cost. The artists pay back by working on charitable projects in the city. (Grbac family collection.)

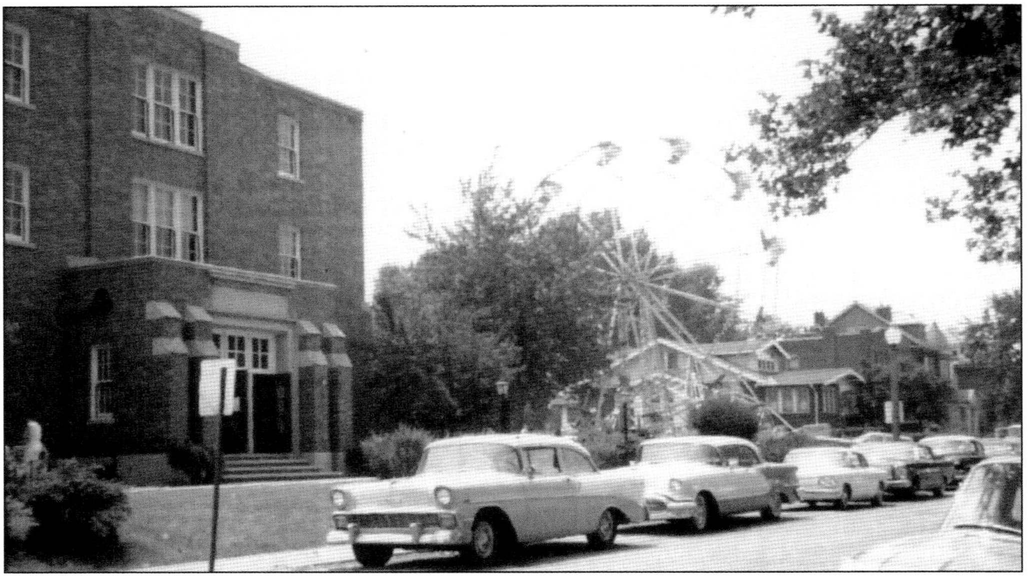

The former Holy Innocents School at 4926 Reber Place is now Epworth City School. The Epworth Children and Family Services has been part of the community for more than 140 years. It provides emergency shelter, treatment, family therapy, special education, and foster care. The organization was founded after the Civil War by the United Methodist Church to care for orphans. Today Epworth serves all children and families regardless of their religious beliefs. (Grbac family collection.)

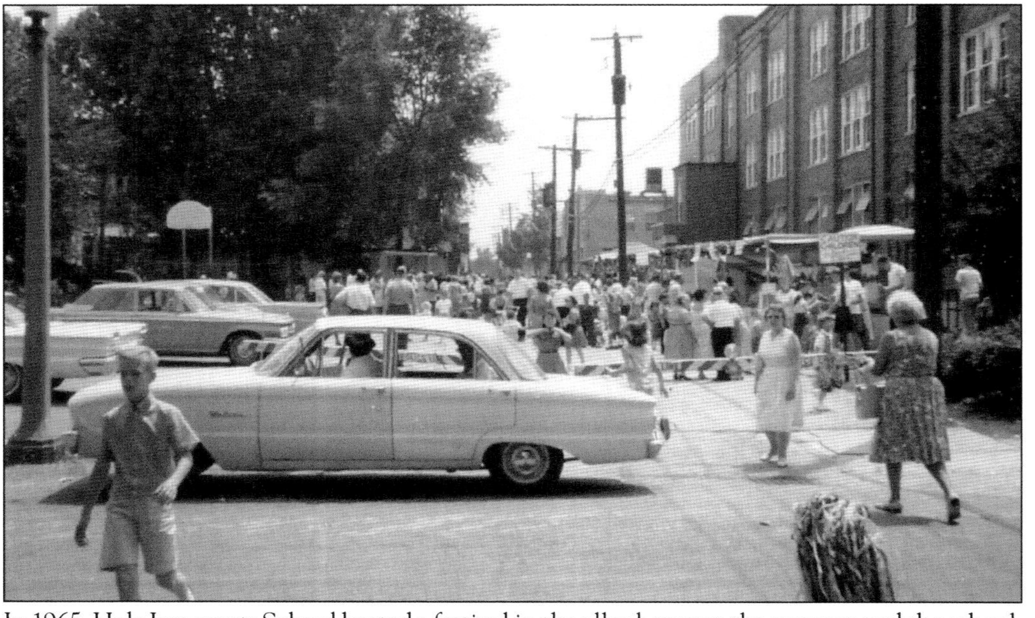

In 1965, Holy Innocents School hosted a festival in the alley between the convent and the school. In 2005, the last year the school was open, it had 94 students. In a 2005 private school report, the school had students ranging from prekindergarten to the eighth grade. The student-teacher ratio was 1 to 26. Of the students, 75.64 percent were white, 17.94 percent were black, and the rest was made up of Asians and Hispanics. (Grbac family collection)

The Gorman house (site B13) at 2823 South Kingshighway Boulevard was built in 1891. This is a Victorian Romanesque house. Through the 1880s, most of the houses being built in South St. Louis were town houses. Since most city lots measured 25 feet wide by 120 to 140 feet long, houses built on those lots had to be narrow and long. As the city grew, the lots were platted at a width of 50 feet, allowing architectural change. (Derek Cadzow Photography.)

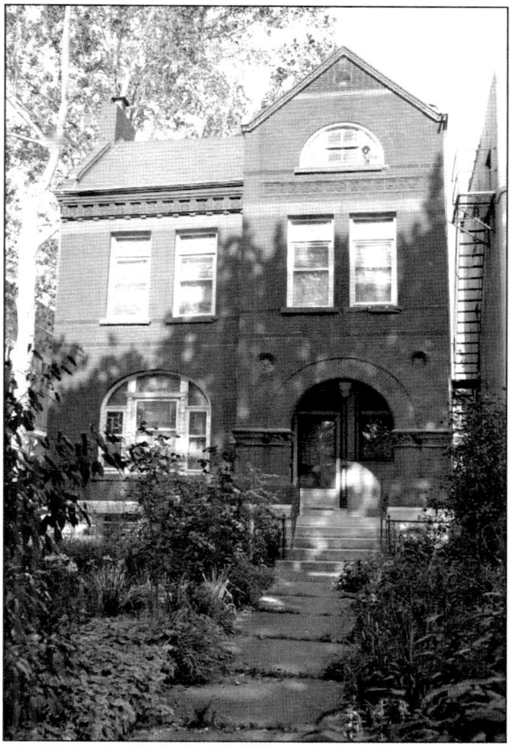

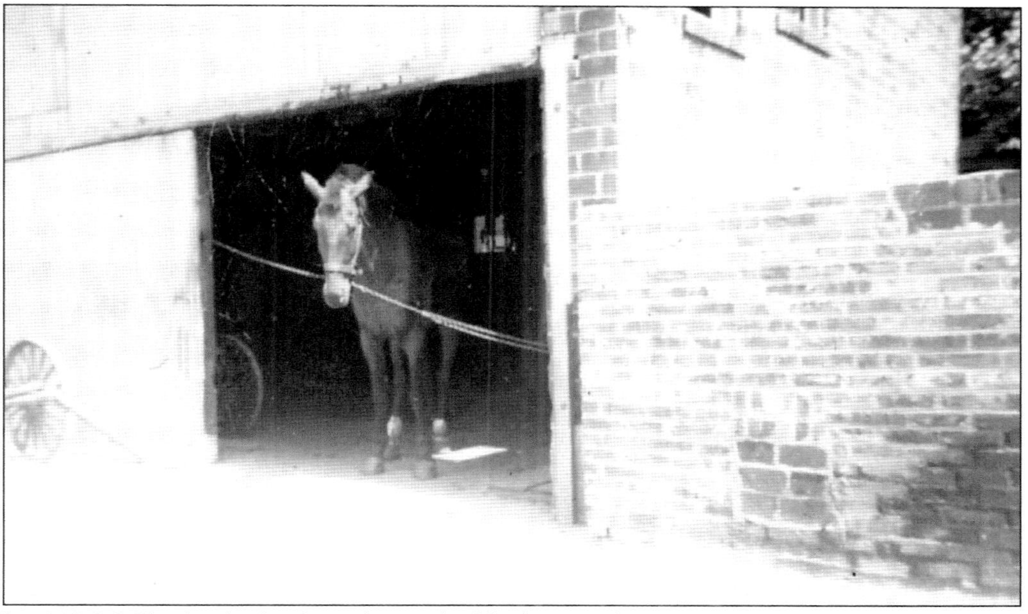

In 1907, J. J. Fletcher built a frame buggy shed for $100, and in 1924, Keyran Gorman built a brick garage for $400. The structure where the Gormans' horse was kept seems to be a combination of the two. Gorman and his son John delivered the *St. Louis Post-Dispatch* and the *Globe Democrat* newspapers in a horse-drawn wagon. By the 1950s, most of the other barns in the city were converted to just garages or apartments. (Grbac family collection.)

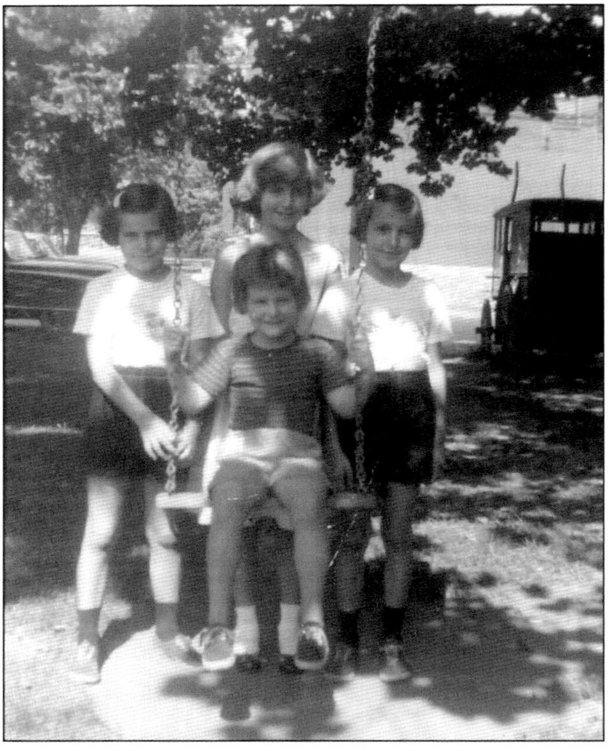

The newspaper delivery wagon was no longer in use, so it was parked on Reber Place. This photograph, taken in 1957, shows childhood friends who lived in the neighborhood. From left to right are Bebe Daniels, Sandra Gavwiner on the swing, unidentified, and Barb Daniels. The girls' picture was taken in the Gavwiners' yard at 4917 Reber Place. The Gavwiners rented the carriage house in back of 2737 South Kingshighway Boulevard. (Grbac family collection.)

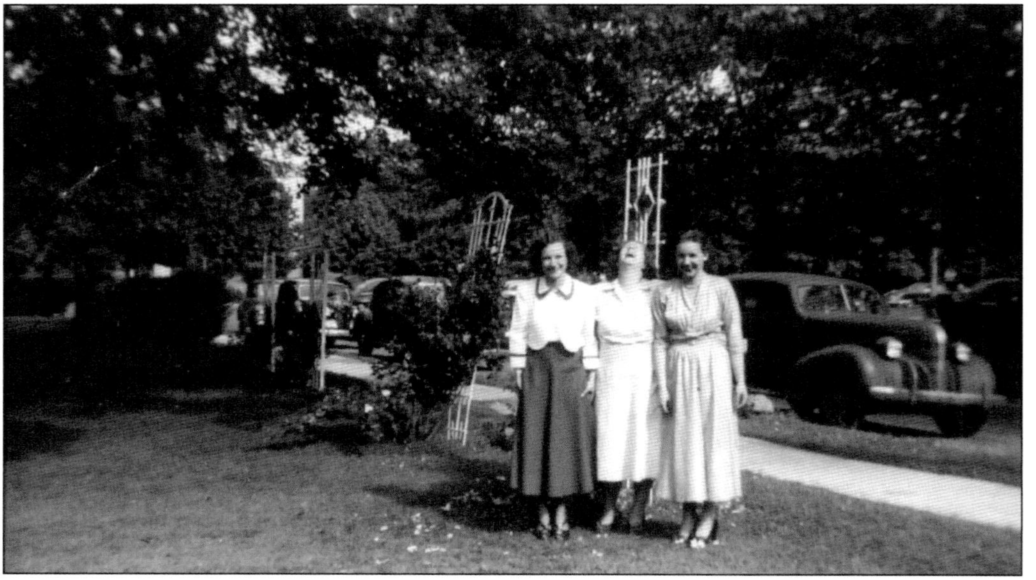

Pictured from left to right, these young ladies, Marian Rieper, Juanita Sternamm, and Audrey Gavwiner, are enjoying each other's company as they pause for a photograph in the 1950s. Residents of the Southwest Garden, as is true of most South St. Louis residents, grew up here, married, and stayed to raise their children in this close-knit community. Audrey and her husband, Leroy, lived at 4917 Reber Place and then at 2737 South Kingshighway Boulevard. (Grbac family collection.)

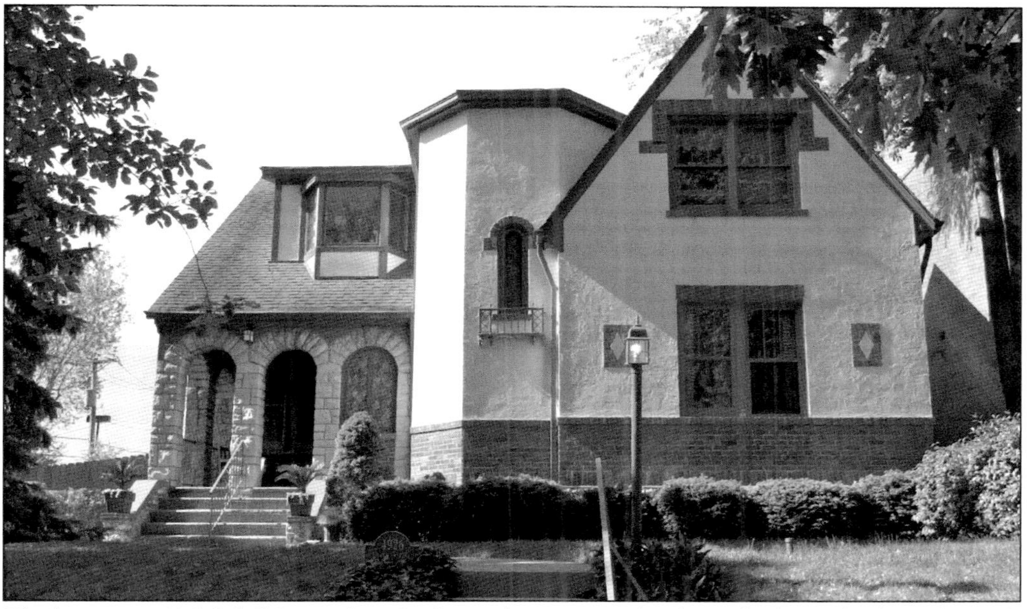

The house at 4926 Odell Street (site B14) is a classic example of a Tudor home built in the early 1900s. The entry is different from most of the other Tudors in this area, as it has a porch. Typical of this design, the exterior is composed of multiple materials with patterned stone, brickwork, and stucco walls. There are many other examples of Tudor houses in the Southwest Garden. (Derek Cadzow Photography.)

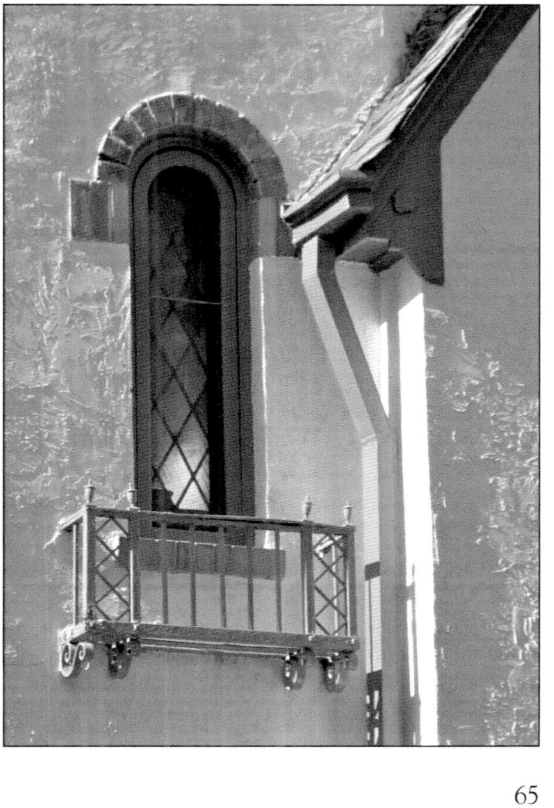

In 1930, the city directory lists Edward A. and Irene Doerr as residents of the home pictured. Edward was a part owner of Doerr and Engel Oil and Supply. The company's office was at 2642 Michigan Avenue, and the station was at 2702 Brannon Avenue. In 1940, Edward was still living there, but Irene is not listed. By 1952, there were new residents, Earl H. and Margaret M. Gimple. Earl owned a grocery at 1817 Tower Grove Avenue. (Derek Cadzow Photography.)

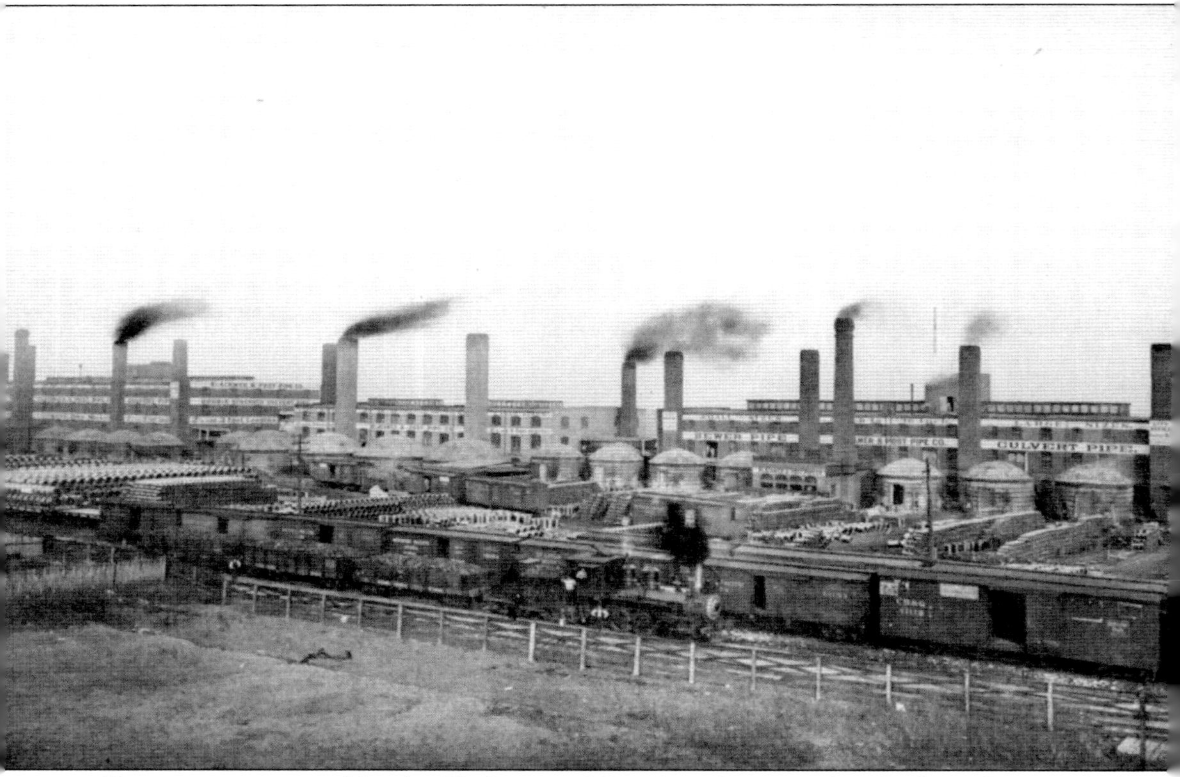

Here is acreage owned by the Blackmer and Post Pipe Company (site B15) at 2701 Hereford Street. This photograph, taken by George Stark around 1906 for *St. Louis Today*, shows the expanse of the factory at the Missouri Pacific Railway and Arsenal Street. The Laclede-Christy Granview No. 17 Mine was on Southwest Avenue. The Arrow No. 1 Mine Van Cleave was close by at 6500 Southwest Avenue. The Laclede-Christy Mine No. 11 was at Columbia Avenue, Hampton Avenue, Elizabeth Avenue, and Sulphur Avenue. The Laclede-Christy Mines No. 1 and No. 2 were at Hampton Avenue, January Avenue, Columbia Avenue, and Wilson Avenue. The Krummel and Buchner Mine was at Columbia Avenue and Fifty-ninth Street. The Guelker No. 4 Mine was at Stephen Avenue, Sublette Avenue, Elizabeth Avenue, and Bischoff Avenue. The Laclede-Christy No. 4 Mine was at Columbia Avenue, Sublette Avenue, Wilson Avenue, and Edwards Street. The Edwards and Hereford Mines were at Marconi Avenue, Southwest Avenue, and Kingshighway Boulevard. The largest mine was Blackmer Post at Arsenal Street and the railroad, Columbia Avenue, and Kingshighway Boulevard. At one time, Blackmer Post owned 60 acres in the area. (Missouri History Museum.)

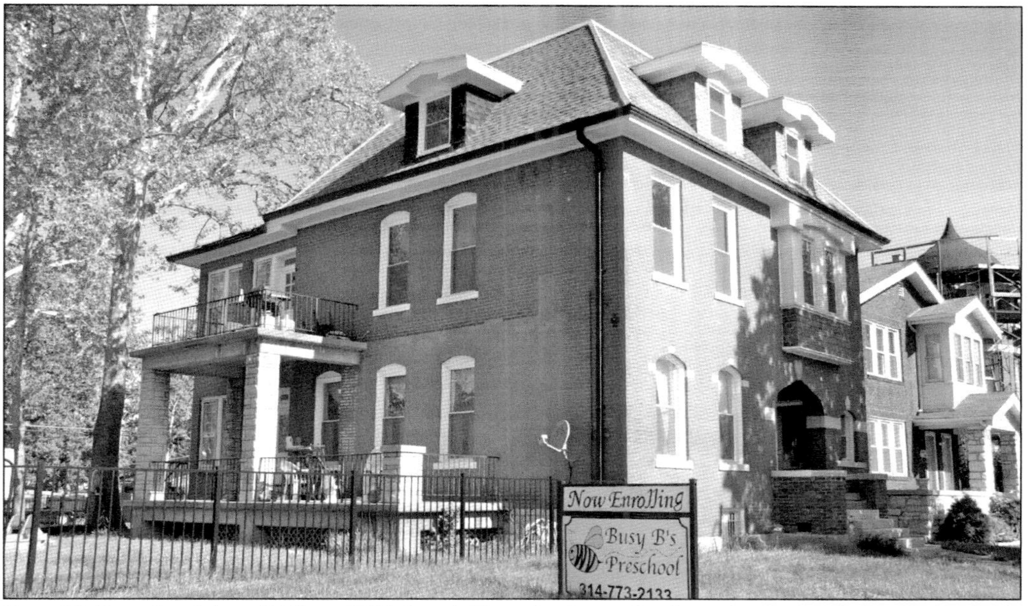


Busy B's Preschool (site B16) at 2737 South Kingshighway Boulevard is located in a house built in 1885. In 1893, owner A. L. Ludwig made repairs. In 1897, he built an addition, and in 1903, he repaired the porch. In 1908, owner Marie Woltman built on to the structure at a cost of $5,300. By 1922, the new owner is listed as F. Ebbler, and in 1930, the new owner and resident was Julia Noonan. (Derek Cadzow Photography.)

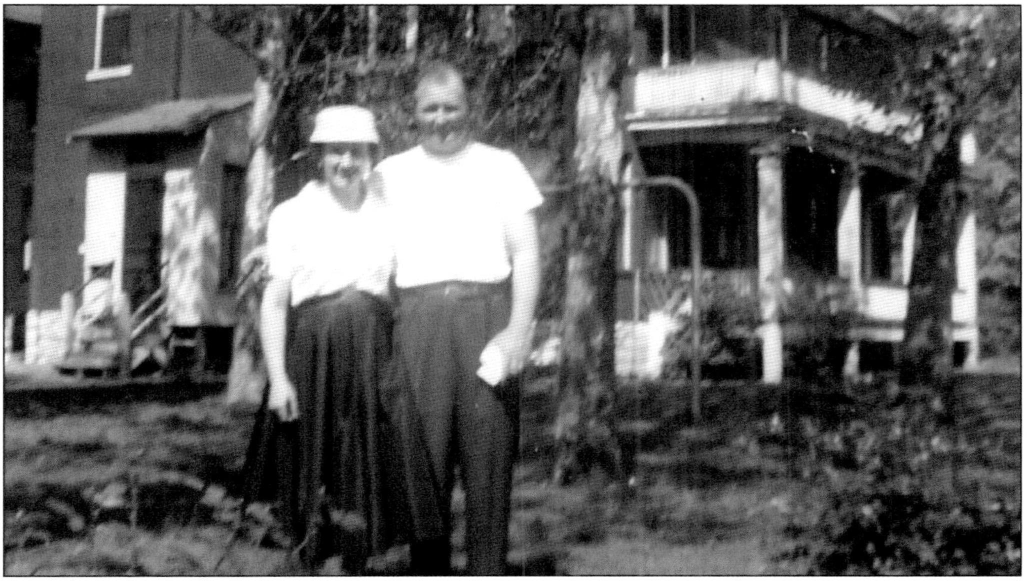

Audrey and Leroy Gavwiner lived in a home on South Kingshighway Boulevard in 1958. Before that, they rented the carriage house in back of the property. The current owners, Kenneth and Barbara Garthe, bought the property in 1984 and continued to operate the units as rentals. Recently they made renovations and converted the structure into two separate spaces. The preschool is on the first floor, and the townhouse consists of the second and third floors. (Grbac family collection.)

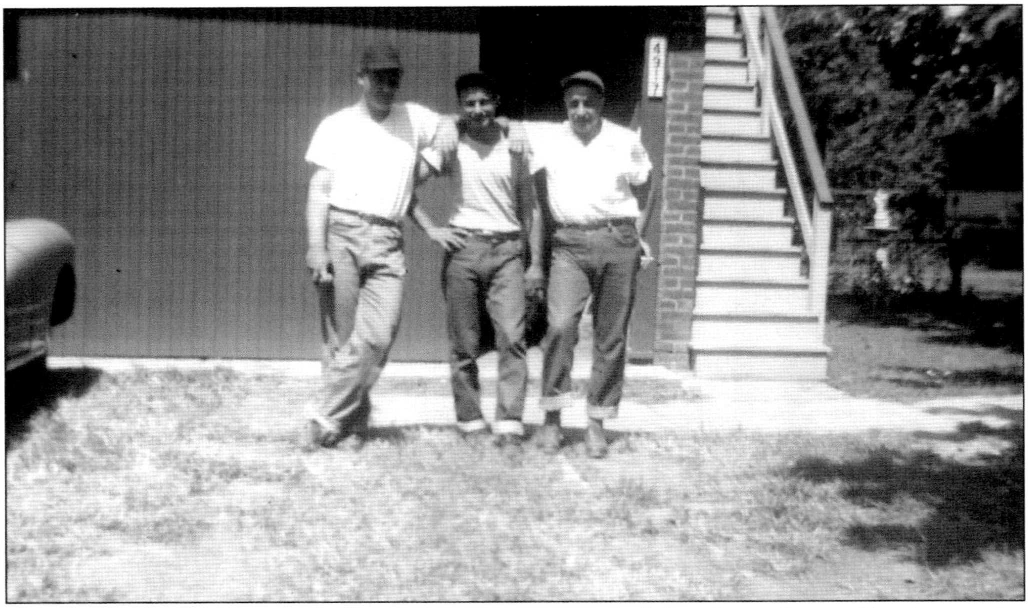

Leroy Gavwiner (left) takes a break with his unidentified friends in front of his home, the carriage house on Reber Place. This location was originally a two-story horse stable built in 1899 for A. L. Ludwig for $400. Later the first level of the stable was turned into a garage, and the second level became an apartment. Many carriage houses in the city have been turned into homes, with their entrances located in the alley. (Grbac family collection.)

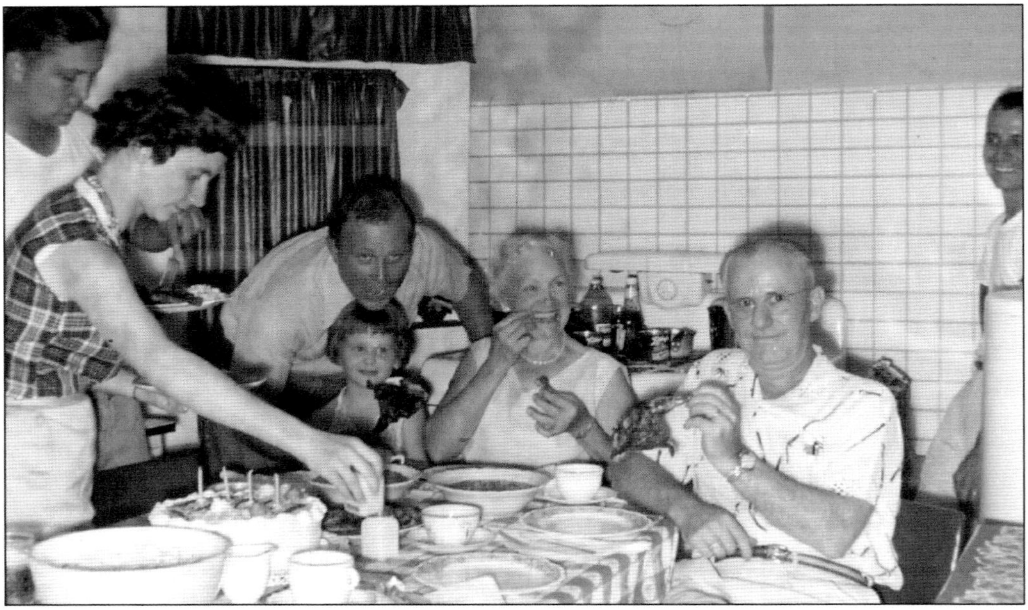

Sandra (Gavwiner) Grbac celebrates her birthday surrounded by family at Reber Place. From left to right are Bob Gavwiner, Marian Rieper, Leroy Gavwiner, Sandra, May Rieper, Harry Kaufmann, and unidentified. The Gavwiners lived in the carriage house until Sandra was eight, then they moved to the house in front of the carriage house. Sandra still lives in the neighborhood on Botanical Avenue. (Grbac family collection.)

The Wofford house (site B17) at 4940 Magnolia Avenue was built in the late 1800s. The original owner was a Mrs. Wolff, who is listed as the owner in building permits that were issued in 1901 and 1904. In 1908, Mrs. Wolff had an addition built to the dwelling for $1,500. Photographed in the living room are Anne and Ted Ferguson, the grandparents of Theodore J. Wofford. George H. and Dorothy G. Wofford bought the house in 1953. (Stephen Burns collection.)

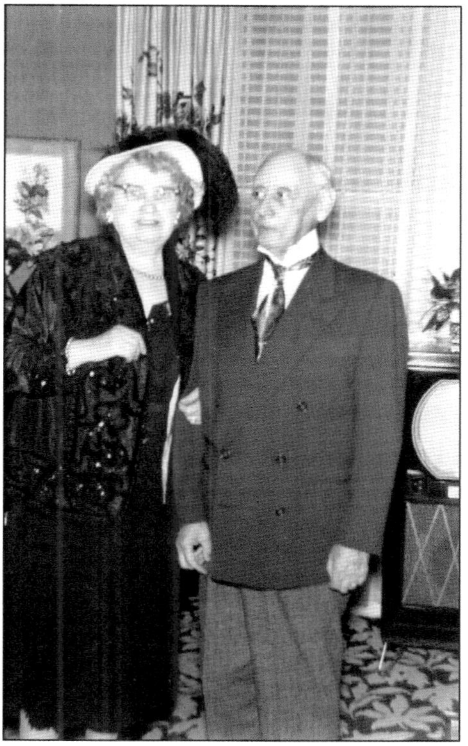

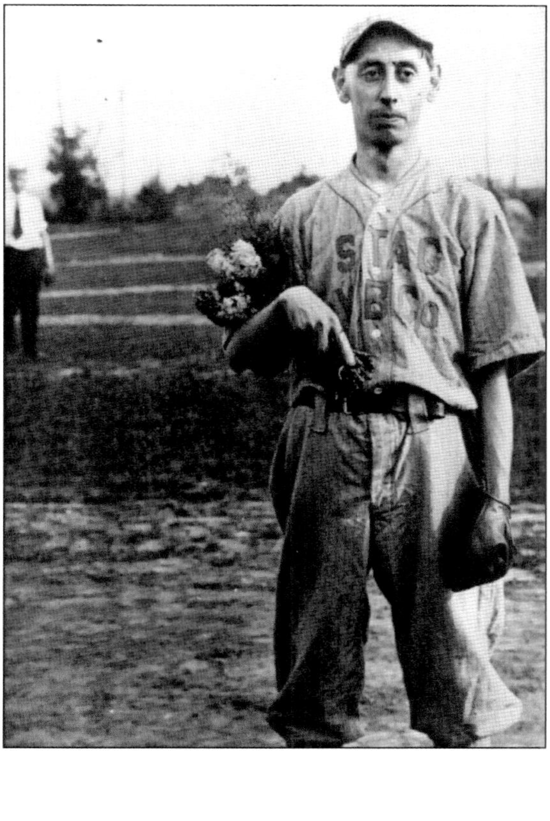

Ted Ferguson, in uniform, poses for the camera in the early 1900s. Ferguson played for an amateur baseball club in St. Louis, similar to today's minor-league baseball. He is cradling a bouquet of flowers given to him by his teammates for pitching a no-hitter in the ninth ending. He was offered a chance to play for the St. Louis Cardinals but turned it down. His wife, Anne, reminded him, "No God fearing man should play baseball on Sundays." (Stephen Burns collection.)

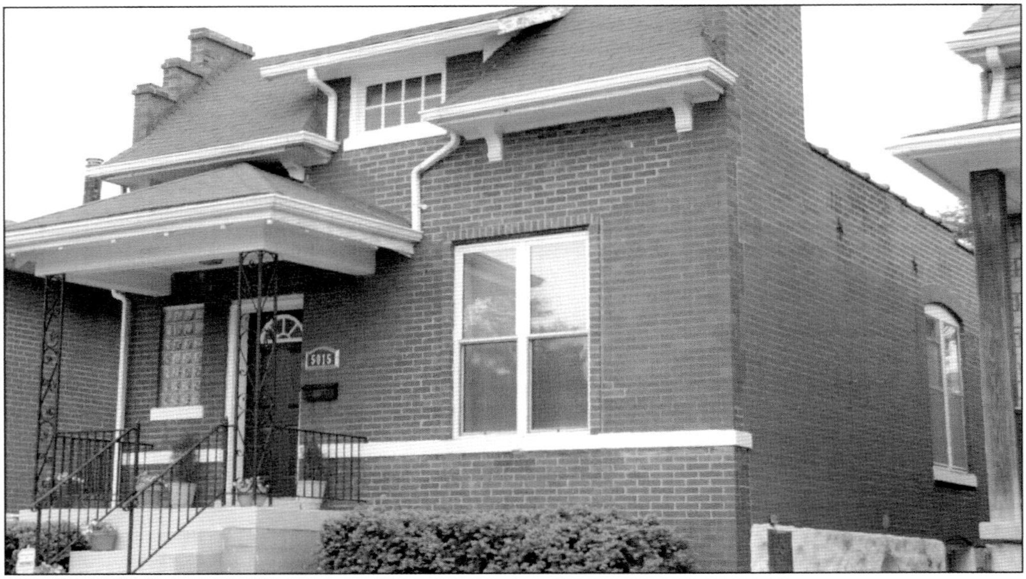

The one-story house with the illusion of having two stories (site B18) was built in 1912 at 5015 Columbia Avenue. The city granted owner Sam Koplar permission to build six houses from 5009–5023 Columbia Avenue for $12,000. Houses designed in this style were built to make them look larger. The illusion is possible when viewing the house head-on, as evidenced in this photograph. When the house is viewed from the side, it is clear there is only one floor. (Photograph by Renée Crane.)

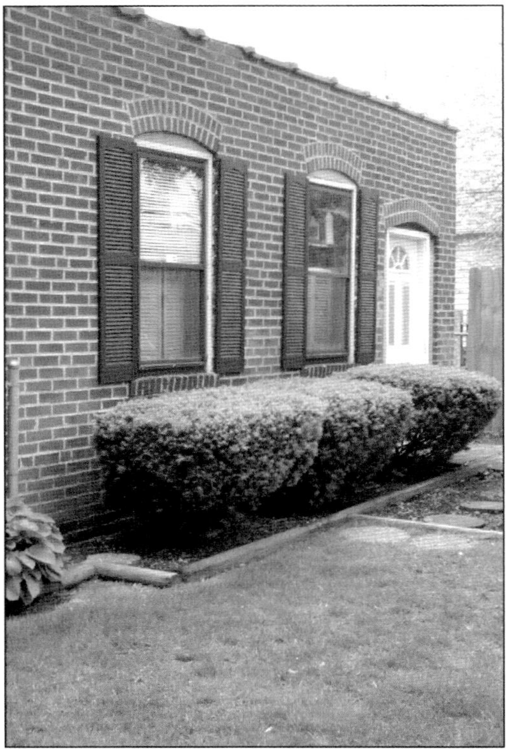

This old mule barn on Columbia Avenue from the early 1900s is now the garage of current owners John and Carolyn Stelzer. Carolyn remembers her grandfather Ernest Ranzini working for the Blackmer and Post Pipe Company that was located in this area. The company used teams of mules for hauling materials. On the lawn in front of the old barn, the Stelzers built a boccie ball court and an Italian courtyard for family gatherings. (Photograph by Renée Crane.)

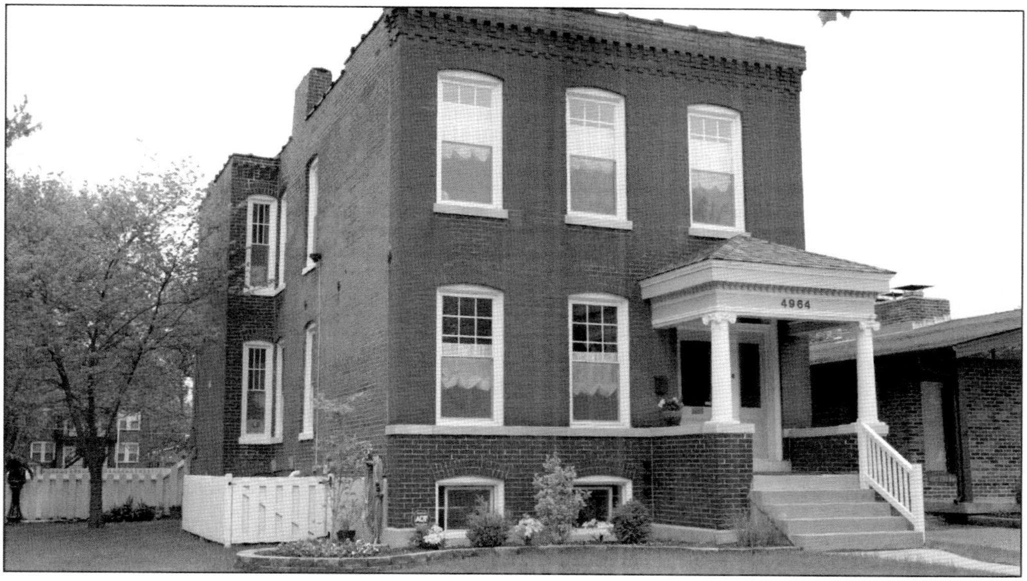


Pictured is the Evans home (site B19) at 4964 Columbia Avenue. The home was built in 1908 for $4,000 by William Evans, a local contractor. He also built a stable the same year. By 1920, it was a two-family residence; William and Elizabeth Evans lived in one part, and William B. and Erma Robinson lived in the other. By 1930, the Robinsons moved downstairs, and Elizabeth moved upstairs after being widowed. (Photograph by Renée Crane.)

In the 1940s, the house was still a two-family dwelling with the Robinsons residing downstairs and Anna Gautsche living upstairs in 4964A. William B. Robinson was a clerk at Shapleigh Hardware and Company. This neighborhood, like other city neighborhoods, has a large stock of houses that were once two- and four-family apartments being converted into single– and two–town house units in recent years. The larger houses were once boardinghouses catering to young professional men and widows. (Derek Cadzow Photography.)

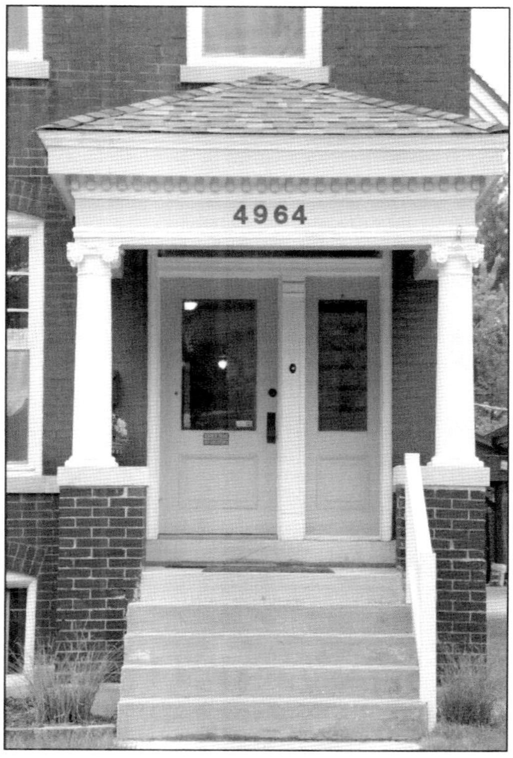

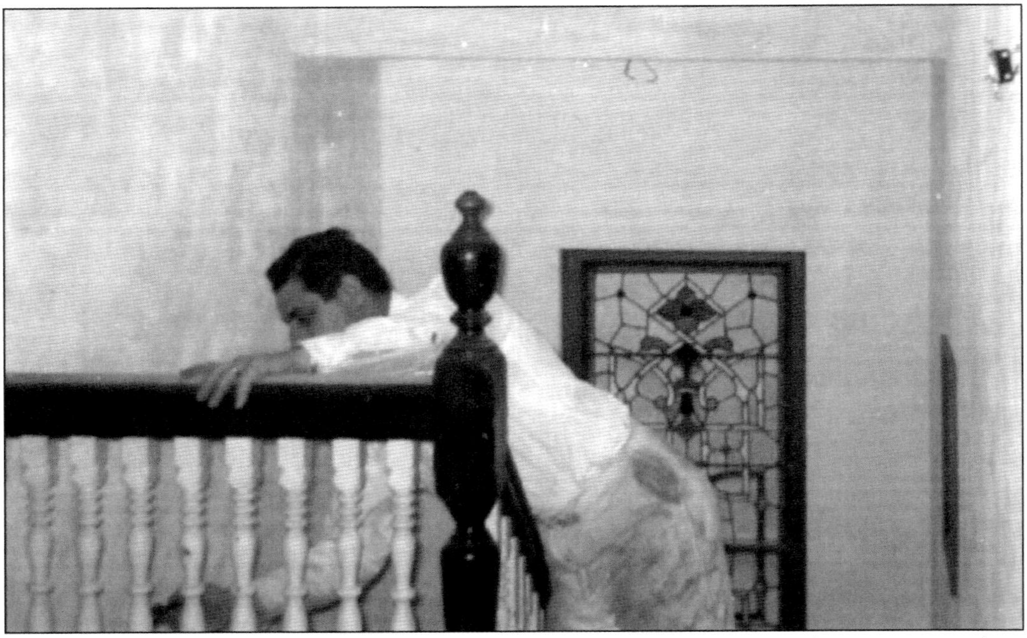

In 1965, the owners of 4934 Columbia Avenue (site B20) decided to have the staircase in their house painted. Friend Pat Pisani, the painter, is leaning over the staircase, and in the background, one of the two original stained-glass windows left in this house is visible. The house was built in the late 1800s for Thomas A. Tobin. Tobin and his business partner, George J. Iggens, had a poultry company at 921–923 North Broadway. (Madalon family collection.)

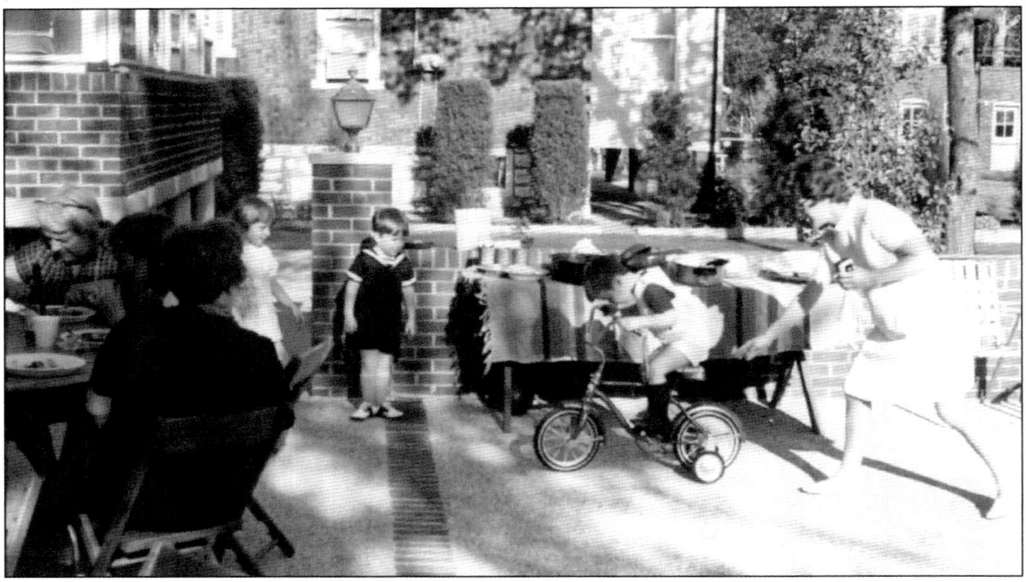

The Madalon family gathers in the backyard to celebrate Lenny's third birthday in 1970. The ladies sitting at the table are, from left to right, Dena Madalon, unidentified, and Estelle Madalon. The others are, from left to right, Jill Madalon, Jerry Daues, Lenny Madalon, and Carol Madalon. Today most of the family lives in the neighborhood, and there are relatives on Columbia Avenue and South Kingshighway Boulevard. (Madalon family collection.)

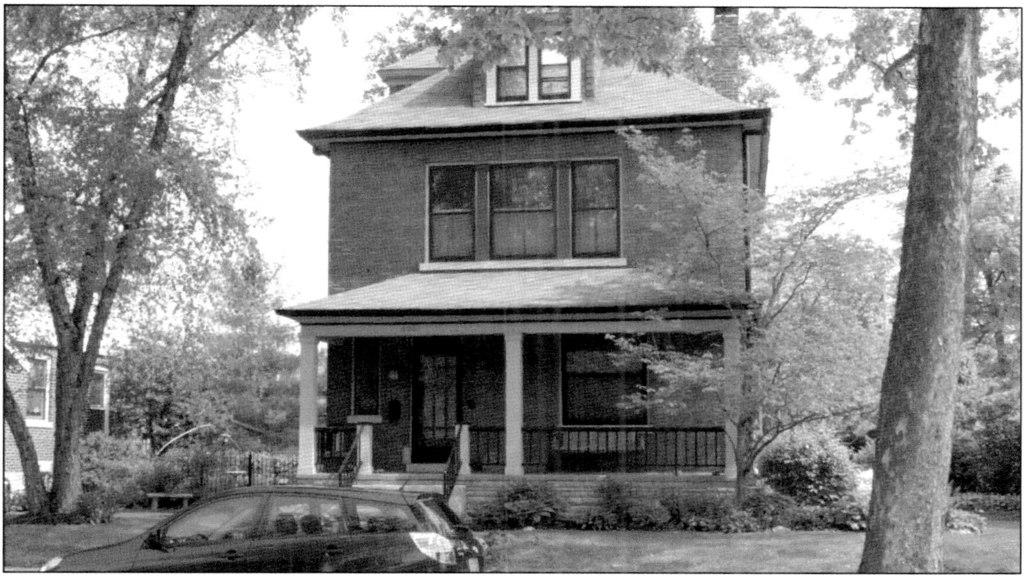

This house on Columbia Avenue, along with No. 4921, No. 4925, and No. 4927, was built in 1906. The city issued a building permit to W. E. Jones to build four houses for $14,000 and four one-story frame coal sheds for $120. In the 1930 city directory, Paul R. and Adeline V. Dolvin are listed as the residents here, and in the other half of the house, the residents were Homer B. and Lillie McKnight. Paul was a purchasing agent, and Homer was a salesman. (Derek Cadzow Photography.)

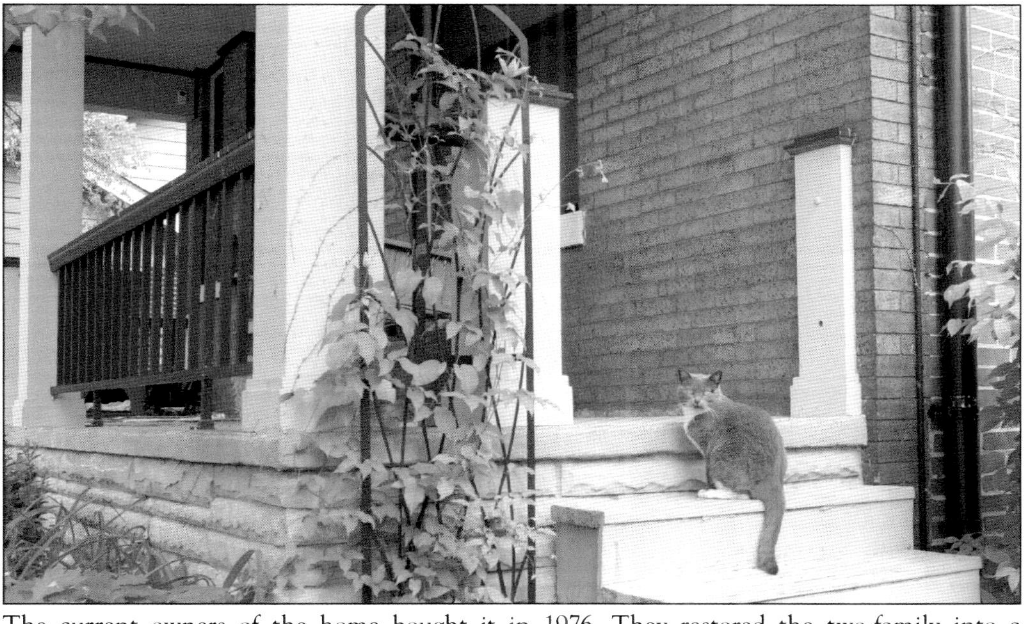

The current owners of the home bought it in 1976. They restored the two-family into a single-family home. This house is a good example of the prairie style. Prairie homes were built between 1900 and 1920. This one is one of the most common forms: vernacular. The porch, front door, and third floor dormer are typical of this style. After World War I, this style became less popular. (Derek Cadzow Photography.)

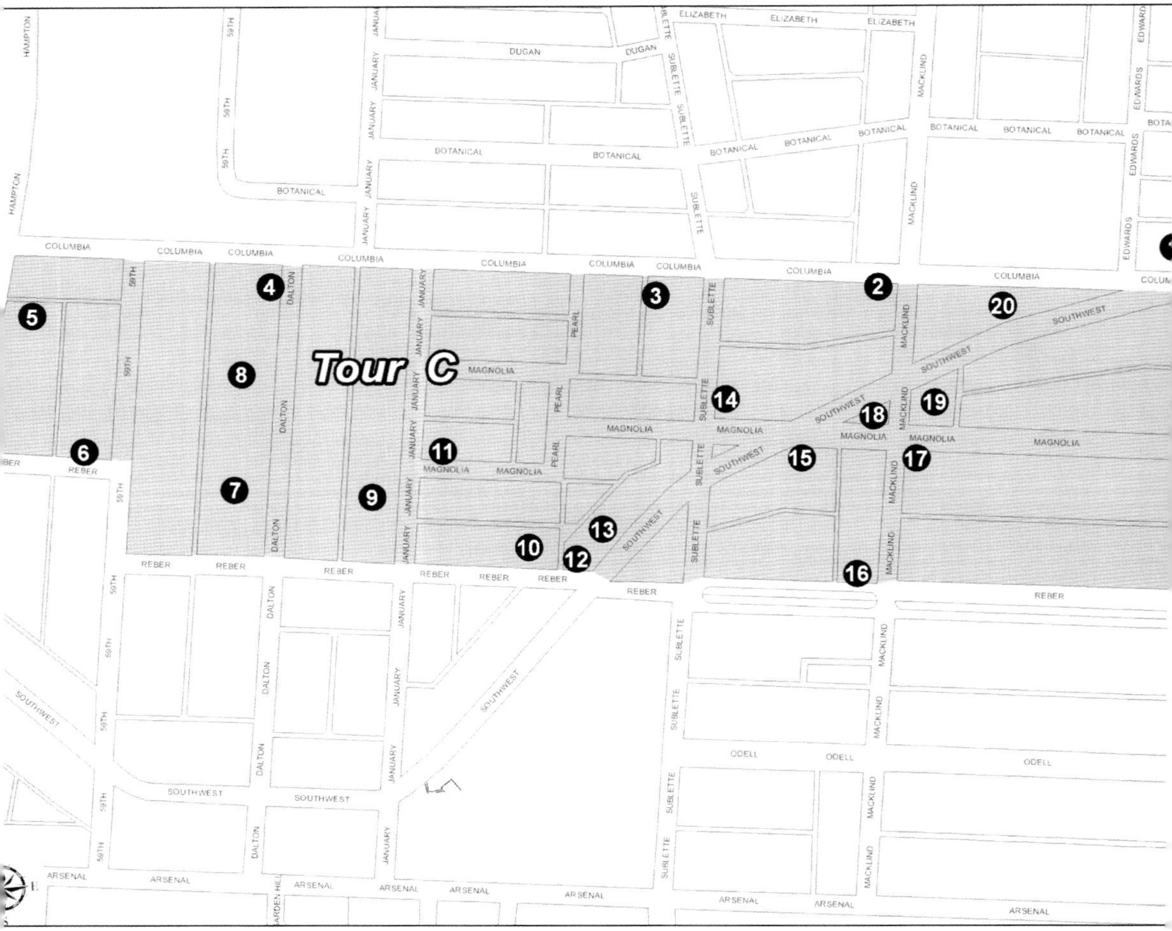


This is a map of Tour C by Shari L. Maxwell-Mooney. (Planning and Urban Design Agency City of St. Louis.)

# *Three*

# Tour C

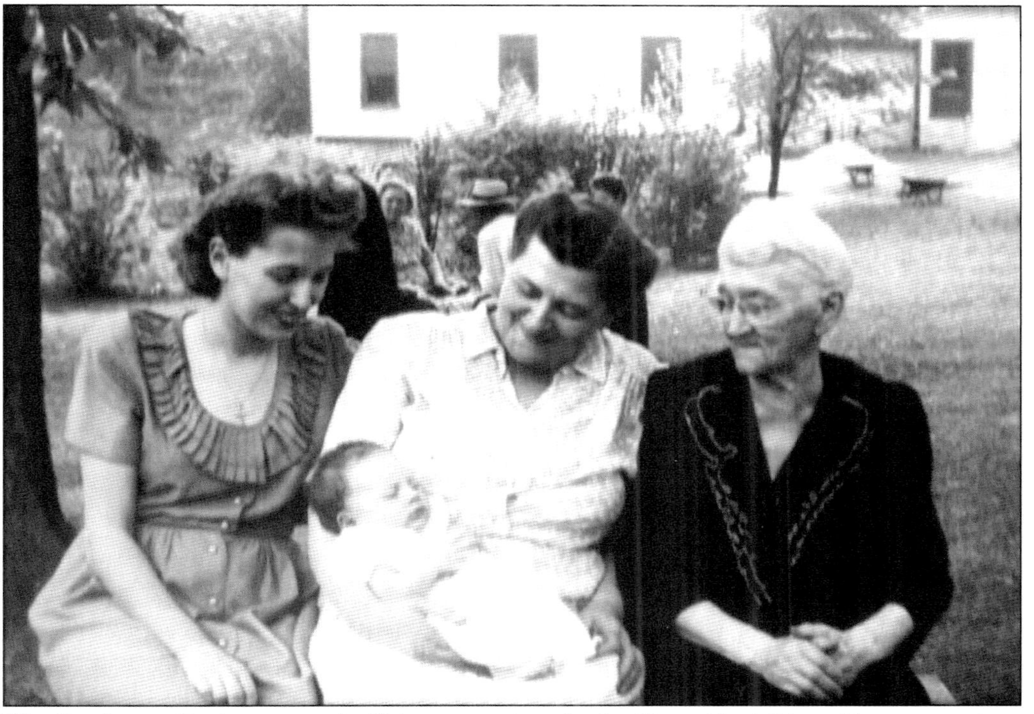

The Southwest Garden was and still is a great place for families with children. Four generations of the Wolf family are represented in this photograph: from left to right, Clara Seibel, Elizabeth Wolf holding infant Conrad Seibel Jr., and Anna Ulrich. The neighborhood had a movie theater, several confectioneries, groceries, churches, a park, a shoe cobbler, and a drugstore. Today there are markets, restaurants, retail shops, and the park, plenty of fun places to entertain kids and grown-ups. (Owens family collection.)

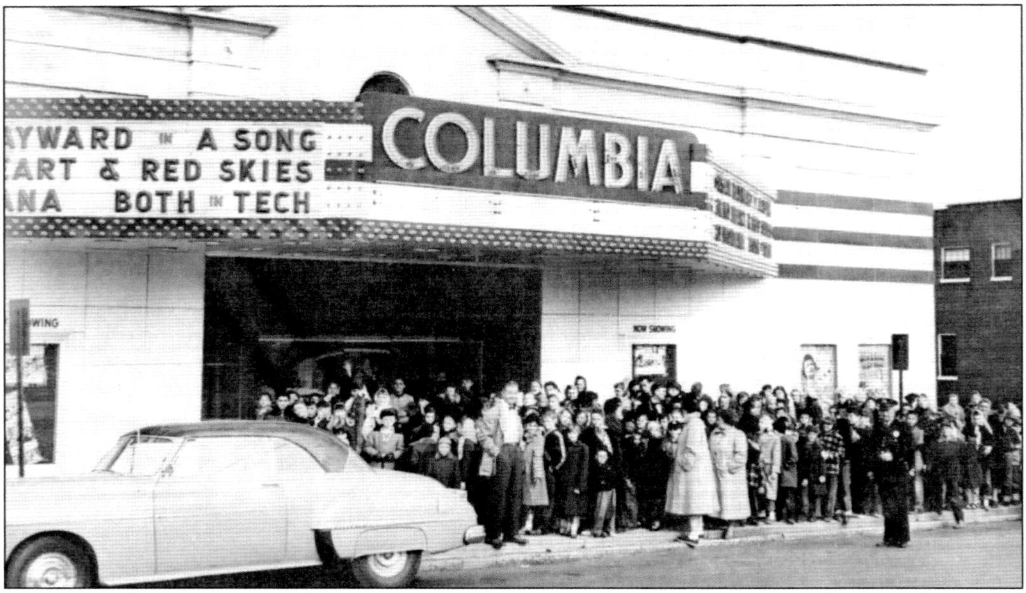


The Columbia Movie Theatre (site C1) at 5333 Columbia Avenue has a new face. This photograph was discovered by Rose Tappella while she was going through some family papers. Joann Arpiani gave the photograph to the current owner of the property, artist Frank Schwaiger. The theater had the support of the community. According to an article in the July 1984 *Hill 2000*, Carl Hanneke of Hanneke Hardware sponsored matinees at the theater. (Frank Schwaiger collection.)

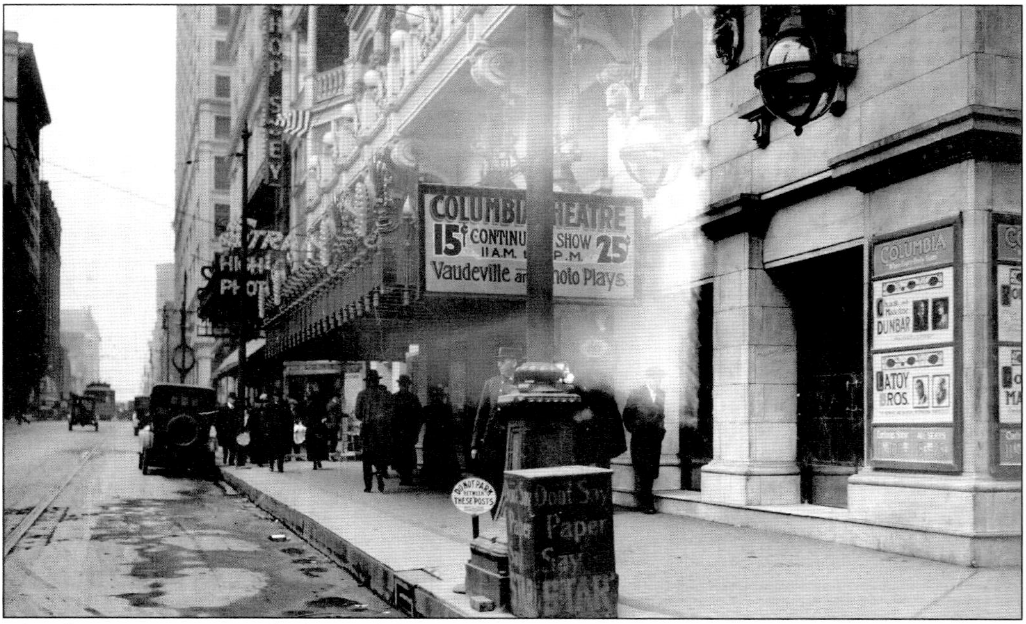


The theater was originally located downtown at 425 Sixth Street. In an article titled "Home Theater," written by Jeannette Cooperman for the May/June 2008 issue of *At Home* (a publication of *St. Louis Magazine*), the inside of Schwaiger's home is shown. He transformed the old movie house into a living space large enough to accommodate his sculptures and an indoor swimming pool. The old space has found a new audience. (Missouri History Museum.)

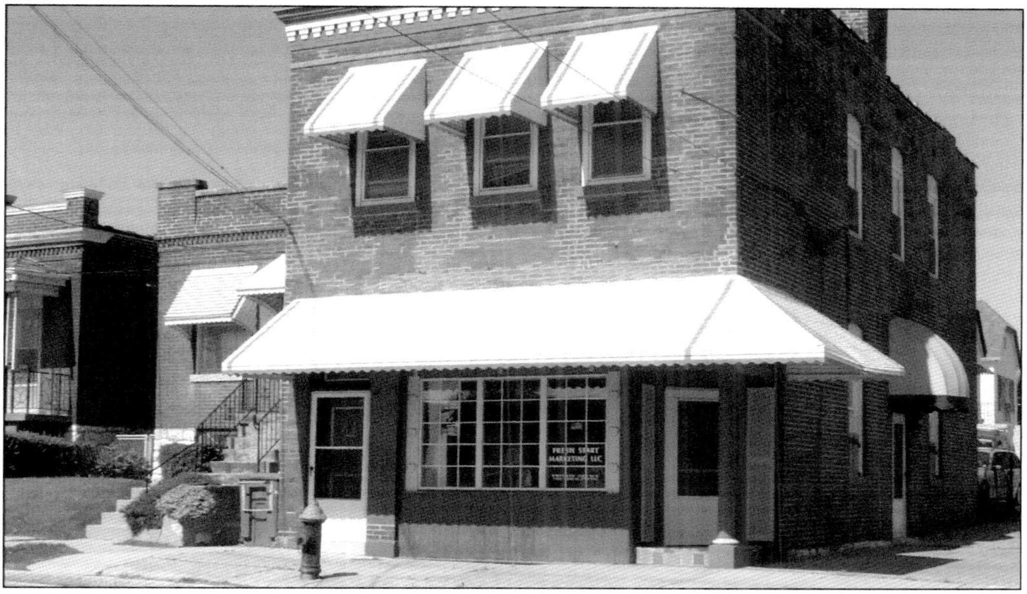


The old confectionery (site C2) at 2601 Macklind Avenue was built in 1910. The city granted a building permit to the Alexander Building Company and to architect G. J. Dan to construct the two-story storefront and dwelling for $3,000. In 1920, Charles and Lena Kaufmann owned the confectionery; in 1930, the owner was Ambrose Gianella; and in 1940, James Karda owned it and lived in the upstairs apartment. Today this property is a private office. (Photograph by Janice Markham.)

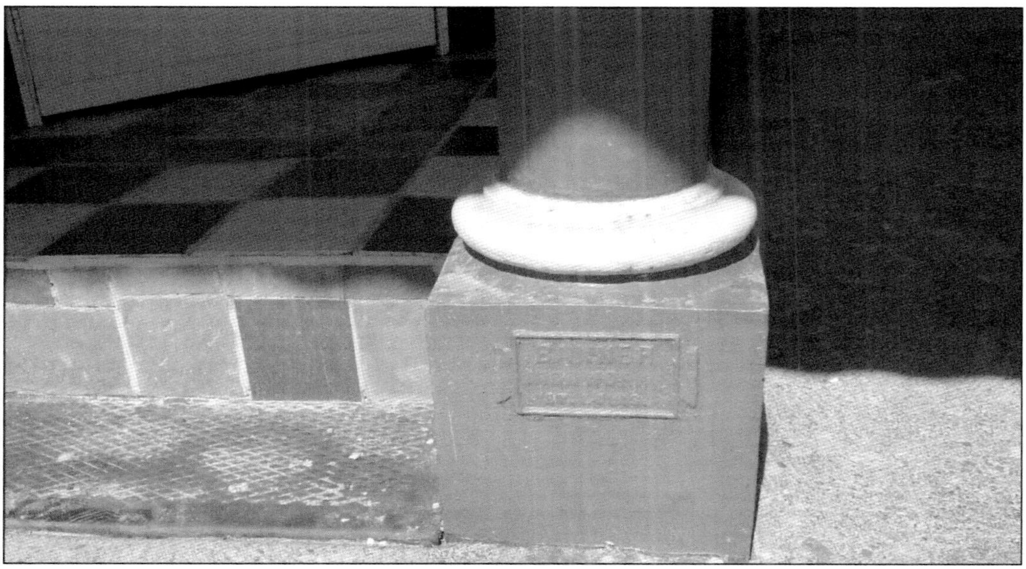

The iron storefront was manufactured in the neighborhood by Banner Iron Works. The company was located at 1926 South Kingshighway Boulevard and 4630 Shaw Avenue. Building permits make reference to the business back to 1905. Banner added a two-story brick foundry for $6,500 in 1910. Besides the foundry, it built brick ovens and a three-story brick shop in 1909 and 1910. The foundry continued to grow, and in 1921, a concrete factory was added. (Photograph by Janice Markham.)

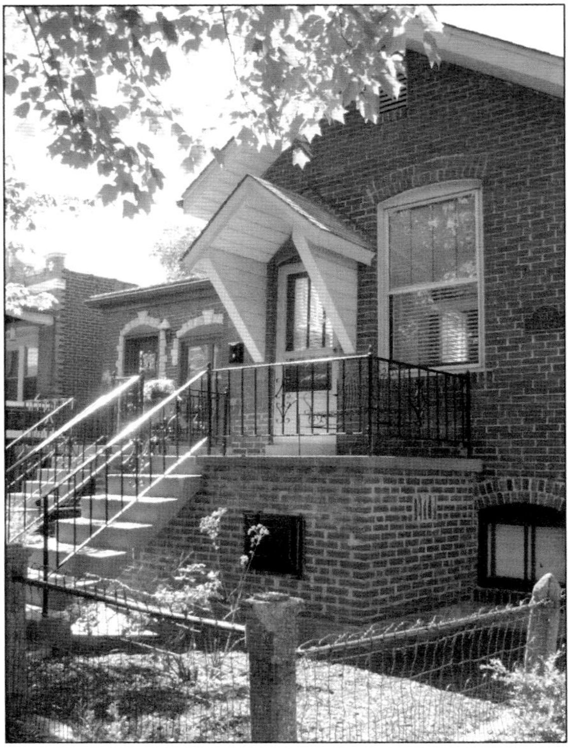

The cottage at 5512 Columbia Avenue (site C3) was built in 1925. On October 24, 1924, T. J. Grabb obtained a permit to build five houses between 5506 and 5514 Columbia Avenue for $5,000. In 1934, owner Charles Lavazzi altered the dwelling. The job cost $180. The marking on the coal chute cover reads "Majestic." Walking around the neighborhood, one will notice that most of the covers in this area were manufactured by the Majestic Company. (Photograph by Janice Markham.)

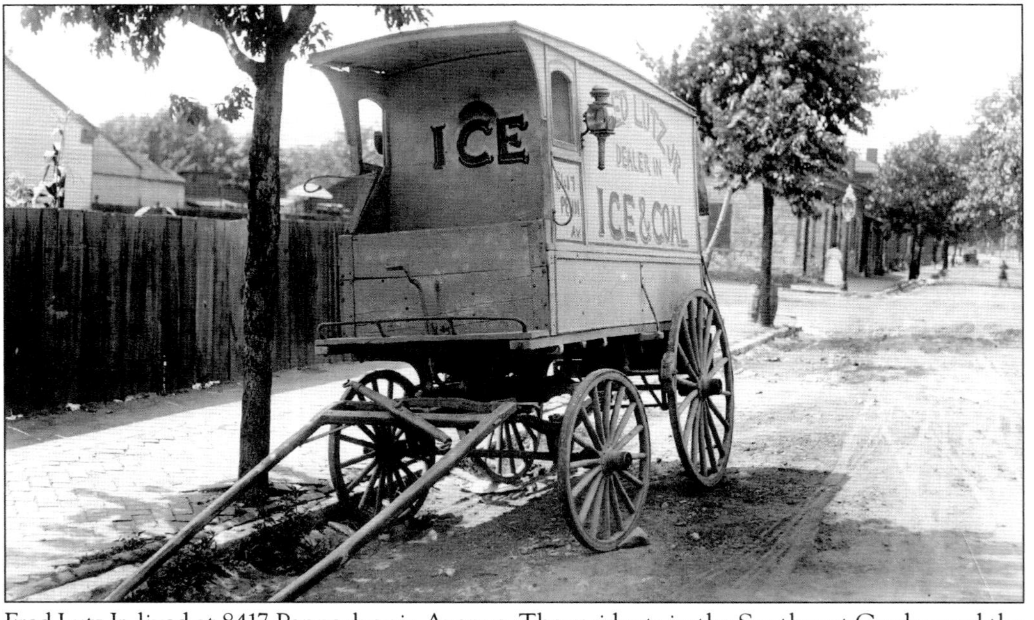


Fred Lutz Jr. lived at 8417 Pennsylvania Avenue. The residents in the Southwest Garden and the Hill got their ice from the Polar Wave Ice Branch located at 4500 Shaw Avenue. At the Missouri Historical Society, in "Bulletins," it stated, "Polar Wave ice man who presented us with a card to be placed in the window to indicate whether we needed 25, 50, 75 or 100 pounds of ice that day." (Missouri History Museum.)

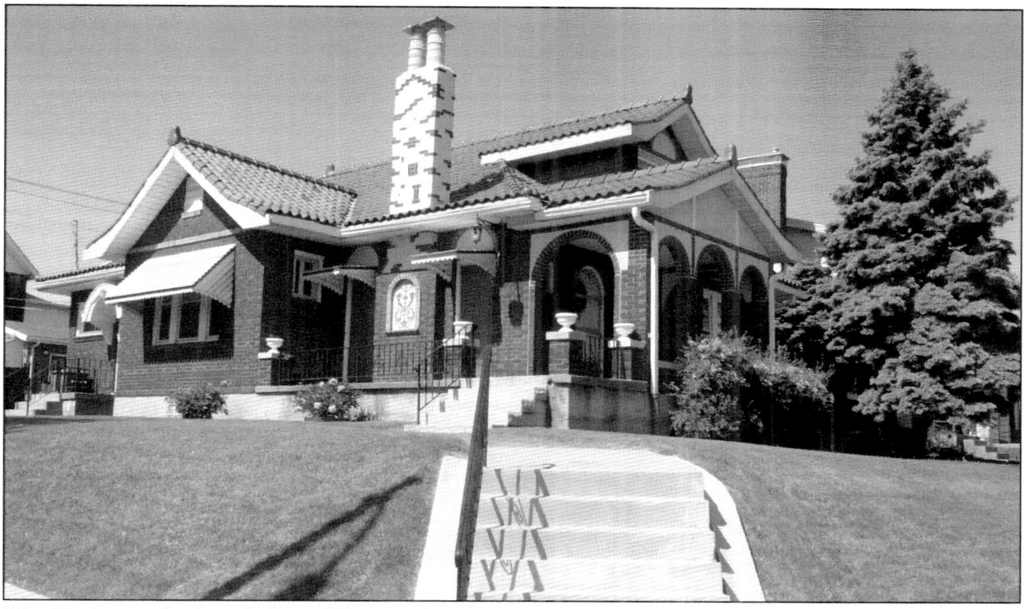

The Tudor with the tiled roof (site C4) at 5002 Columbia Avenue was built for L. Donate in 1926 for $3,000. The tall, patterned chimney crowned with decorated chimney pots is typical for this design. There is just enough exterior stucco to set it apart from the Tudors in the 2600 block of Hampton Avenue. The house sits on a low hill, as so many of the houses do in this neighborhood; this appealed to Italian immigrants. (Photograph by Janice Markham.)

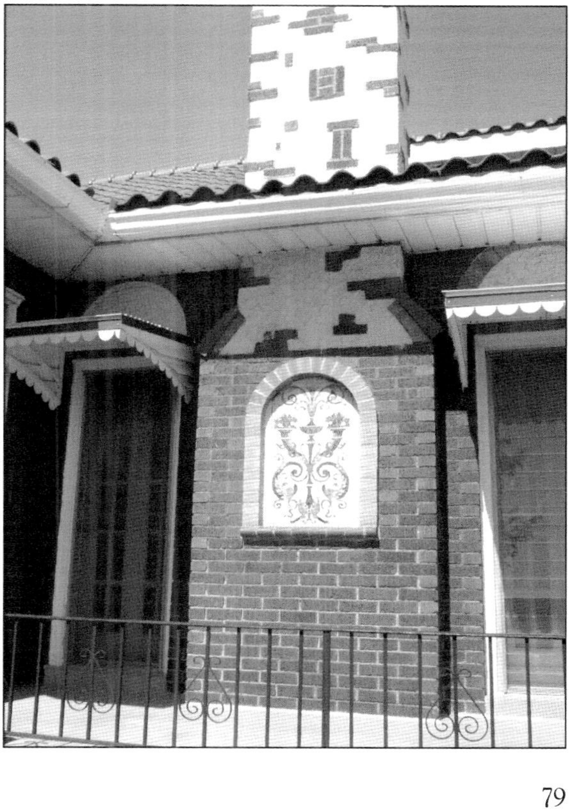

The exterior art adds to the charm of this eclectic Tudor, and it is one of the smallest mosaic scenes in St. Louis. On the corner of Lindell Boulevard and Newstead Avenue one will find the world's largest collection of mosaic art in the Cathedral Basilica of St. Louis, which is known as the new cathedral. The new cathedral opened in 1914. The old cathedral is downtown and celebrated its first mass in 1834. They are both designated as basilicas. (Photograph by Janice Markham.)

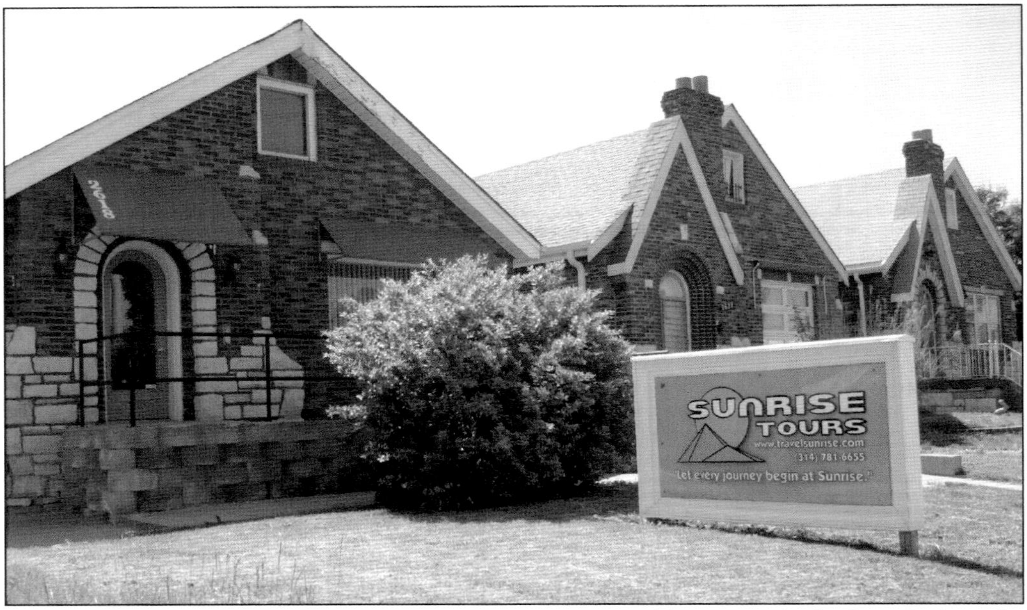


Sunrise Tours (site C5) at 2618 Hampton Avenue is owned by Jim and Charlene Dalrymple, whose travel agency has been in business for 15 years. The Tudor-style houses were built in 1938 at a cost of $4,000 each. They were built for W. J. Abbott. The first residents at the location were Michael and Rose Percelli. Michael was a salesman for C. B. Company. By 1958, the Percellis were gone, and the new resident was Rose Szodo. (Photograph by Janice Markham.)

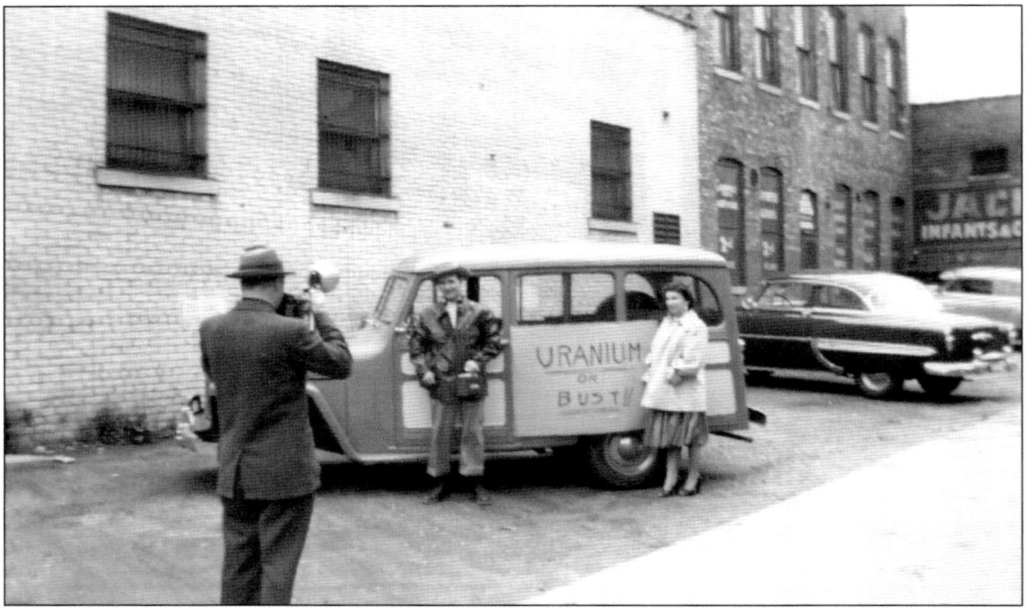


This photograph was found in the collection of the Grbac family. It was taken in the neighborhood, but the exact location is unknown. The state of Missouri was not known for uranium. Looking at the photograph, it seems the couple is leaving St. Louis to seek their fortunes elsewhere. In the early 1950s, there was a uranium boom in the western part of the United States. (Grbac family collection.)

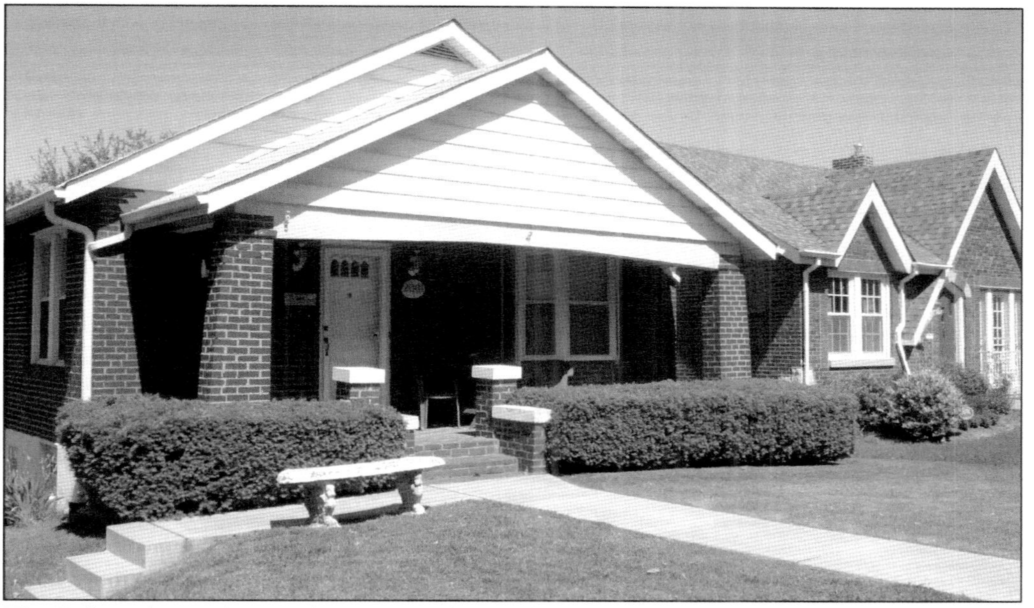

The Rebore house (site C6) at 2661 Fifty-ninth Street was built in the 1920s. Edward G. and Norma Rebore were the first residents. Edward was a lieutenant with the St. Louis Fire Department at Engine Company No. 41. There is a fire hydrant manufactured by the A. P. Smith Company in front of the house that leads one to wonder if it was planned or just a coincidence. (Photograph by Janice Markham.)

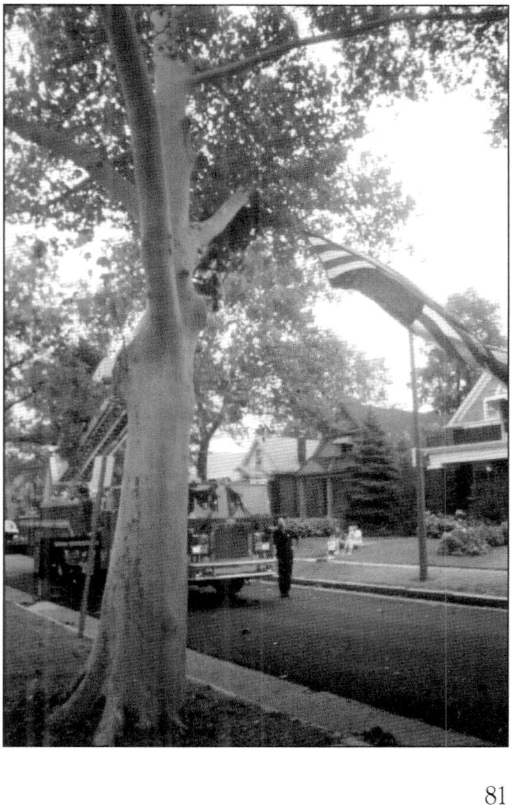

Firefighters hang the flag for National Day Out in the 4900 block of Botanical Avenue. The residents invited policemen, firefighters, and paramedics to a block party honoring them as their community heroes. In a letter dated August 6, 2002, addressed to the Southwest Garden Neighborhood Association from Capt. Bob Oldani, commander second district, he wrote, "We sincerely appreciate your thoughtfulness and hard work in taking an entire day out of your busy schedules to honor us." (Grbac family collection.)

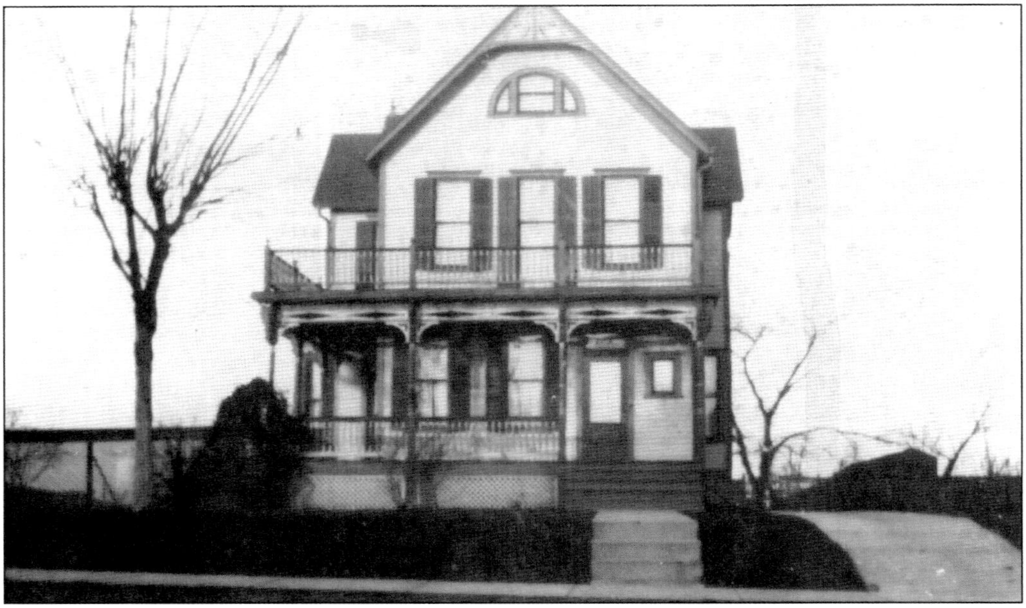

The Queen Anne house (site C7) at 2715 Dalton Avenue was built in the late 1800s. In 1901, Jessie Keyhoe had L. B. Wright build her a frame stable for $300. In 1906, the new owner, Eliza Barnett, had a two-story frame chicken shed built for $10. It is unknown who built the barn/carriage house, as the building permit has not been found. This city treasure was rehabilitated by Ronald and Teresa Bozikis. (Ronald and Teresa Bozikis family collection.)

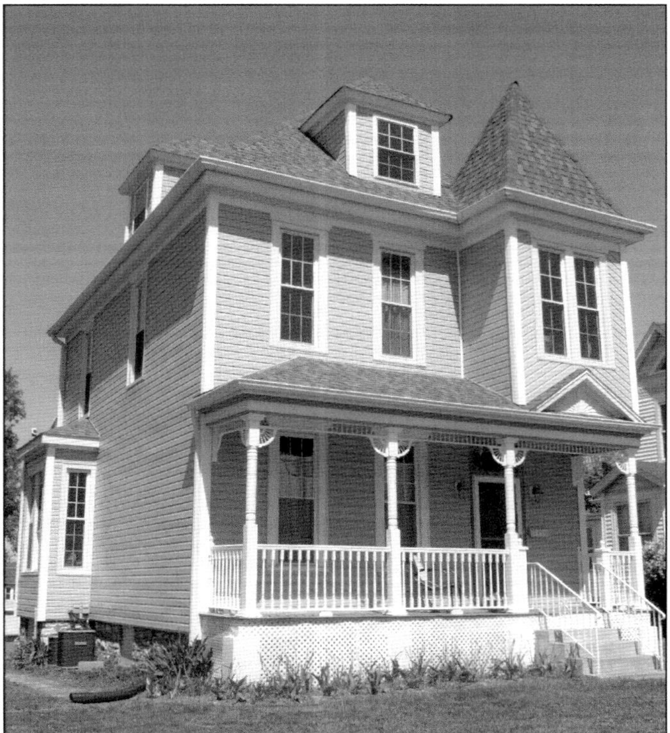

Another Victorian Queen Anne house on Dalton Street was also rehabilitated by the Bozikises. This home, built in the late 1800s, is the residence of the Bozikis family. The house across the street was built for John A. Bryers. The building permit was issued on December 14, 1891. The current owners are Rosemary and James Schriefer. Dalton Avenue on this block is all brick, which is a rare sight since most city streets are paved. (Photograph by Janice Markham.)

This two-family Tudor-style home at 2633–2635 Dalton Avenue (site C8) was built in 1940 for Paola Negro for $6,000. In the alley behind the property, there is an ash pit marked "PA Shore." Walking around the neighborhood, there are many reminders of the days when coal was used in these houses. There are numerous coal chute covers visible from the street and a good stock of ash pits in the alleys. (Photograph by Janice Markham.)

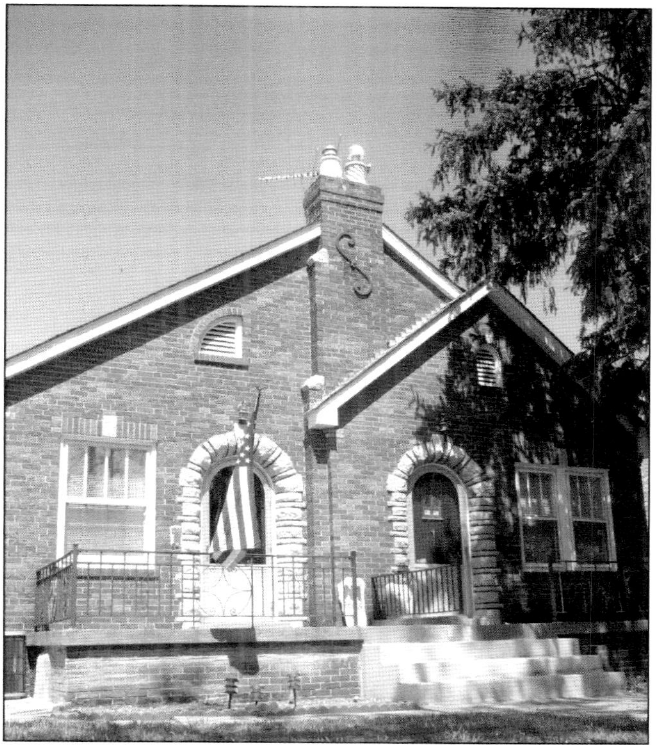

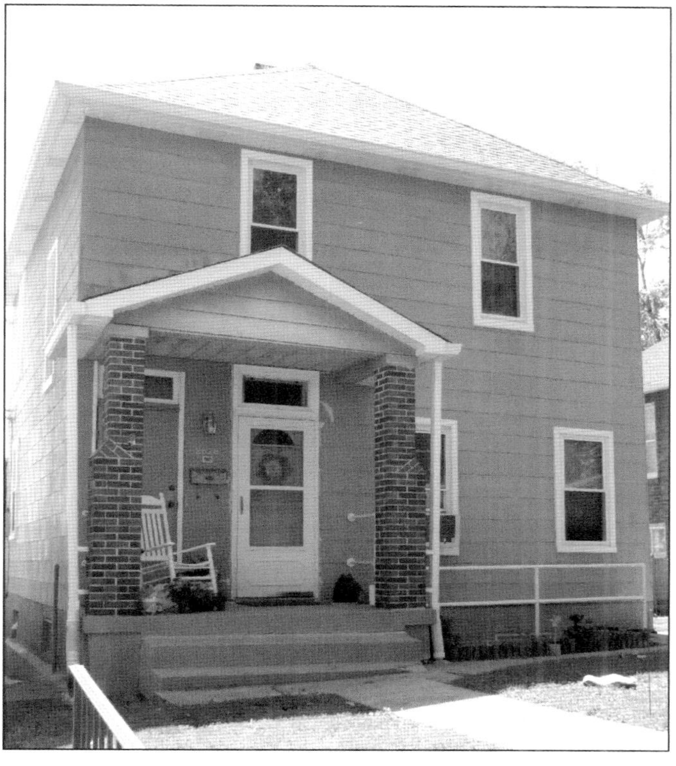

This house at 2628 Dalton Avenue was a rental in 1910. The census records list John E. Ashworth, his wife, Gertrude, and their children. John E. was in insurance. In 1920, it was the home of John and Mary Wheeler. John was the assistant secretary of the Kieselhorst Piano Company. By 1930, the house became a two-family. Herman A. and Theresa Koettker lived in one part, and John A. and Nora Lasley lived in the other. (Photograph by Janice Markham.)

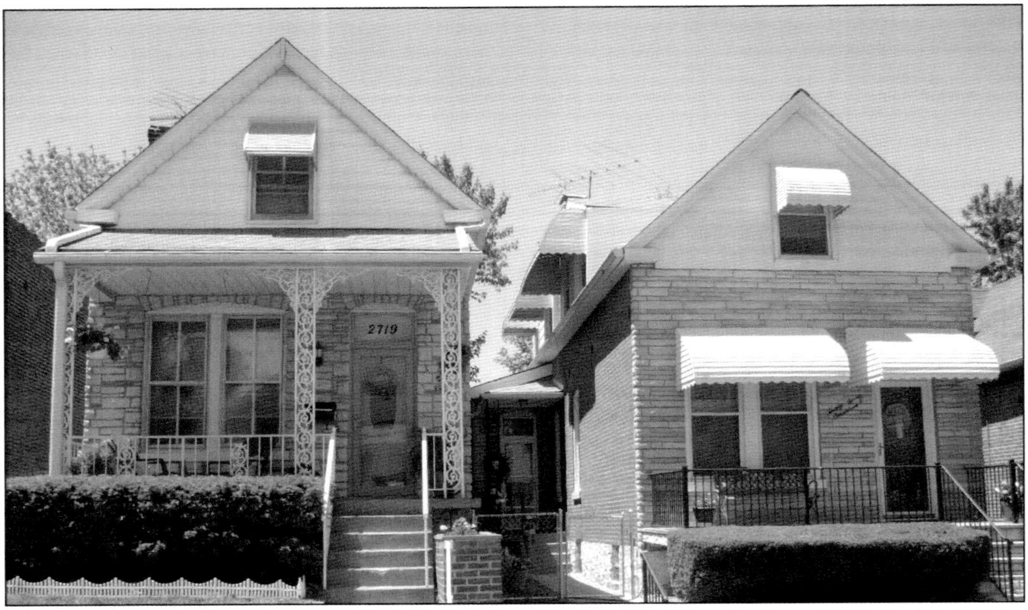


The twin houses (site C9) at 2717 and 2719 January Avenue were built in 1902 for $2,600 for the Investment and Loan Company. The building permit listed them as one-and-a-half-story dwellings. In 1914, there was an addition built to No. 2717 for C. Walling at a cost of $175. Walling was still there in 1924. There was a building permit issued to build a one-story frame shed for $75. (Photograph by Janice Markham.)

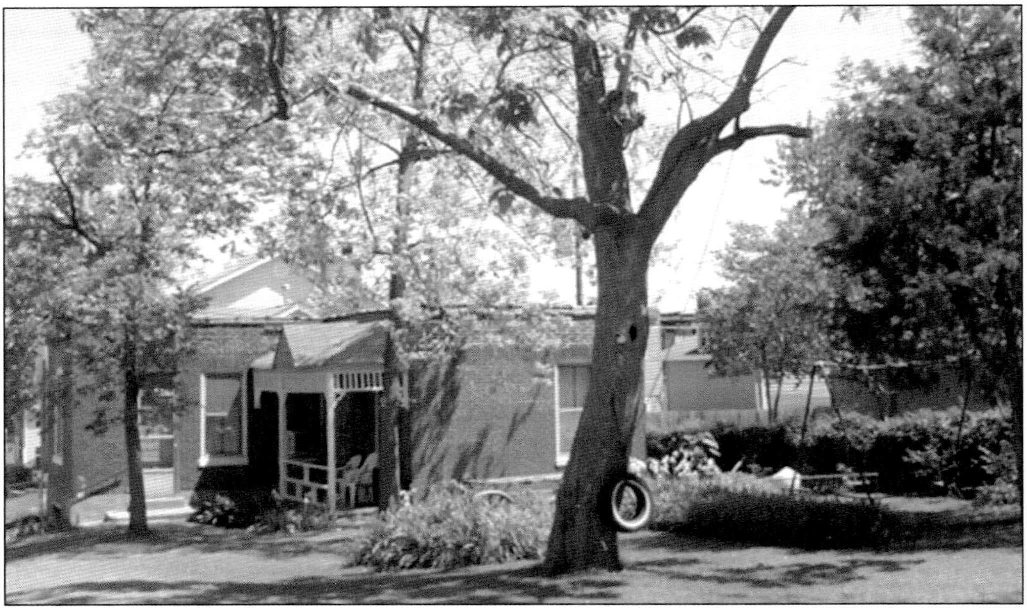

In 1910, the cottage at 2714 January Avenue belonged to William J. Maslters, a tinner who did shop work. In 1920, Marie and Ferdinand Hausleithner were the residents. Ferdinand was a waiter. In 1930, there were new residents, Paul L. and Anna Stroupe. Paul was a bricklayer. The tire hanging from the tree is a reminder of a different time—the days when swings and toys were made from materials that had been discarded. (Photograph by Janice Markham.)

The former Metz house (site C10) at 5617 Reber Place was built for $2,000 in 1905. The 1910 census records list William and Olivia Metz and their children William, Olivia, Charles, and Milton. William was a factory inspector, and, according to the 1920 city directory, he became a constable for the Ninth District court. By 1930, Arch and Dorothy Gates were the residents at this address. Arch was a foreman for the department of public utilities. (Photograph by Janice Markham.)

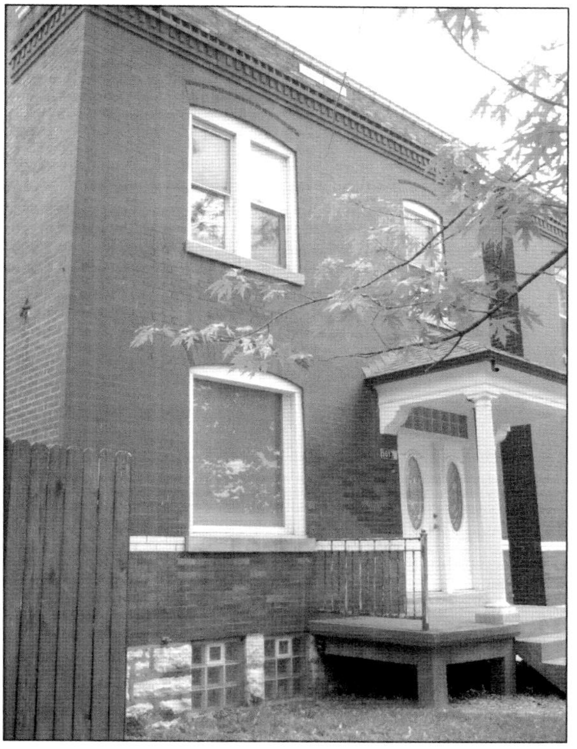

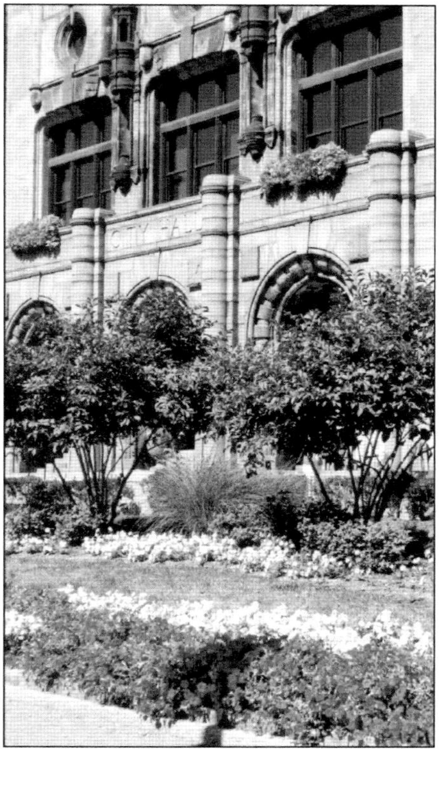

St. Louis City Hall is located downtown at the corner of Tucker Boulevard and Clark Avenue. It is a great resource for researching historic homes and neighborhoods. A title transfer search can be done in the tax assessor's office. Original building permits issued by the St. Louis Commissioner's Office are found on the fourth floor in the building division, and the other building permits issued by the city are found in the basement in the comptroller's office and microfilm section. (Operation Brightside.)

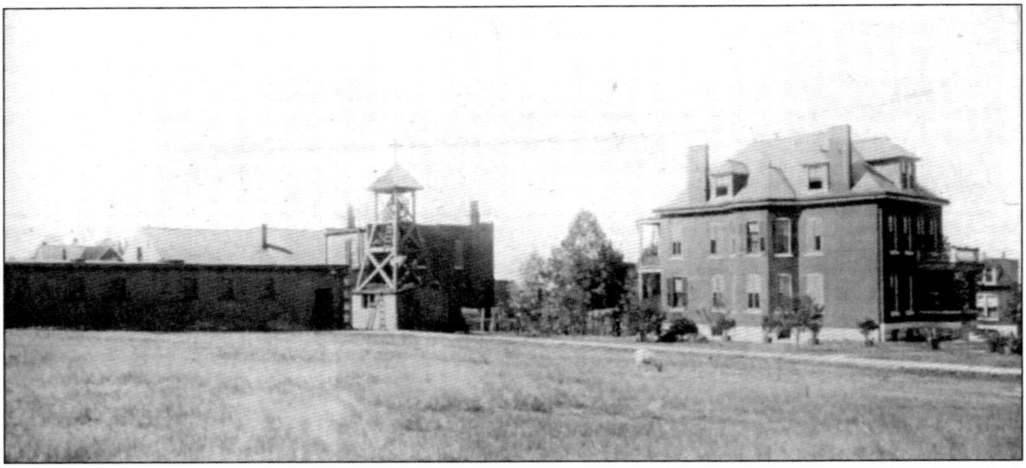

St. Aloysius Gonzaga Church (site C11) at 5608 North Magnolia Avenue was completed in 1925 and torn down in 2006. The stained-glass windows were designed by Emil Frei. The original frame church was built in 1892. It was established to serve the German immigrants who settled in Blue Ridge, the area bordering the Italian community now known as the Hill. The last mass was celebrated on June 26, 2005. (Diane Rademacher collection.)

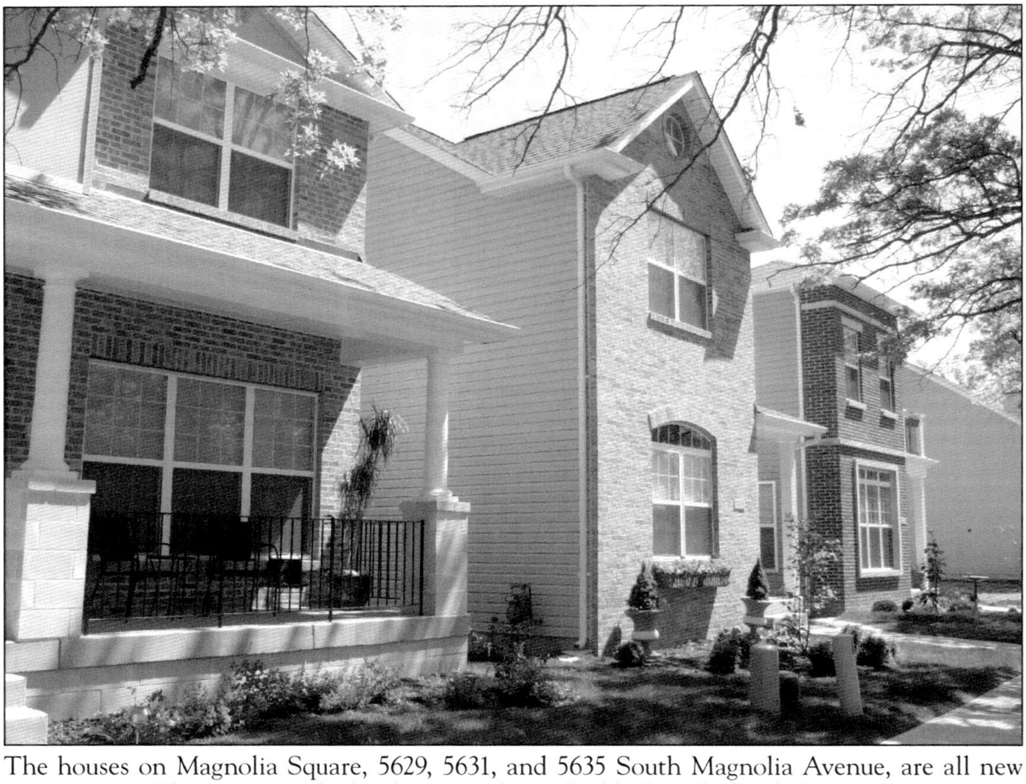

The houses on Magnolia Square, 5629, 5631, and 5635 South Magnolia Avenue, are all new construction. They are part of a development plan to build 25 single-family homes. Construction started in the spring of 2006. A slice of history about the church that stood on this block has been preserved as a feature in the book *House of God: The Historic Churches and Places of Worship of the St. Louis Area* by James J. Schild. (Photograph by Janice Markham.)

The Owens children are pictured in 1917 at their home at 5539 Southwest Avenue (site C12). They are, from left to right, Bernice, Frank, and Fred. On March 31, 1915, a building permit was issued to owner F. Owens and contractor Dawson Brothers to build a two-story brick tenement for $5,000. On June 19, 1915, they obtained a building permit to build a two-story frame stable for $300. The house is still in the family. (Owens family collection.)

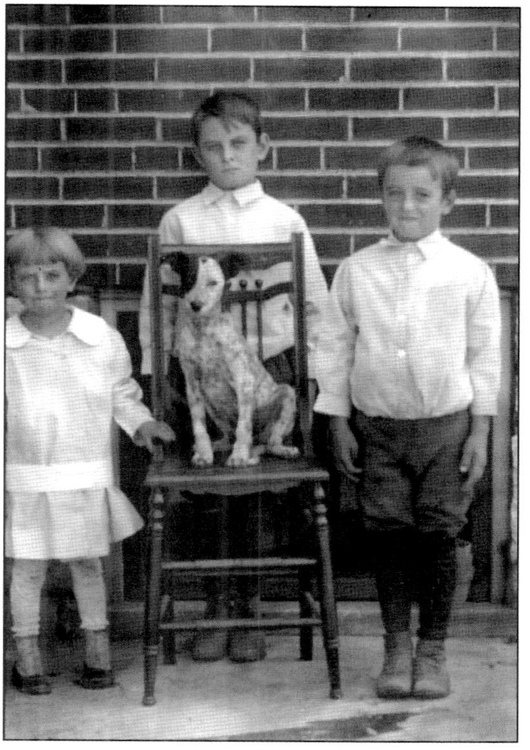

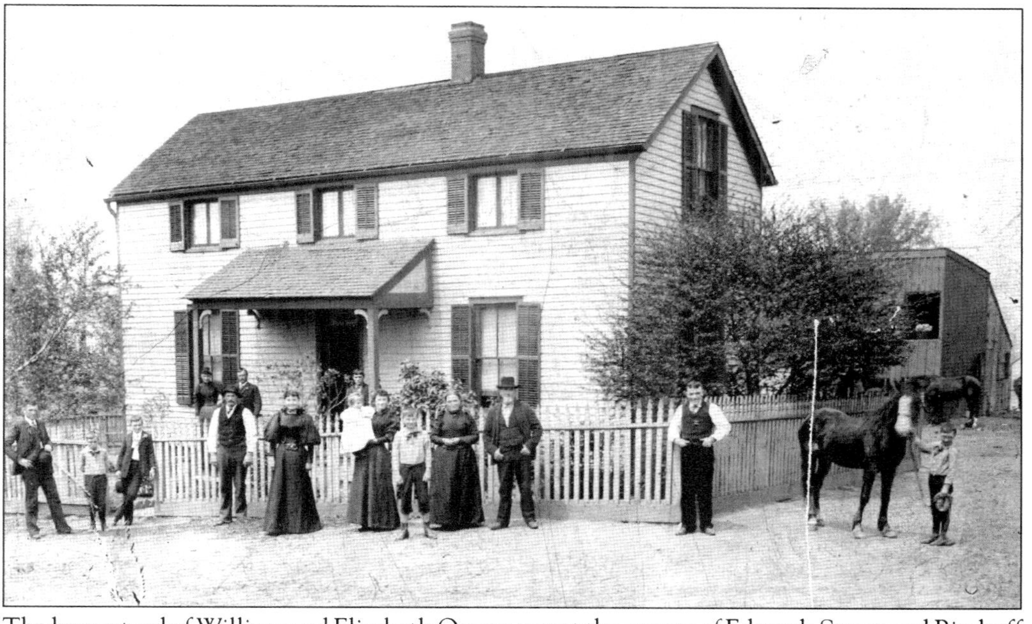

The homestead of William and Elizabeth Owens was at the corner of Edwards Street and Bischoff Avenue. In the 1880 census, William is listed as a 45-year-old miner born in Wales. Elizabeth is listed as his wife. She was 33 at the time and was born in Wurtenberg, Germany. Their children are listed as John, age 16; Elizabeth, age 13; William, age 11; Annie, age 10; Frank, age 8; Joseph, age 7; Martha, age 5; Richard, age 3; and Edward, age 1. (Owens family collection.)

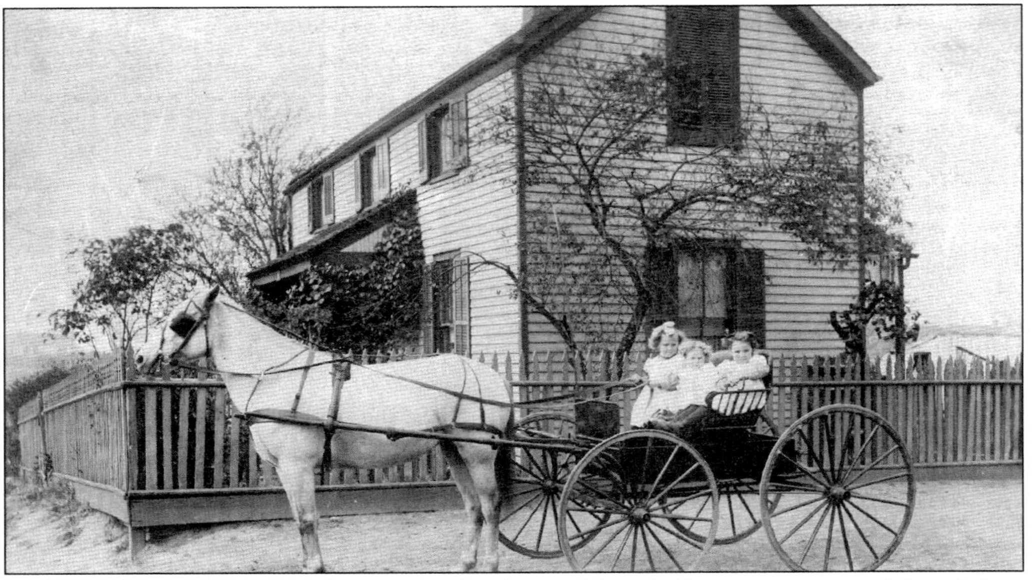

Evelyn, Helen, and Marjorie Owens, the daughters of Joseph Owens, are pictured from left to right in 1905 at the Owens homestead on the Hill at 5303 Bischoff Avenue. According to the 1930 city directory, William and Elizabeth Owens' sons were living on Bischoff Avenue at the time. There is no occupation listed for William Owens Jr. Edward and Frank Owens are listed as drivers, George and Richard Owens are listed as teamsters, and Henry Owens worked with terra-cotta. Henry probably worked in the neighborhood. There were several clay mines in the area. (Owens family collection.)

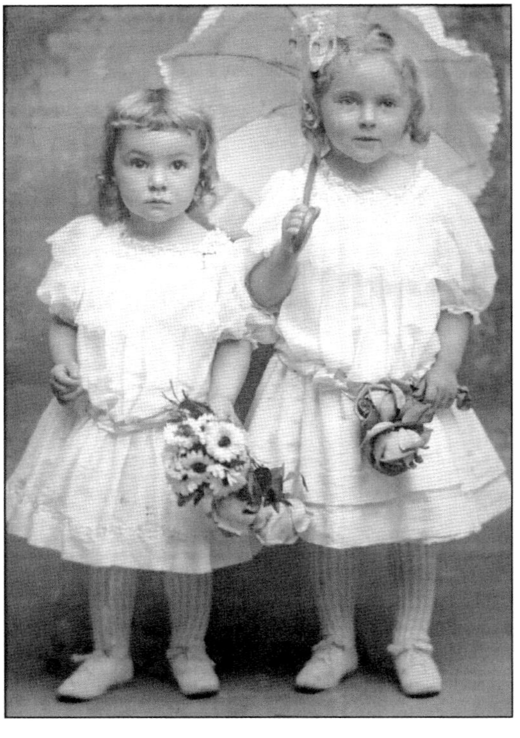

Pictured in this 1905 photograph are two of Joseph Owens's daughters, though it is unclear which two are seen. According to the 1910 census records, Joseph and Margaret Owens were living at 5615 Old Manchester Road (Southwest Avenue). Their children are listed as Evelyn, Marjorie, Helen, and Joseph. Joseph Sr.'s occupation is listed as "saloon keeper—selling liquor." In 1910, Joseph Sr. was 36 and Margaret was 27. They had been married eight years. (Owens family collection.)

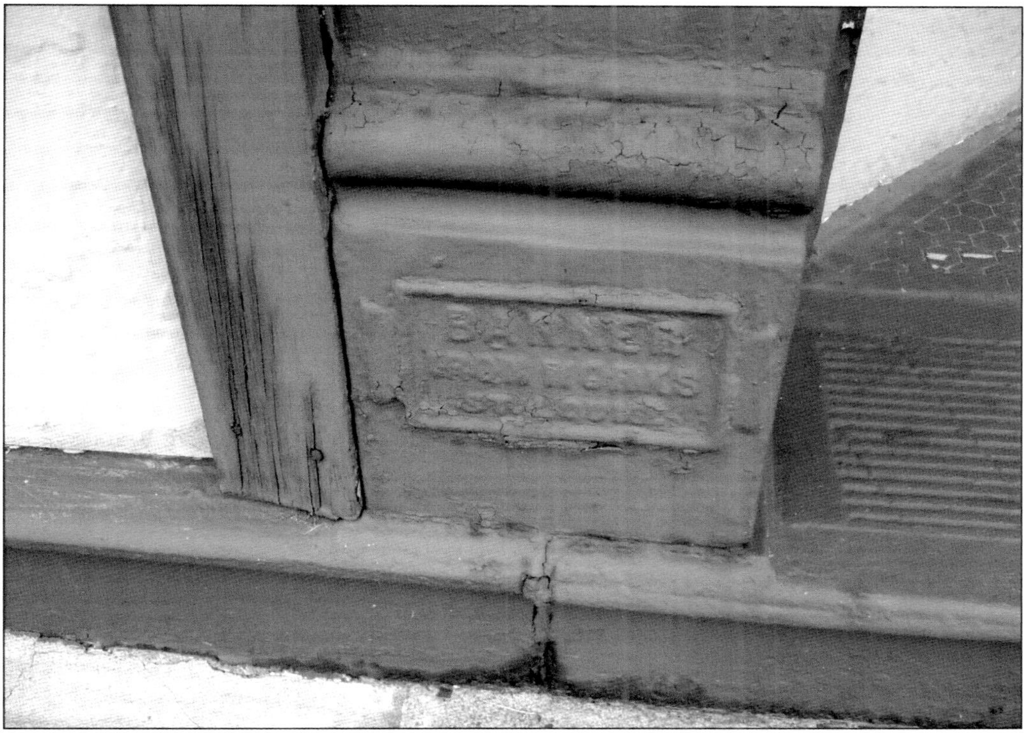

The Banner Iron Works storefront (site C13) at 5529 Southwest Avenue was built in 1908. A building permit for a two-story brick store and residence was issued to owner Xavier F. Hanneke and contractor L. Koppf. In 1904, Hanneke obtained a permit to build a frame horse stable for $170. In 1894, Hanneke obtained a building permit to build a one-story frame store for $450. Hanneke was a shoe cobbler. (Photograph by Janice Markham.)

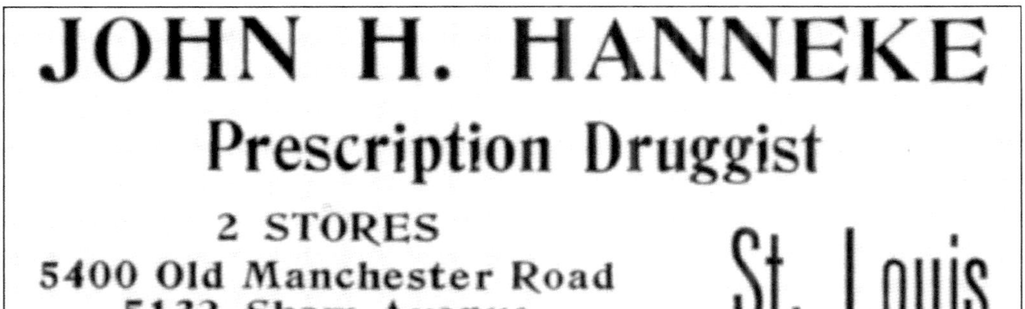


The Hannekes also built the house next door. In 1908, Hanneke obtained a building permit to construct a dwelling for $3,600 at 5527 Southwest Avenue, and A. C. Uthoff was the contractor. In the 1910 city directory, Ignatius F. Hanneke is listed as a butcher who lived at 5527A Southwest Avenue, and X. Frank Hanneke is listed at 5529A Southwest Avenue. He was a clerk at 5132 Shaw Avenue. John H. Hanneke owned drugstores at 5132 Shaw Avenue and 5400 Old Manchester Road (Southwest Avenue). (Diane Rademacher collection.)

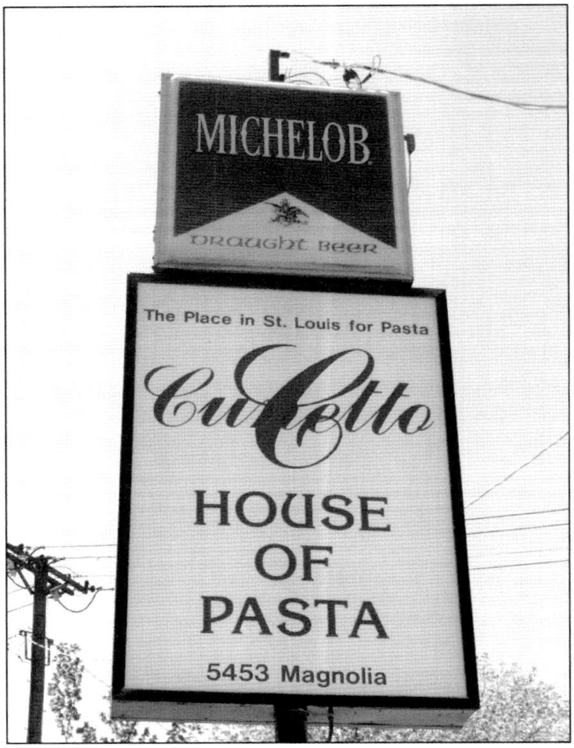


Cunetto House of Pasta (site C14) at 5453 Magnolia Avenue has been in business since 1974. The building dates to the 1930s. A building permit was issued to owners Camillo and Lena de Bartoli to construct a store and flats on September 2, 1936. Before brothers Vince and Joe Cunetto opened the restaurant, they had a pharmacy at this location. The business is owned by the Cunetto family and operated by Vince's son Frank. (Photograph by Janice Markham.)

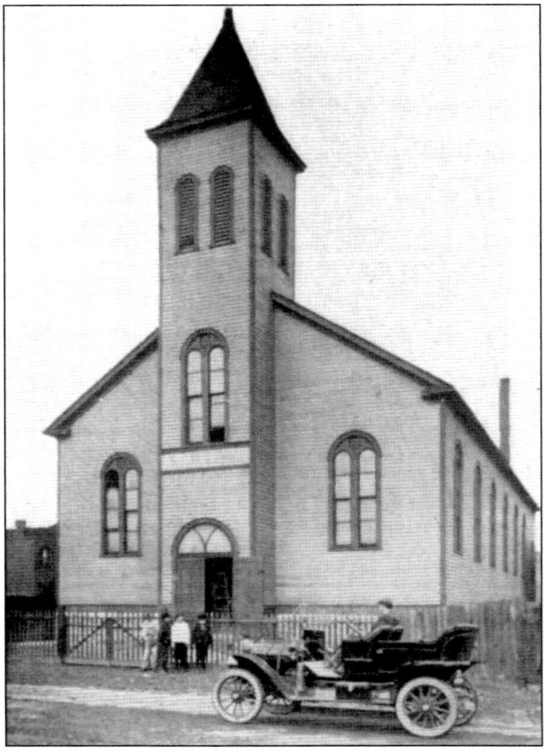

St. Ambrose Church at Wilson and Cooper Avenues in 1903 served the Italian Catholics who lived in southwest St. Louis. The parish was led by Rev. Luciano Carotti. Most of the members were attending mass at St. Aloysius Gonzaga Church where Rev. F. G. Holweck held the service in Italian. In 1911, the parish school had around 150 students. This church building was replaced by a new one in the 1920s at 5130 Wilson Avenue. (Diane Rademacher collection.)

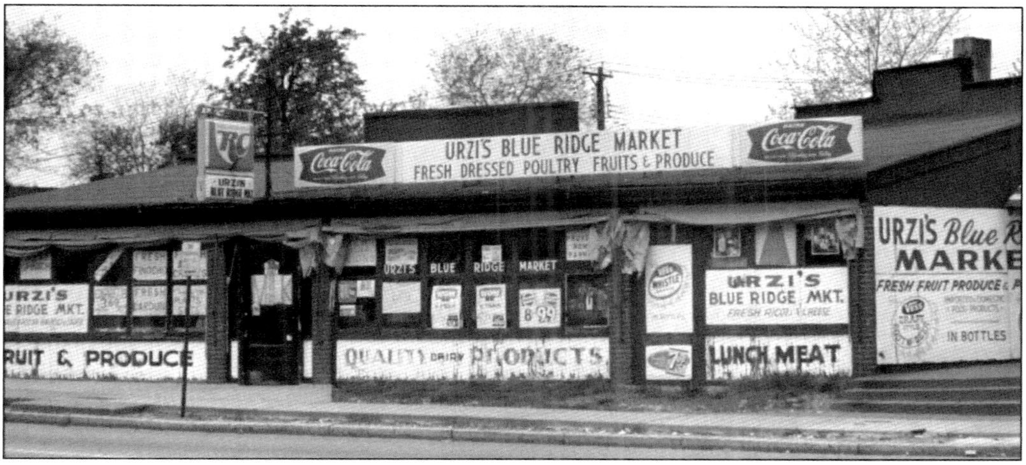


Urzi's Market (site C15), before moving to its present location at 5430 Southwest Avenue, advertised its products to passersby. The original Urzi's Market was located at 5354 Southwest Avenue and owned by Joseph and Vencente Urzi. The *Hill Day Commemorative Issue* of the St. Louis bicentennial from August 15, 1965, a copy provided by Ann Collora, talks about the Blue Ridge area: "A ridge of blue clay, weaving from the west side of Hereford Street to Sublette Avenue, gave this area it's name." (Urzi family collection.)

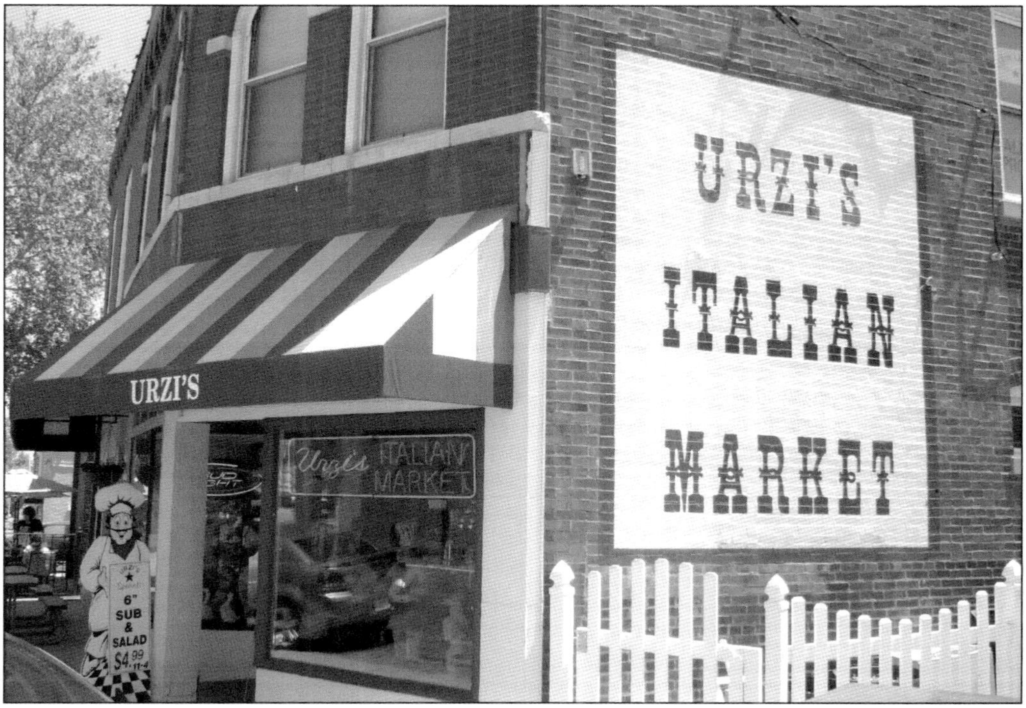


The building Urzi's currently occupies was owned by L. A. Scala in 1905. In 1922, it was owned by B. Grauagna, and in 1926, the owner was R. Russe. Joseph Urzi is listed as a meat cutter in the 1930 city directory. Today the market has a delicatessen, a great selection of Italian foods, and sidewalk tables set up for those who want to eat food there. The market is still owned and operated by the Urzi family. (Photograph by Janice Markham.)

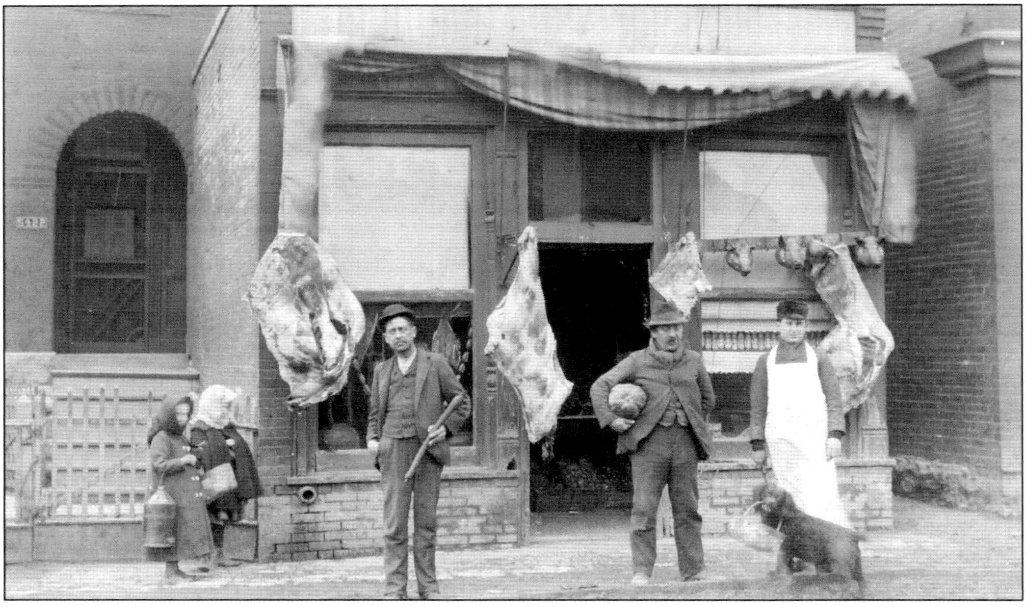

The former O. C. Haenni's Market at 5424 Magnolia Avenue is now Lou Boccardi's Restaurant. In this photograph from about 1900, Otto Haenni is to the far right in the apron. The others are unidentified. The dog holding the basket in its mouth seems to belong to Haenni. The market sold meat and vegetables and appeared for the first time in the city directory in 1900. The Haenni family lived next door at 5422 Magnolia Avenue. (Jennifer Guidici collection.)

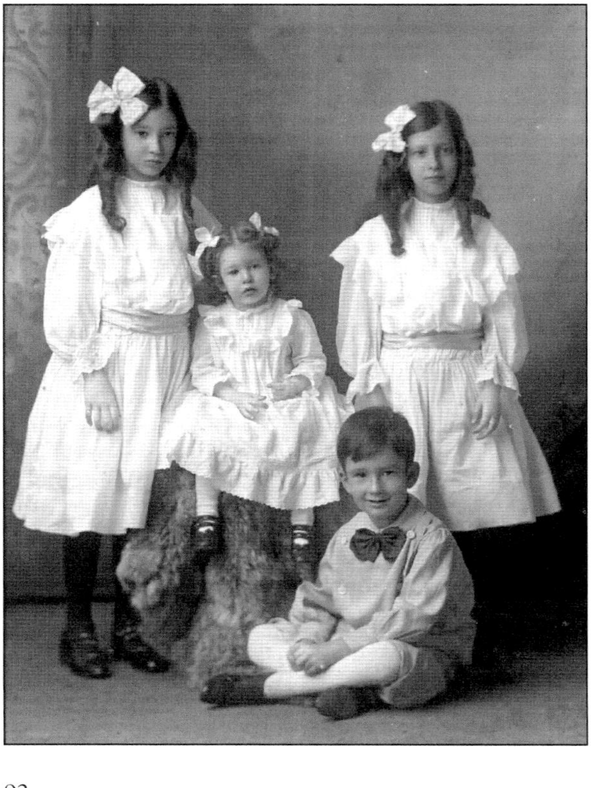

The Haenni children are, from left to right, Clementine, Ida, Otto, and Edna. When Otto was two years old and Clementine was four, they survived falling from the second floor at 5422 Magnolia Avenue. The children were playing by a window with a loose screen when they fell 15 feet below. Dr. L. W. Sherman, who lived across the street, came right away. Otto had a bruise on his forehead, but Clementine took longer to recover from her internal injuries. (Jennifer Guidici collection.)

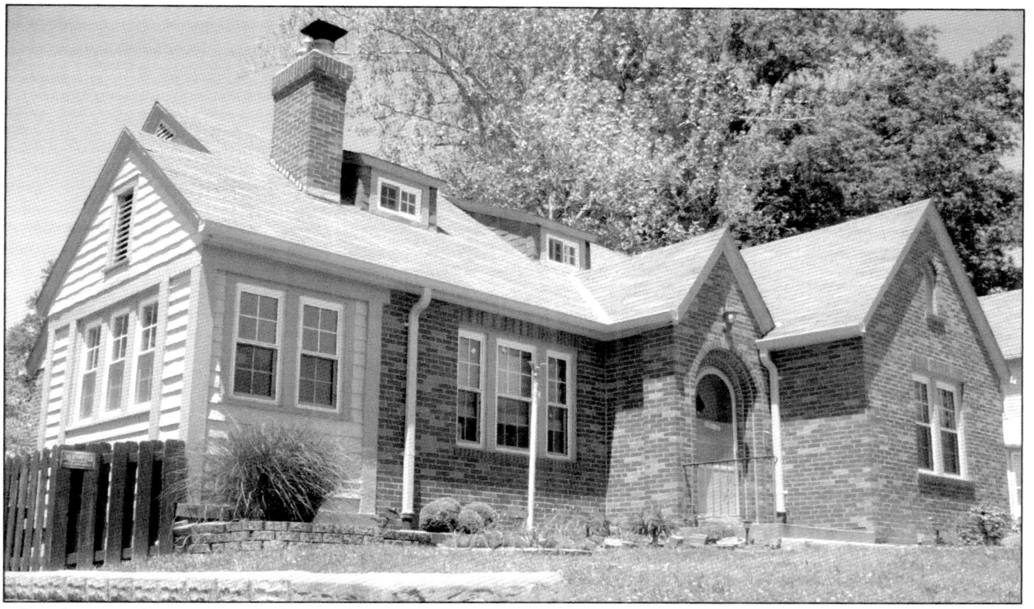

The former location of the Reber Place Congregation Church (site C16) at 2737 Macklind Avenue started out as a chapel in 1891, and then a two-story frame structure was built for the Congregation City Missouri Society. The church was moved to this location in 1903, and in 1904, a frame addition was made for $3,000. More alterations were made in 1916 and 1932. A brick house stands there today. (Photograph by Janice Markham.)

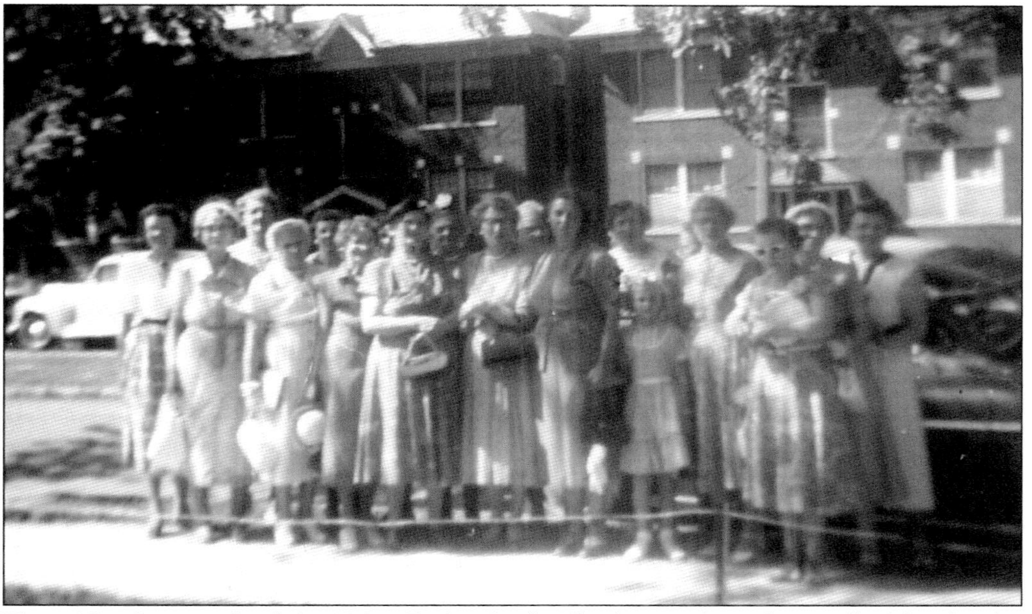

This 1954 photograph of the Helen Bodey Circle Third came from the Wofford family who lived at 4940 Magnolia Avenue. In the group is Dorothy G. Wofford, the author of the book *Thou Hast Given a Banner.* The book tells the history of the Third Baptist Church of St. Louis. It was published in 1985 for the centennial celebration of the church. The church is located at 620 North Grand Boulevard. (Stephen Burns collection.)

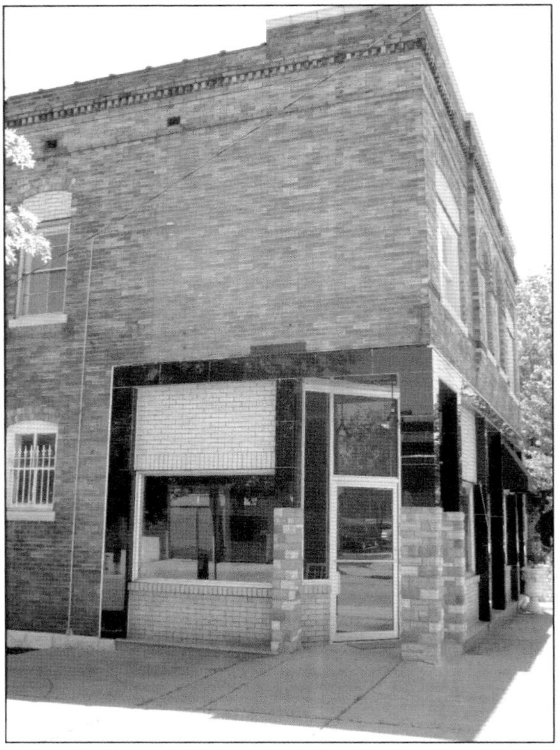

This is the former Grana Market (site C17) at 2700 Macklind Avenue. In 1895, the city issued a building permit to H. Causmann for two adjacent brick stores and dwellings to be constructed for $4,800. In 1926, a bakery brick oven was built by H. Grana, and in 1935, Tony Grana had some work done on the building. Today the property is still being used as it was originally planned. (Photograph by Janice Markham.)

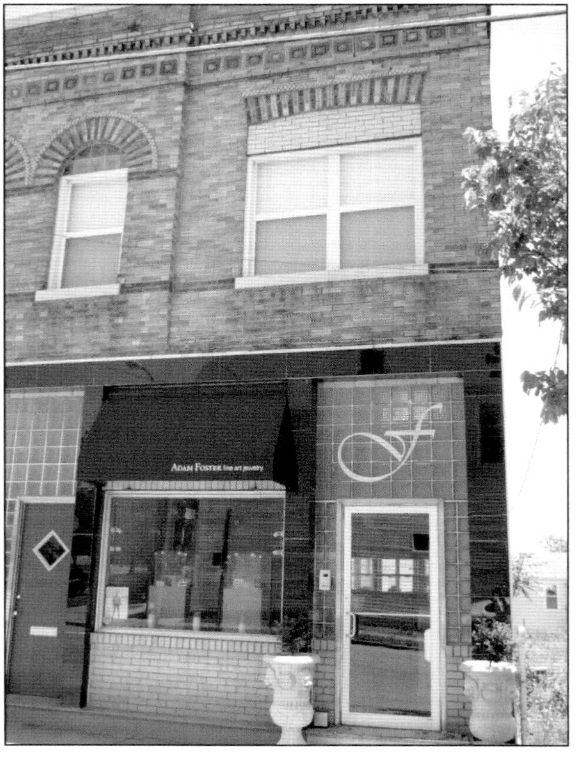

This is a commercial and residential storefront. Since the market served the neighborhood for so many years, this site is still referred to as the Grana Market. The business here today is Gestalt, Inc. The second floor has been converted into modern loft apartments featuring the original refinished oak floors and exposed brick walls. Unique features are the marble windowsills. (Photograph by Janice Markham.)

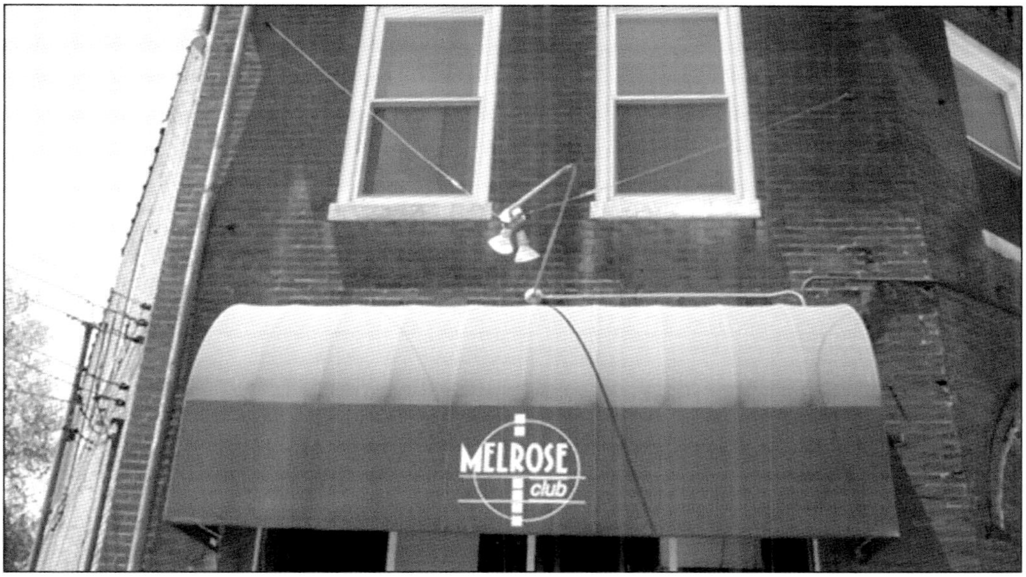


The Melrose Club (site C18) at 5400 Southwest Avenue was in a building constructed for John H. Hanneke by W. H. Gladish as a two-story brick office and dwelling in 1909 for $1,500. Hanneke Hardware was across the street at 5390 Southwest Avenue. According to the 1880s census records, the Hannekes in Missouri came from Hanover, Germany, and sometimes the name is spelled Haneke. The current owners of the building and Melrose Club are Stanley and Patricia Ponciroli. (Photograph by Janice Markham.)

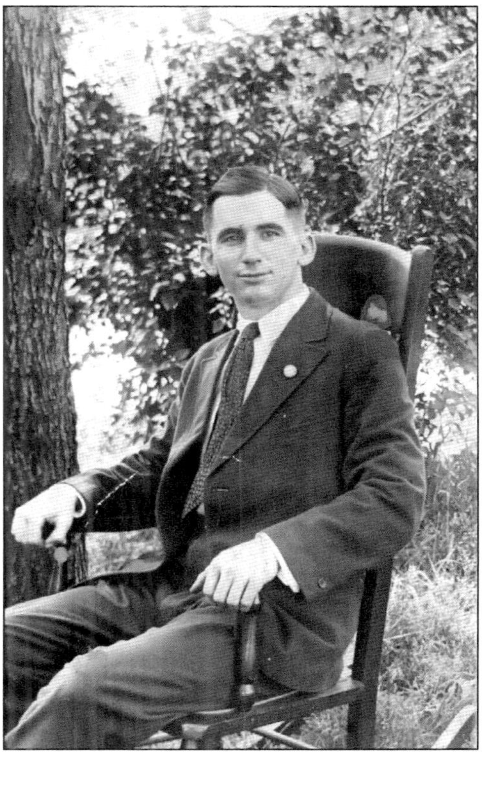

Most of the neighborhood residents were of German and Italian descent, but there were also some Irish in the mix. Arthur English, photographed in 1920, was the son of Annie and John T. English. Annie was the daughter of John W. and Julia Fleming. John T. was born in Westport, Ireland, in the 1820s. The English family lived on Southwest Avenue. (Mary Ann English Winkelmann and Marella Hardesty Baird collection.)

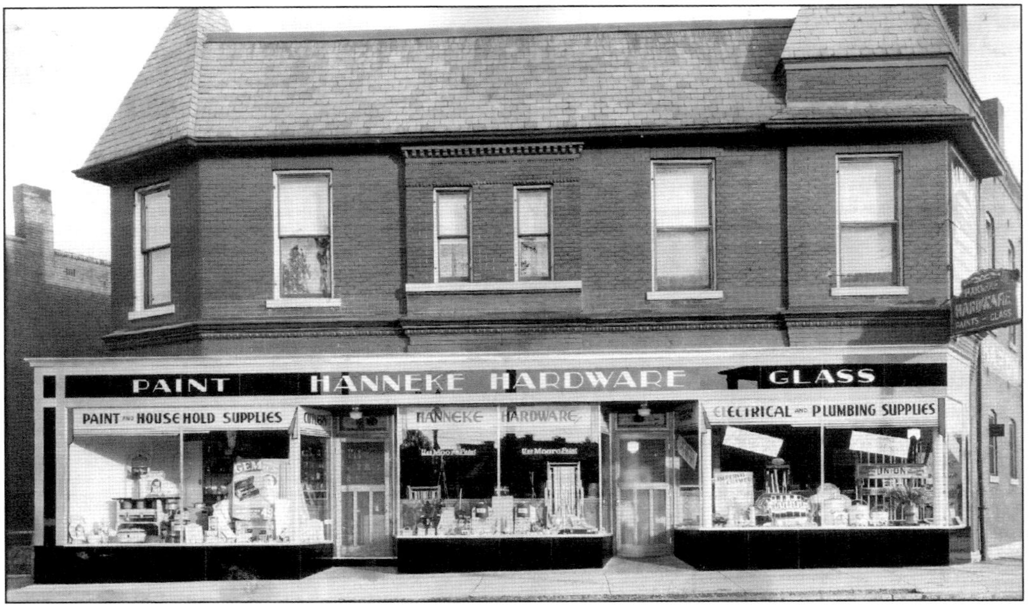


Hanneke Hardware (site C19) at 5390 Southwest Avenue opened in 1927. The original part of the building was built in 1923. In the 1930s, the structure was altered, additions were made to the store, and a garage was added. The early owners on building permits are listed as Ignatius F. and Mollie Hanneke. In 1959, another addition was made, and the entire store was remodeled in 1999 by the new owners. (Hanneke Hardware and Paint Company.)

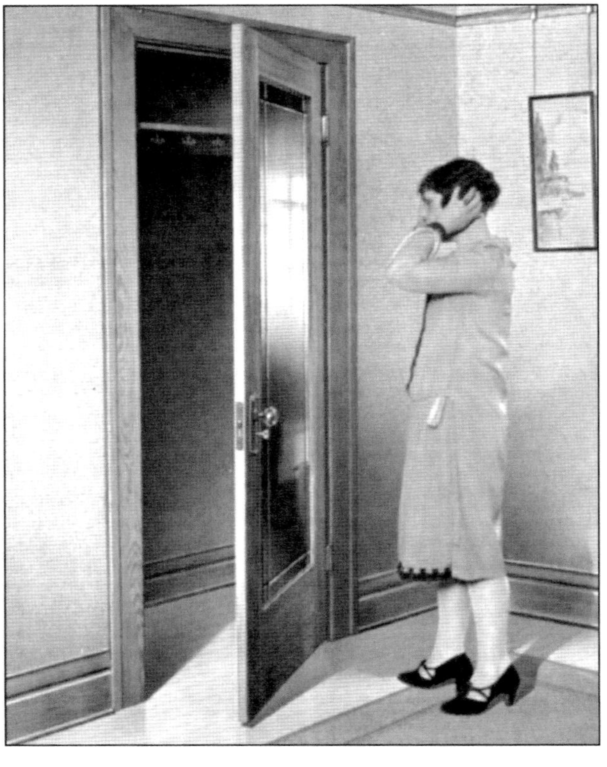

Hanneke Hardware was not the only place to go for lumber or hardware if one wanted to do business with a resident of the neighborhood. Florence Imse, the wife of Robert C. Imse from the Imse-Schilling Sash and Door Company at 4217 Beck Avenue, is photographed for a door advertisement. The Imses lived at 4610 Shenandoah Avenue. Robert, William Lothman, and Edward Schilling were the officers of the business. (Wamhoff family collection.)

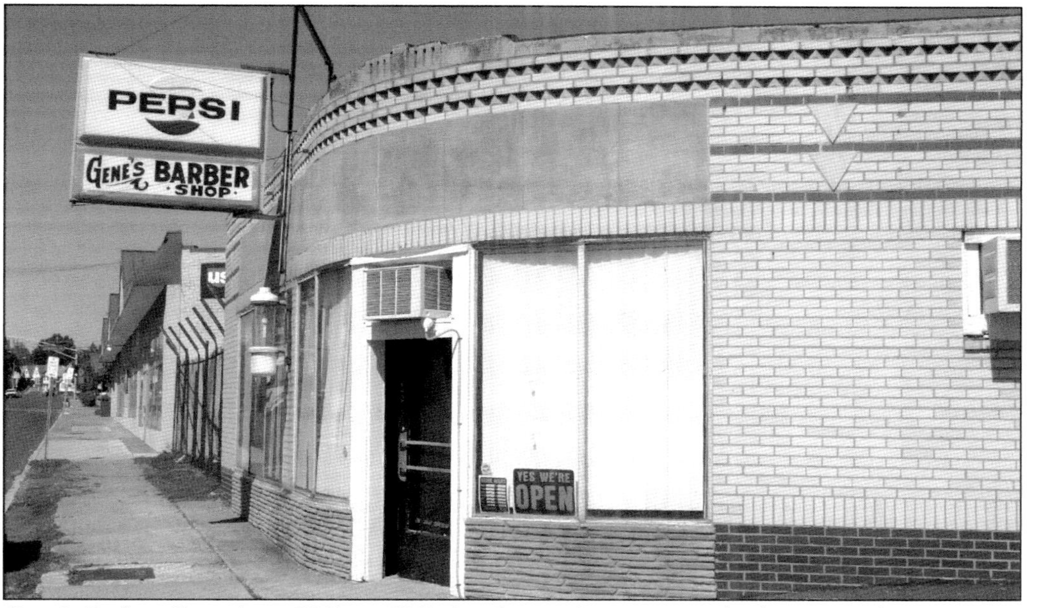


Gene's Barber Shop (site C20) at 5361 Southwest Avenue was the location of a one-pump filling station in 1924. Next door at 5351 Southwest Avenue was also a filling station in 1923. It had two pumps. In the late 1800s, there was a barbershop in this area. A building permit was issued to construct a one-story frame barbershop for $300 to A. Festerbug and his brother. The location was the north side of Southwest Avenue between Macklind Avenue and Edwards Street. (Photograph by Janice Markham.)

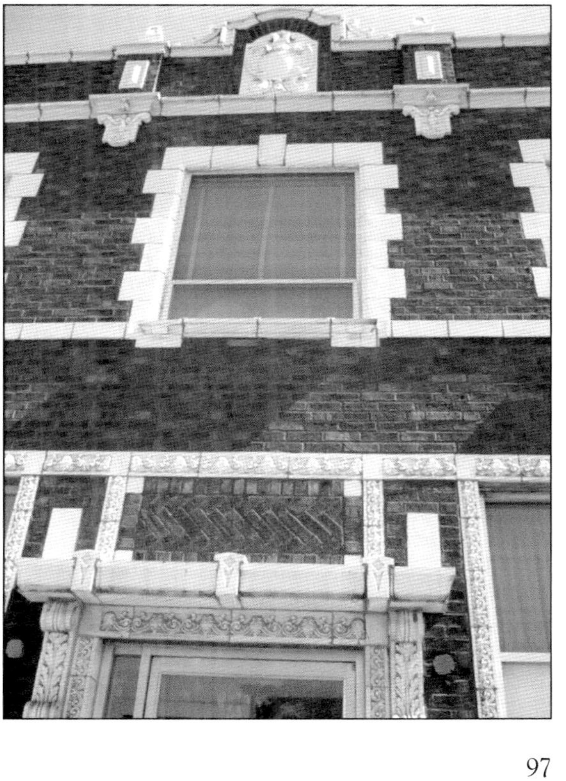

The building at 5241–5243 Southwest Avenue was constructed in the late 1930s. In 1940, Julius Colombo had a barbershop at 5241 Southwest Avenue. He lived at 5256 Botanical Avenue. Daniel and Gertrude Nickels lived in the upstairs apartment. Colombo also owned 5243 Southwest Avenue and had a restaurant there. The upstairs apartment was rented to Matthew and Bess Schulter. Matthew was the president of the Columbia Movie Theatre located at 5333 Columbia Avenue. (Photograph by Janice Markham.)

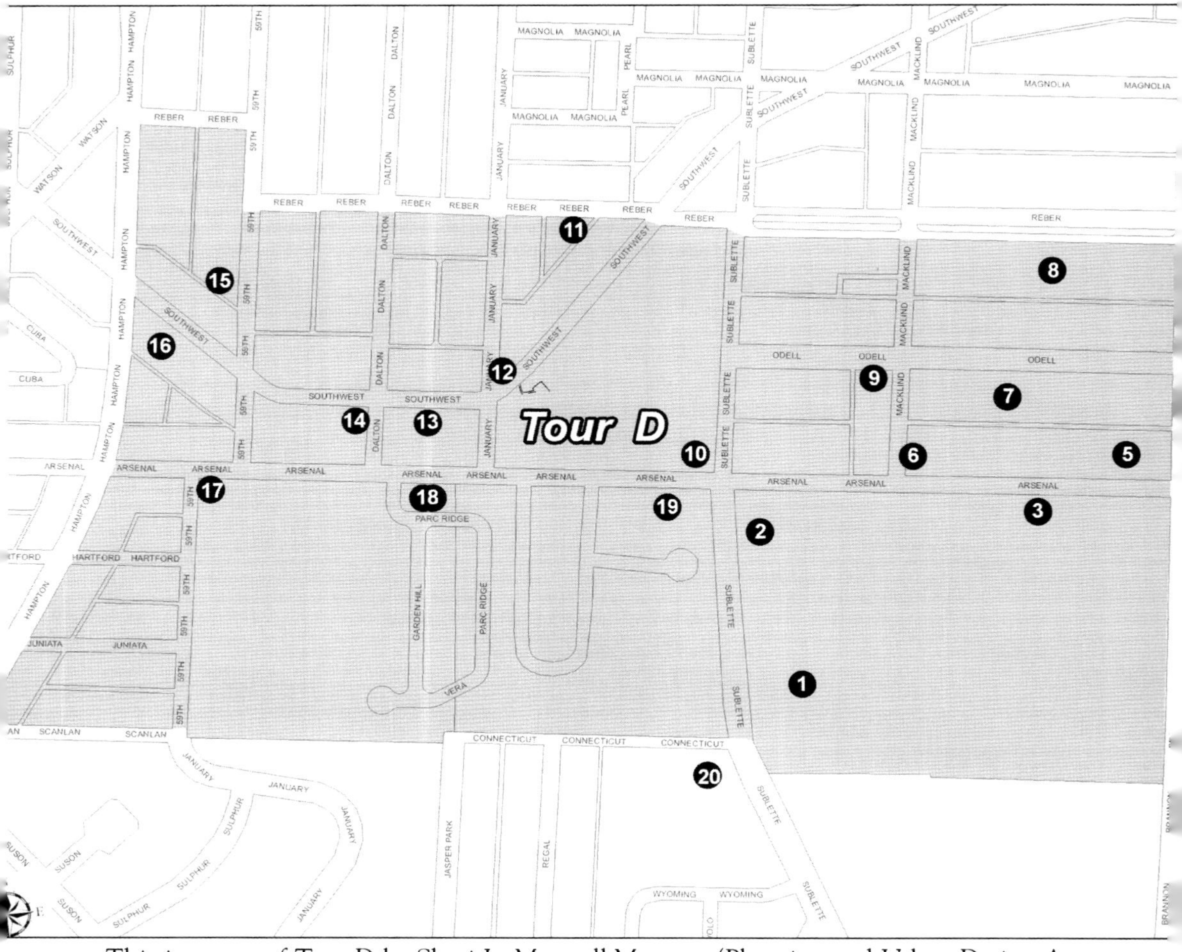


This is a map of Tour D by Shari L. Maxwell-Mooney. (Planning and Urban Design Agency City of St. Louis.)

# *Four*

# Tour D

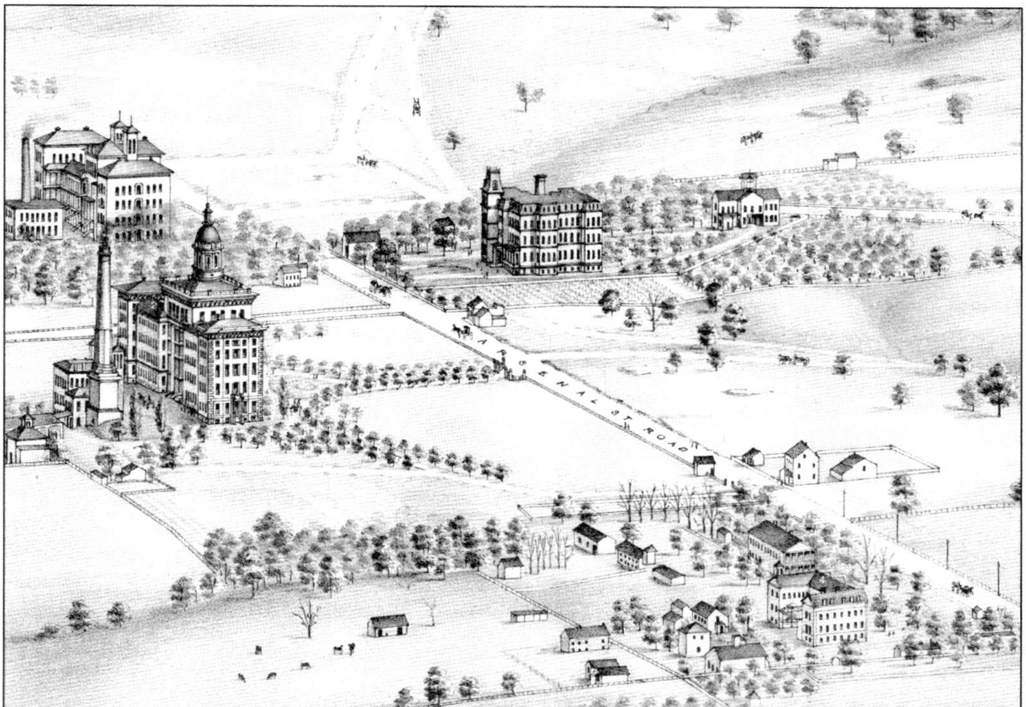


This plate of Arsenal Road, now known as Arsenal Street, gives an idea of what the area looked like at the time and marks the location of the new county poorhouse, the county insane asylum, Social Evils Hospital, and the old county poorhouse. Published in 1875, the plate appeared in *Pictorial St. Louis* by Camille N. Dry. (Missouri History Museum.)

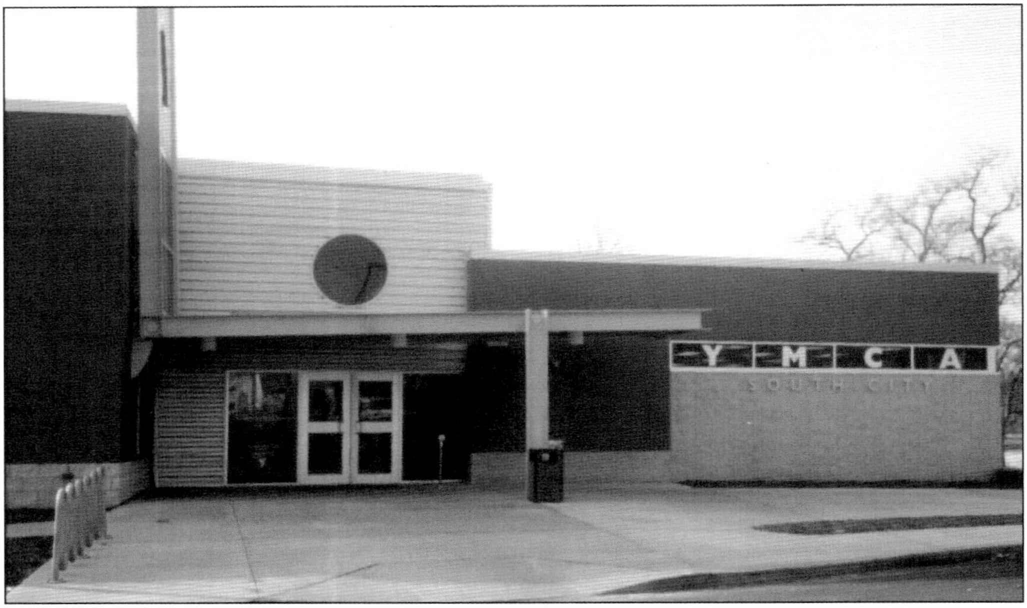


The South City Family YMCA (site D1) at 3150 Sublette Avenue opened in December 2000. From 1879 to 1908, it was known as the German Branch. It was located at several other locations, and then in 1936, the building on Grand Boulevard was built. That building was outgrown. The current structure measures 48,000 square feet. The facility provides families a place to work out, meet, play, and take classes. (South City Family YMCA.)

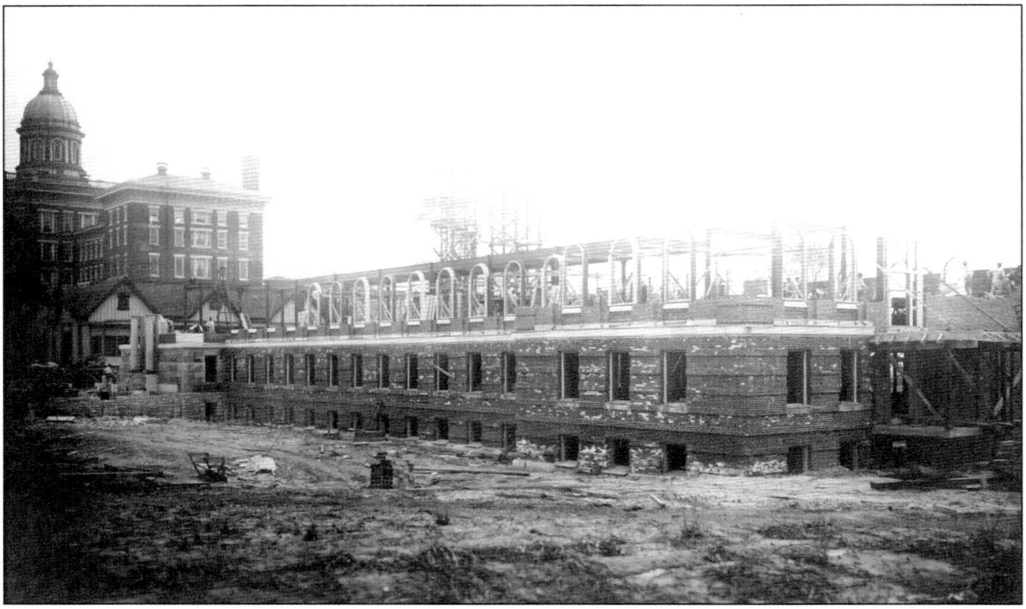

This photograph, taken on May 7, 1909, during the construction of the northwest wing for the insane asylum, gives an idea of what was there and then demolished to build the YMCA. This part of the YMCA is now an outdoor skate park. The YMCA is a great place for kids; there is a full-size gymnasium and a five-lane indoor pool with a waterslide. (Missouri Institute of Mental Health Library.)

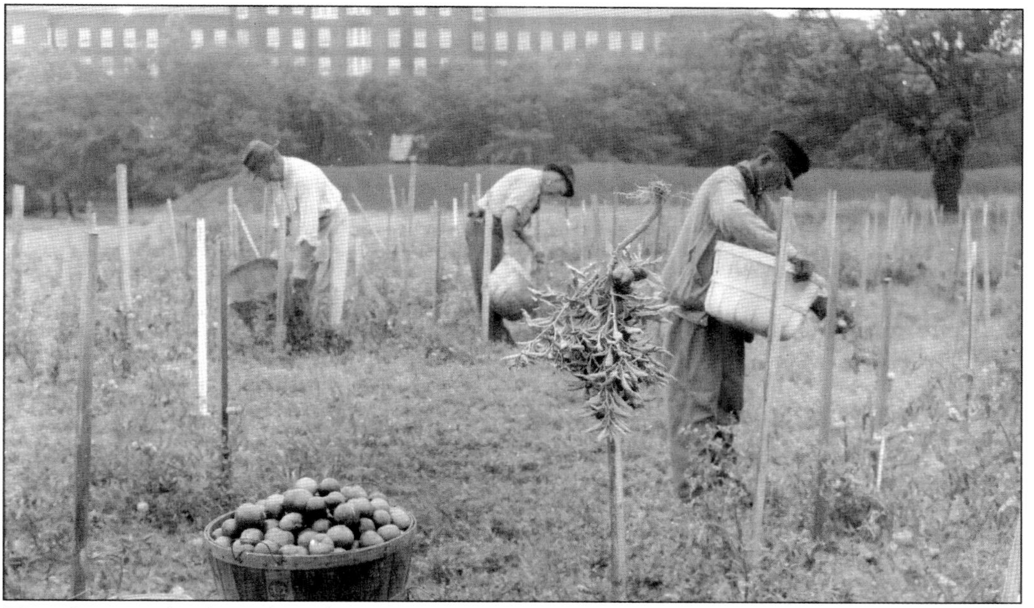

This photograph of people gathering tomatoes on the grounds of the St. Louis State Hospital in the 1940s gives a glimpse of a community that worked together. The fields are long gone, but the location is still a place where people work and stay fit together. The YMCA has meeting rooms, a fitness center with strength training and cardiovascular equipment, a free-weight center, and an aerobic studio. (Missouri Institute of Mental Health Library.)

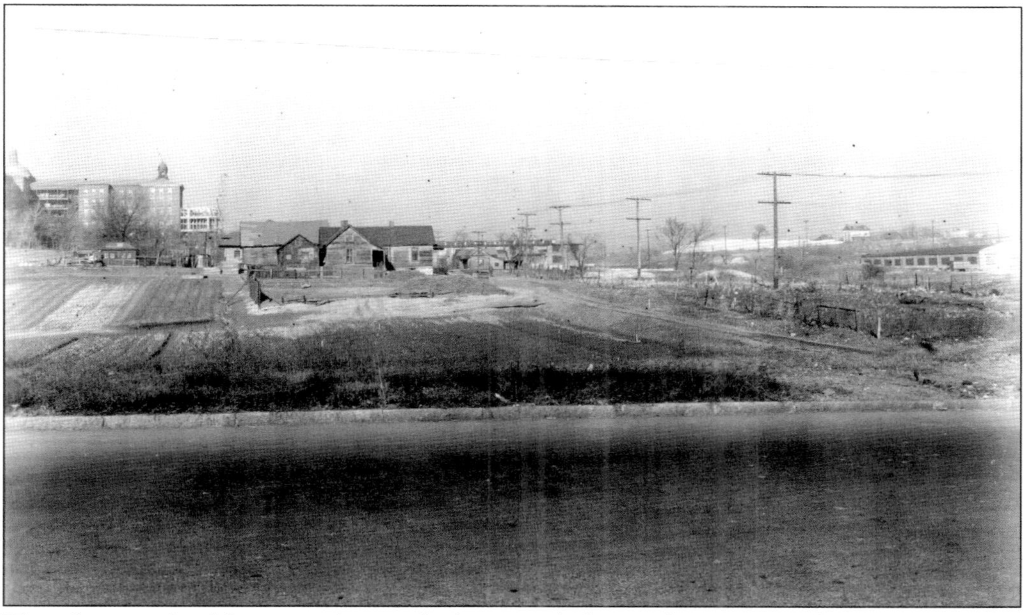

This photograph of Brannon Avenue looking north from Fyler Avenue taken on January 19, 1934, shows the vast acreage of the city sanitarium. It was a self-sufficient community where many of the patients had working skills. The sanitarium had a laundry in the basement, a shop for occupational therapy, a barbershop, and a carpenter's shop. There was even a mule barn. Mule teams were used for maintaining the grounds. (Missouri Institute of Mental Health Library.)

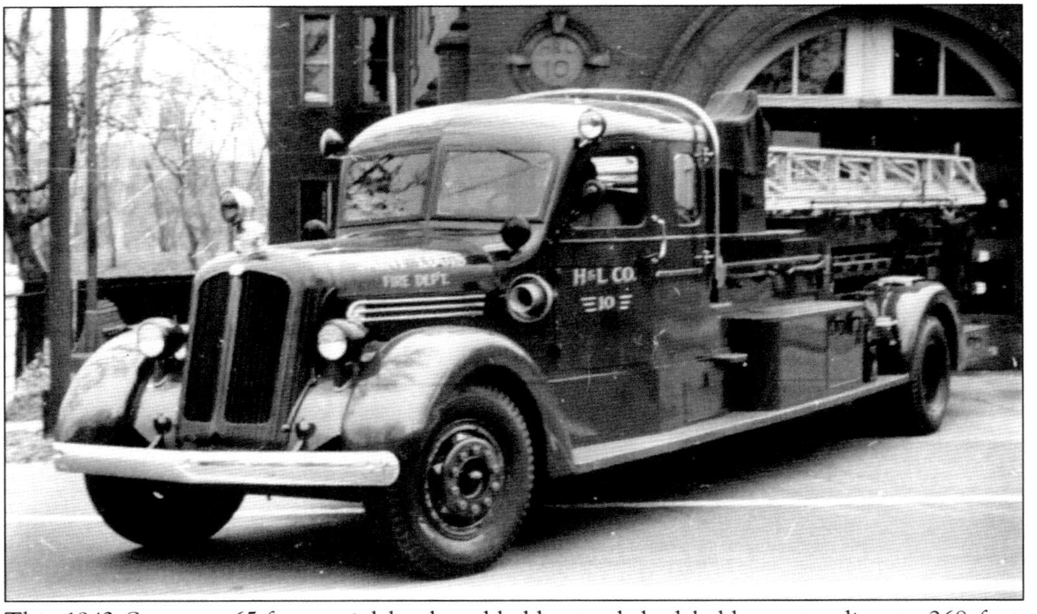


This 1943 Seagrave 65-foot aerial hook-and-ladder truck had ladders extending to 268 feet. Engine House No. 35 (site D2), built in 1895 at 5450 Arsenal Street, is the oldest active fire station in the St. Louis Fire Department. According to Robert Pauly, historian at the St. Louis Fire Department headquarters, Engine Company No. 35 and the Hook and Ladder Company No. 10 were organized at this location. (St. Louis Fire Department Museum.)

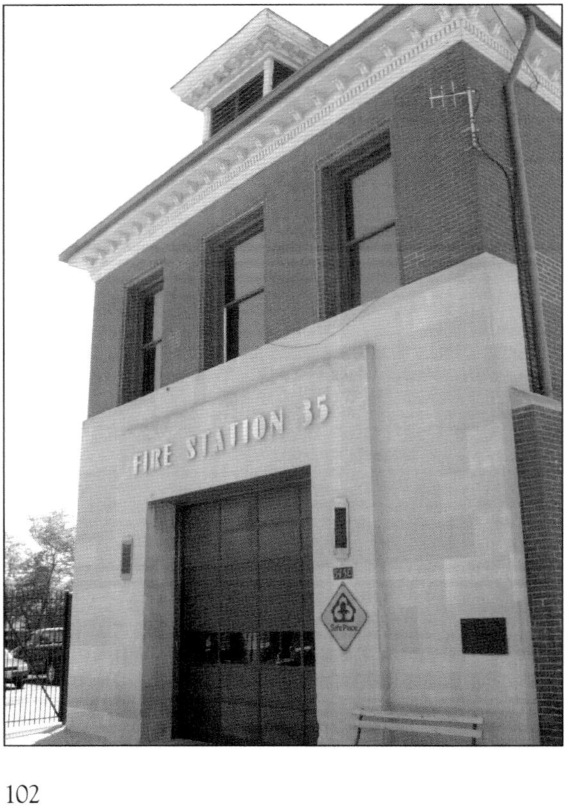


The firehouse was remodeled in 1959. A new front was added to the fire station that proudly serves the Southwest Garden and the Hill neighborhoods. Pauly says, "This station has lost three members who made the supreme sacrifice in the performance of their duty." The St. Louis Fire Department Museum is located at 1421 North Jefferson Avenue. Pauly has been volunteering his time to the museum for 11 years. (Photograph by Janice Markham.)

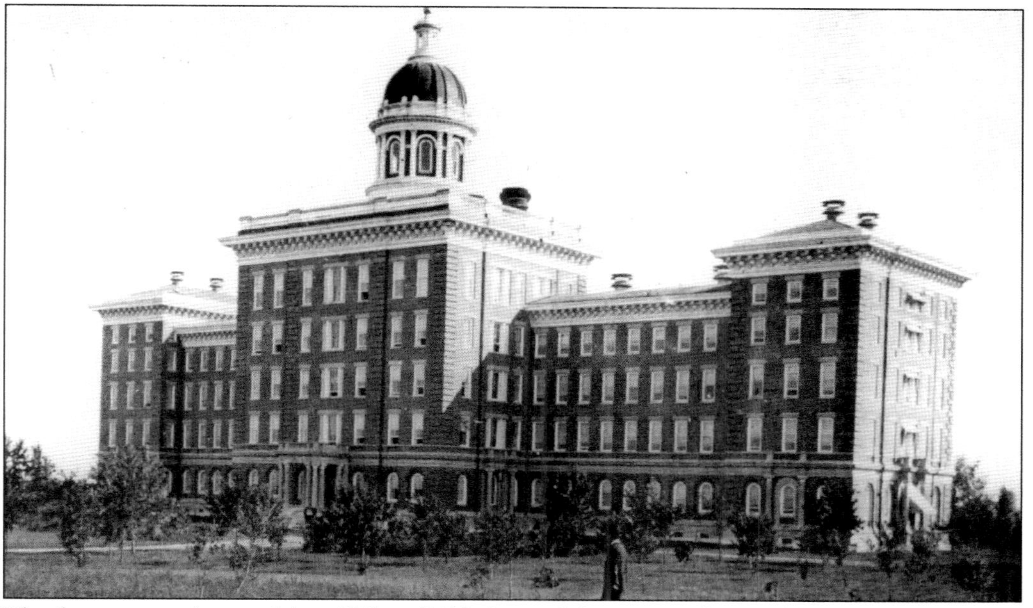

The former state hospital (site D3) at 5400 Arsenal Street was designed by architect William Rumbold in 1864. Dr. Edward C. Runge, the superintendent of the state hospital, is walking the grounds in front of the dome building in this photograph taken around 1900. The asylum opened on April 23, 1869, with 150 patients. By 1907, it was necessary to begin construction of new wings and annexes to the original building. (Missouri Institute of Mental Health Library.)

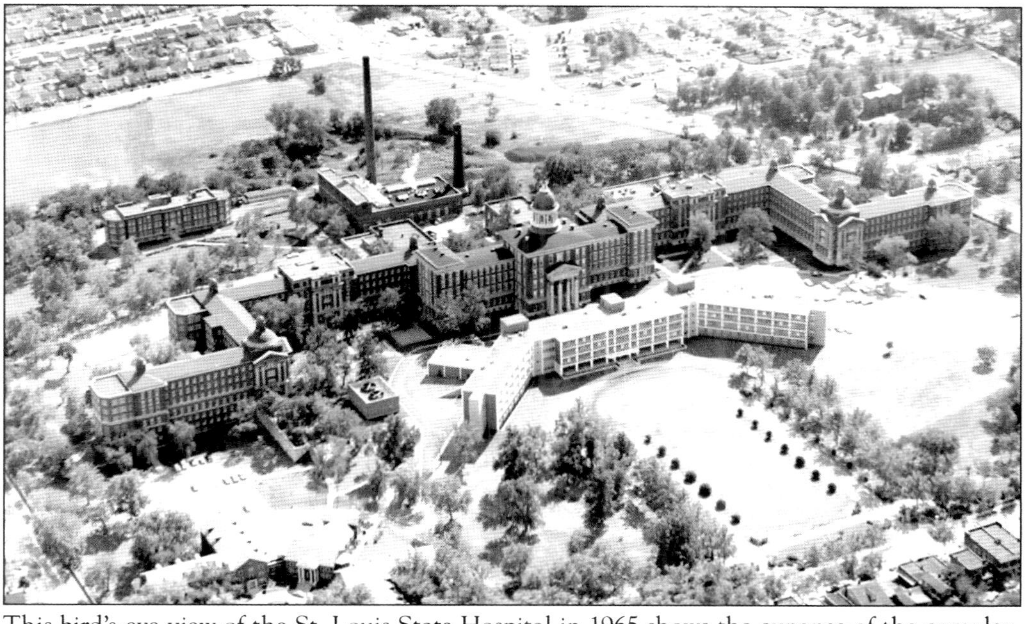

This bird's-eye view of the St. Louis State Hospital in 1965 shows the expanse of the complex. The hospital started with 150 patients and grew to 3,844 patients by 1940. In 1968, two floors were added to the Kohler Building, which was in front of the dome building. The east wing, west wing, and the Kohler Building were demolished in the 1990s. The land west of the dome building was donated to the YMCA. (Missouri Institute of Mental Health Library.)

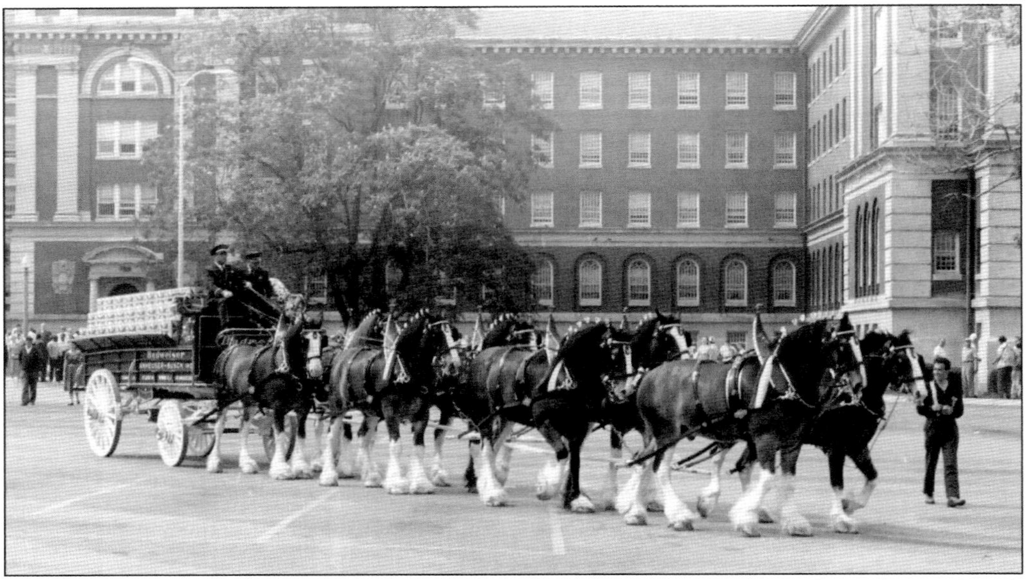

The Budweiser Clydesdale horses visit the hospital on Fun Day in June 1964. The Anheuser-Busch Brewery is located a few miles from the state hospital going east on Arsenal Street. The Clydesdale horse teams came into the Anheuser-Busch picture in 1933 after Prohibition was repealed. To celebrate the event, the first case of beer was carried by the hitch down Pestalozzi Street. Today the Clydesdales are still taking part in celebrations around the country. (Missouri Institute of Mental Health Library.)

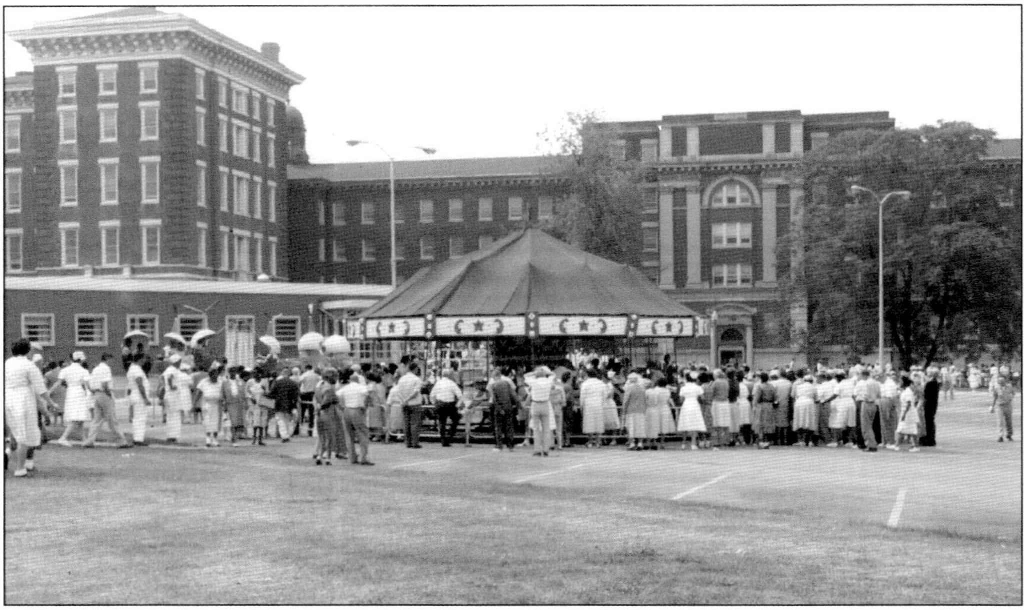

The crowd enjoys a picnic in the foreground of the Kohler Building during Fun Day in June 1964. The groundbreaking ceremony for the Kohler Building was held in October 1959. Speakers at the ceremony included Missouri governor James T. Blair; chairman of the state mental health commission Francis Smith; and Dr. Louis H. Kohler, state hospital superintendent. The building was completed in 1962 at a cost of $5 million. (Missouri Institute of Mental Health Library.)

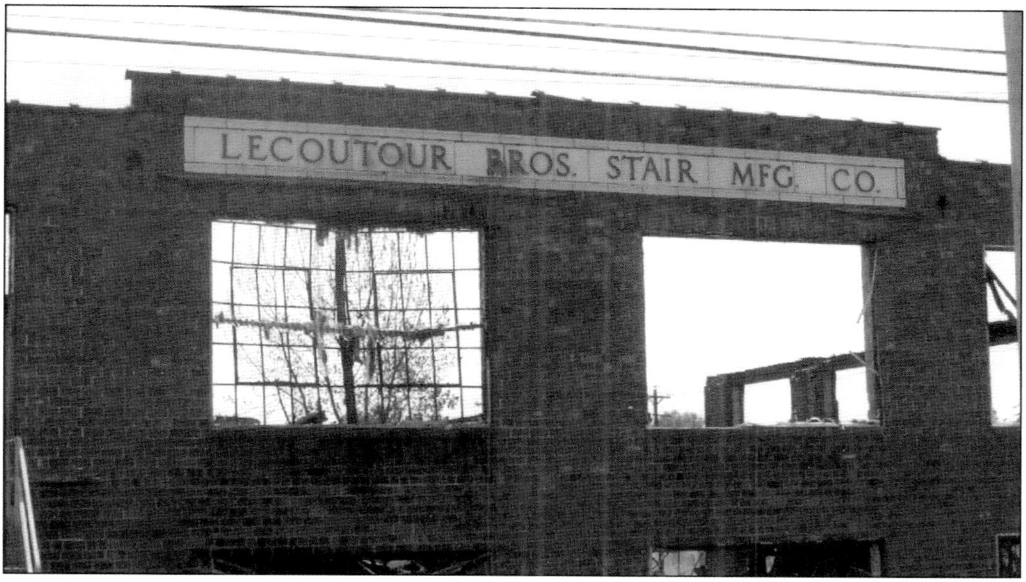


The Sterling Lacquer Manufacturing Company (site D4) at 3150 Brannon Avenue owns the former site of the Lecoutour Stair Company that burned down in 2005. The 1930 city directory lists Lecoutour Brothers Stair Manufacturing and Fred Kralemann, a wood turner, at 3176 Brannon Avenue. In 1975, 3150 Brannon Avenue was the location of Peerless Products, which made storm doors and windows, and the Federal Bag Company, which was a manufacturer of cotton goods. (Kay Mantia collection.)

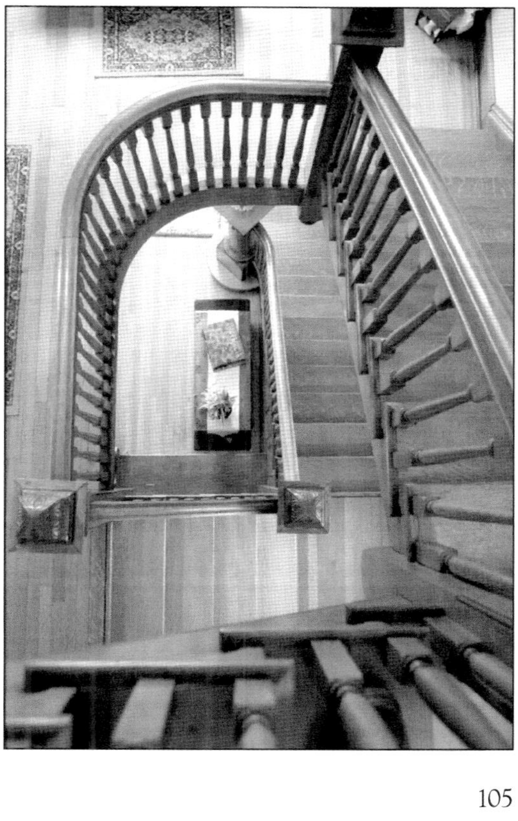

This staircase was built by the Lecoutour Stair Company for president Emil Lecoutour's home at 4533 Tower Grove Place. The Lecoutour company's first factory was in Benton Park at 3015 Salena Street. Next it opened a factory in the Southwest Garden at 4521–4523 Shaw Avenue. This factory at 3176 Brannon Avenue was the last one it built. By 1955, the site became the C. D. Midland Building, where the Mundet Cork Company and the Branchell Company were located. (Derek Cadzow Photography.)

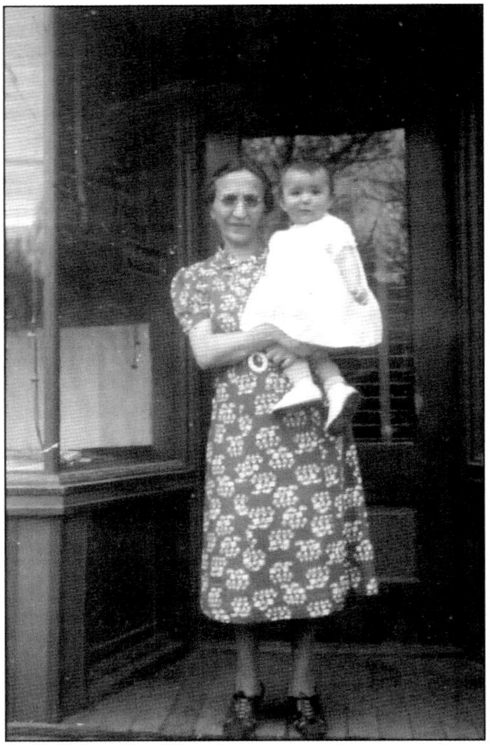

In front of the former site of Your Choice Bakery (site D5) at 5315 Arsenal Street, Carolyn (Ranzini) Stelzer is being carried by her paternal grandmother, Erminia Ranzini. The Ranzini family lived above the bakery. The bakery closed when the master baker went to war in 1942. On Sundays, families with patients at the state hospital stopped by the bakery to pick up pastries to take on their weekly visits to the hospital. (Carolyn Stelzer collection.)

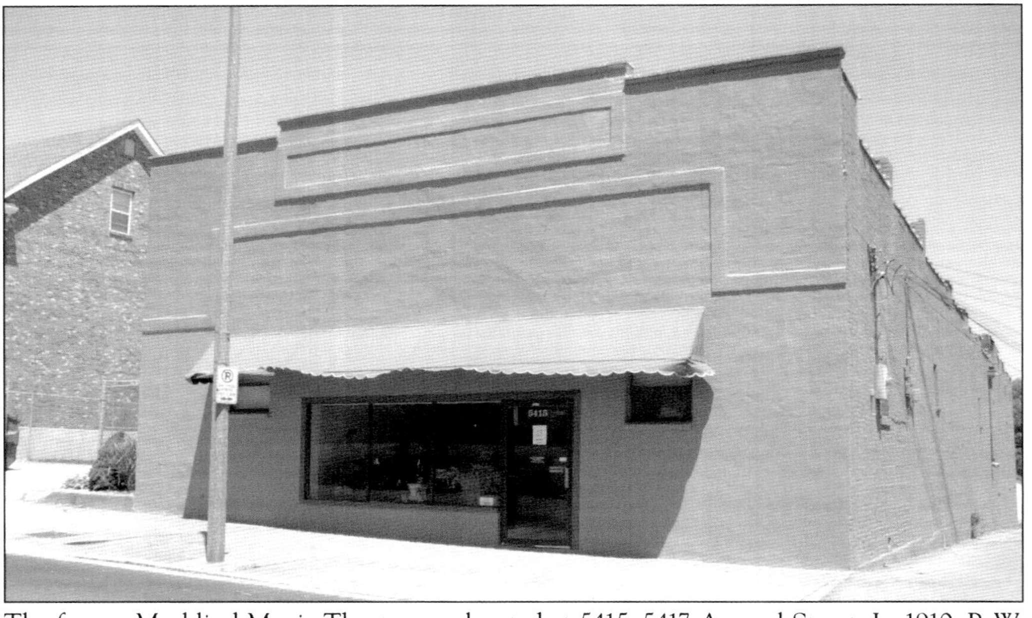

The former Macklind Movie Theatre was located at 5415–5417 Arsenal Street. In 1910, P. W. Steffan obtained a building permit to construct a nickelodeon for $2,000. In 1921, J. B. Lueken turned it into a picture show, and in 1924, he made an addition for $4,000. In 1936, he added a canopy to the theater, and in 1938, he made another addition for $1,000. The building is currently owned by the Theodorou family and is used as office space. (Photograph by Janice Markham.)

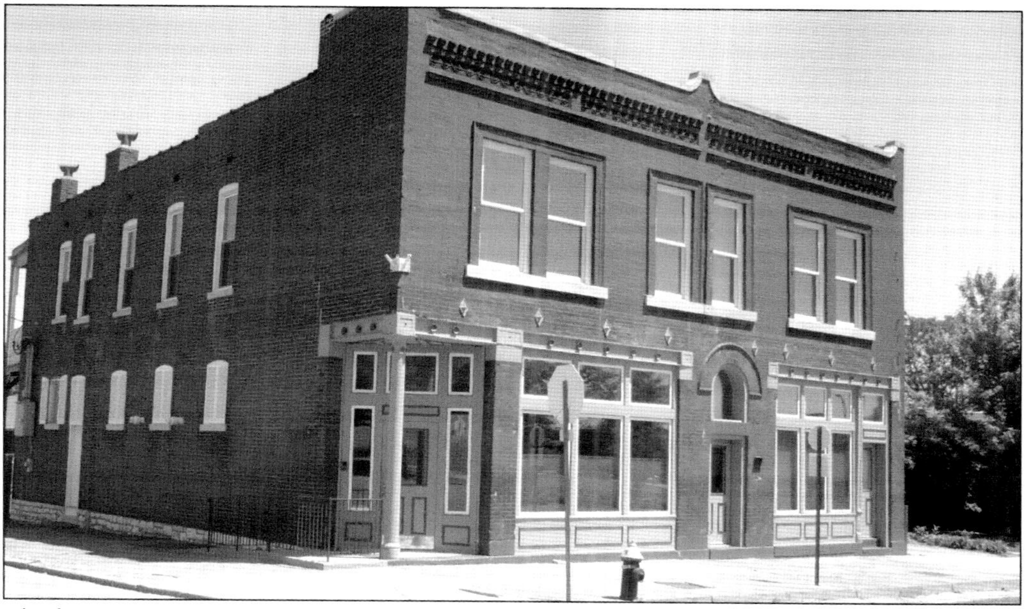

The former Weaver building (site D6) at 5385–5389 Arsenal Street was a confectionery. Currently it is the location of the Butler's Pantry, a catering business established in 1966. In 1901, David Weaver obtained a building permit to construct a store and flats at 5389–5391 Arsenal Street for $8,404. In 1902, he built a wagon shed in back. In 1912, the city issued a permit to G. Weaver to build a two-story dwelling at 5385 Arsenal Street for $3,000. (Photograph by Janice Markham.)

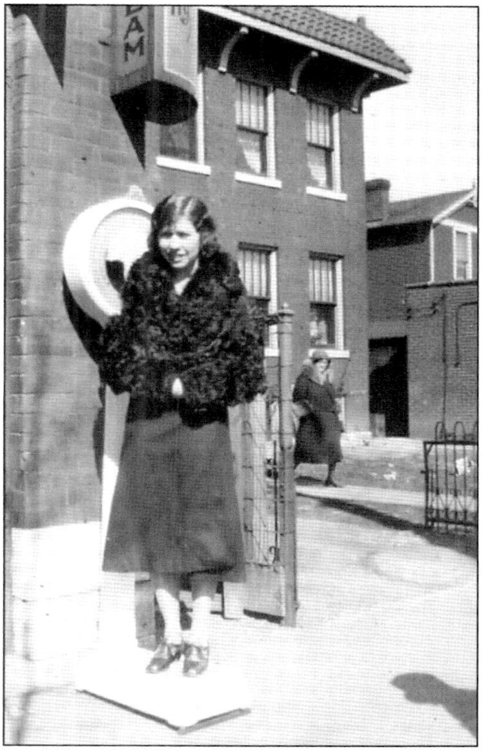

A girl poses on the scale at the corner of 5385 Arsenal Street. The 1930 city directory lists Catherine Rice, dry goods, at 5389 Arsenal Street, and Harry J. and Theresa Powell lived at 5385 Arsenal Street. Frank Kieling's confectionery was at 5391 Arsenal Street. By 1935, Kieling had expanded his confectionery to 5389 Arsenal Street. Photographs were given to the Butler's Pantry of Thompson's Pharmacy; however, in researching the city directories, the pharmacy was not found to have been located in this building. (Butler's Pantry.)

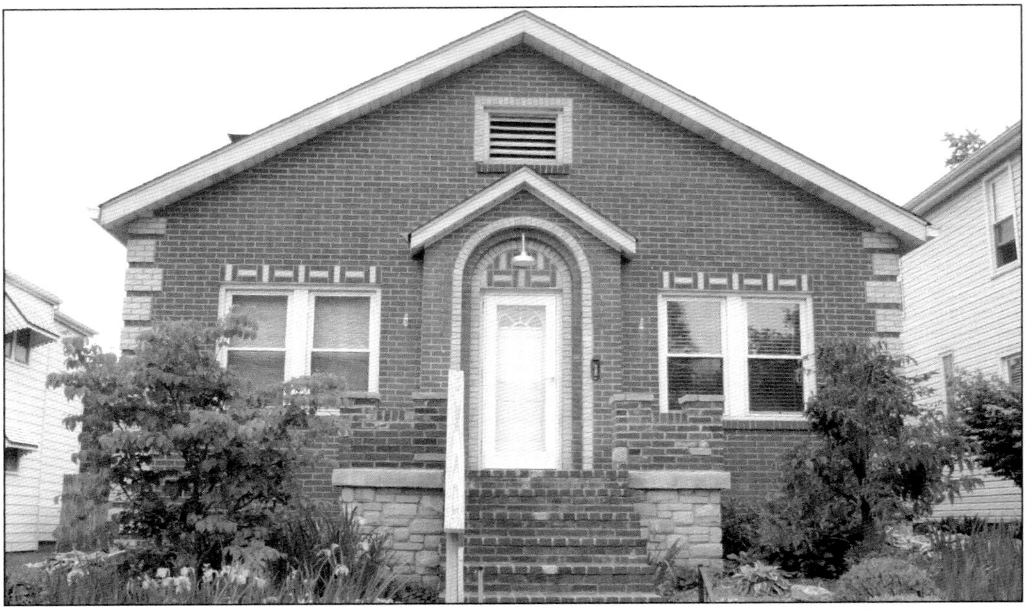

A Tudor-style house (site D7) at 5358 Odell Street stands out among the other houses on this block. The most visible feature is the patterned brickwork. The brick could have come from this area. There were several brick factories here. In 1910, several of the men living on this block worked in the brickyards for Clay Pipe Works as laborers and bricklayers and tending the kilns. (Photograph by Janice Markham.)

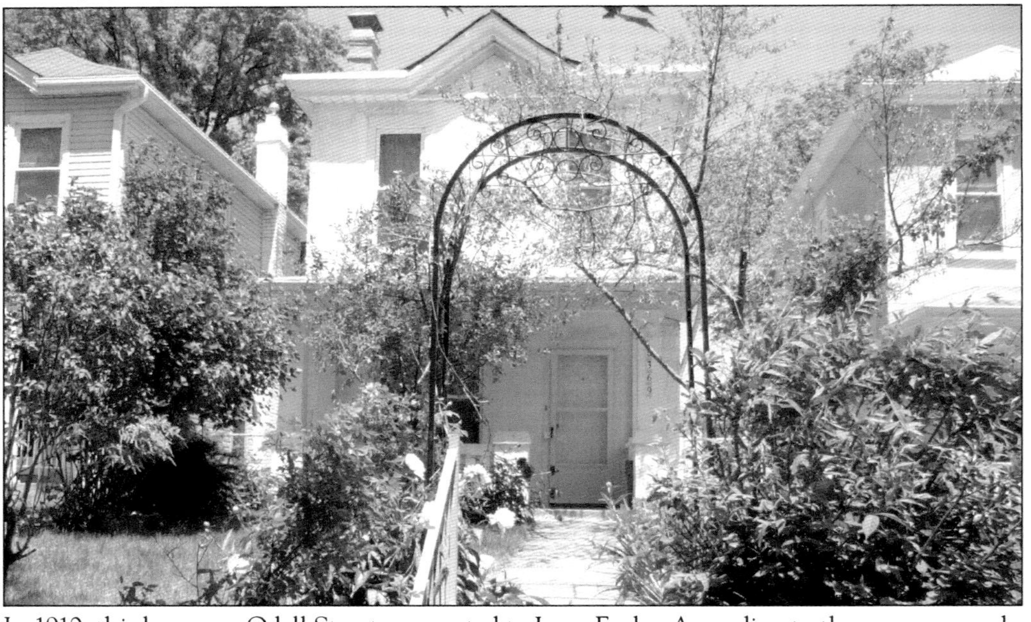

In 1910, this house on Odell Street was rented to Lena Fuchs. According to the census records, Fuchs was a widow and had two daughters living with her: Annie, age 21, and Olga, age 16, who both worked for a supply company. Fuchs was not employed outside the home, but she took in boarders. John Meehan, who came to the United States from Ireland in 1903, rented from her. Meehan was a porter for a dry goods store. (Photograph by Janice Markham.)

The Queen Anne house with the turret (site D8) at 5342 Reber Place was built in 1910. The 1910 census records list households that already existed on this block, including Charles Zurick, who worked for the railroad; John Stockton, who did iron bridge work; George Melick, who was a driver for a furniture company; Clarence Wendell, who was a postal clerk; and Joseph Regelman, who sold shoes. (Photograph by Janice Markham.)

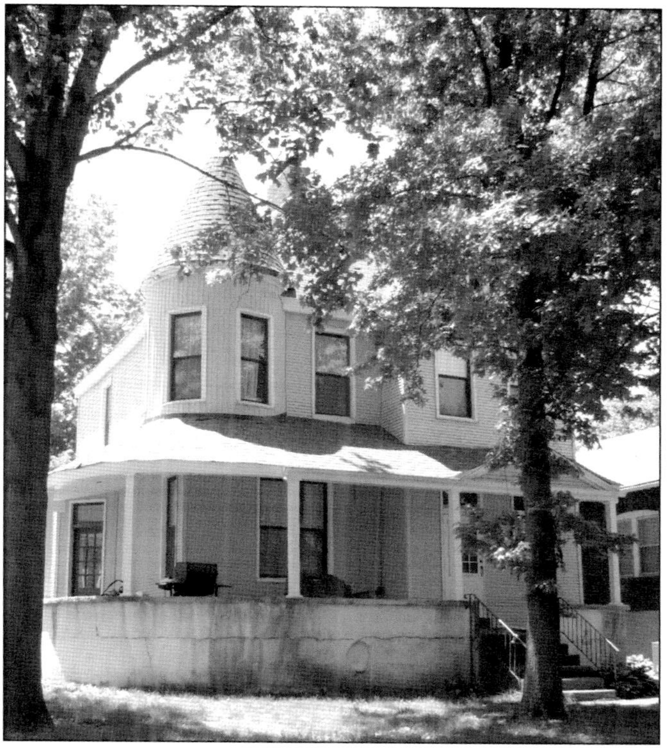

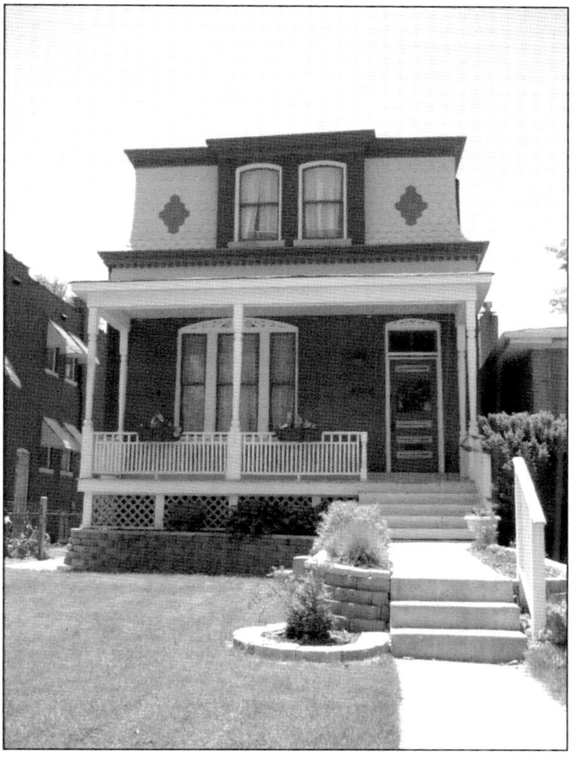

The mansard roof house at 5366 Reber Place was owned by Carl Friedrichs and his sister Augusta in 1910. They were both born in Germany and came to the United States in 1882. Carl was a molder at a foundry. In 1920, the Friedrichs were still there, but by 1930, the residents were Frank F. and Mamie Lauman. Frank was a chauffeur. In 1940, the Laumans were gone, and Joseph Spraul moved in. (Photograph by Janice Markham.)

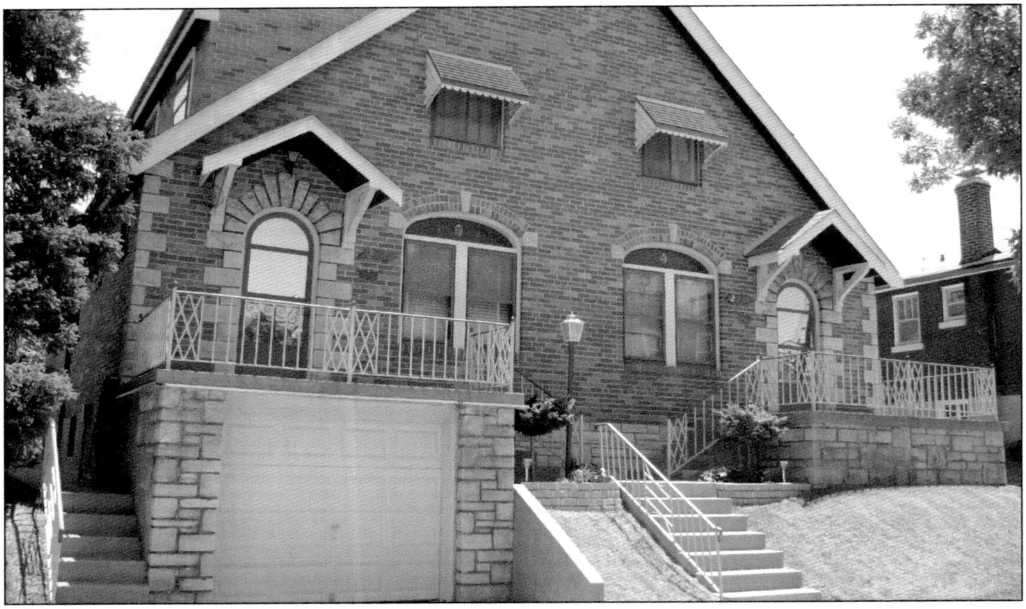

The former Berra homes (site D9) at 2906 and 2908 Macklind Avenue were built for two brothers, John J. and Charles J. Berra. The brothers owned the homes at 2912 and 2914 Macklind Avenue before they moved here. In the 1952 city directory, Charles and Ida Berra are listed at 2906 Macklind Avenue, and John and Rose Berra were listed at 2908 Macklind Avenue. Charles owned the Wayne Café at 901 Market Street. (Photograph by Janice Markham.)

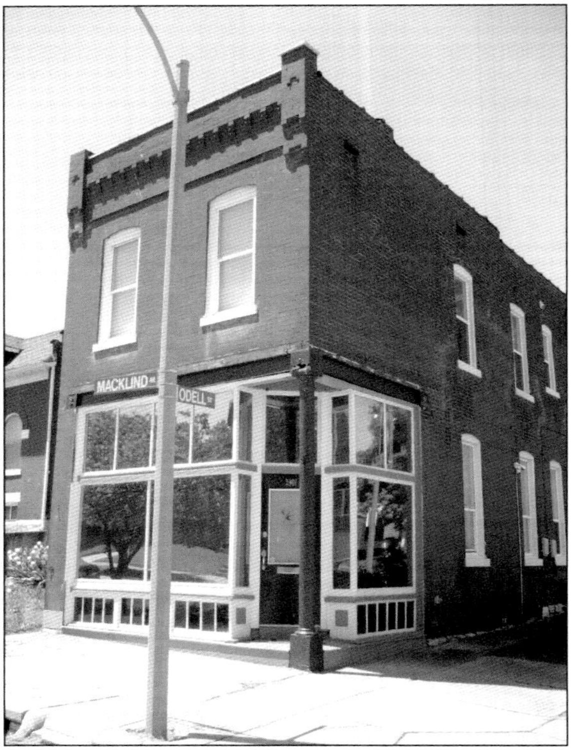


The storefront at 2901 Macklind Avenue was built as a corner grocery with an apartment upstairs by B. J. Charleville for Rudolph Sindelar in 1909 for $3,200. Sindelar was a machinist and his wife, Barbara, ran the grocery store. The 1910 census records list their children as Rudolph, a printer; Emma, a dressmaker; Annie, a stenographer; and Charles, a helper at a machine shop. The younger children were August, Emil, Louis, Marie, and Richard. (Photograph by Janice Markham.)

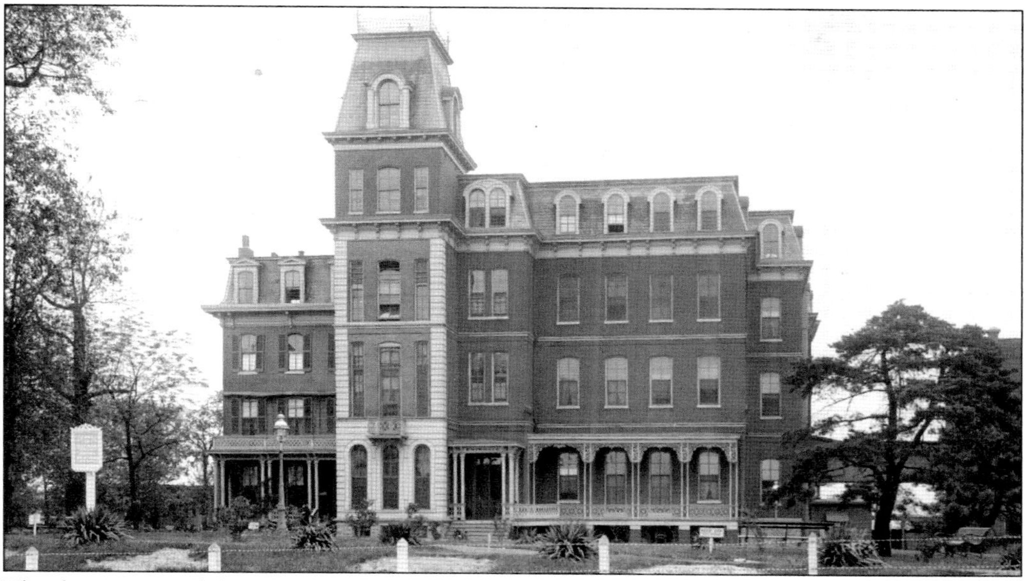

The former site of the Social Evils Hospital (site D10) is now Sublette Park at the northwest corner of Arsenal Street and Sublette Avenue. This photograph was taken by F. D. Hampson around 1900. The hospital was established in 1872 to regulate prostitution. It was modeled after a law in Paris, France. After a year of treating prostitutes who became ill or contracted venereal diseases, the hospital changed its focus to women and children and became the Female Hospital. (Missouri History Museum.)

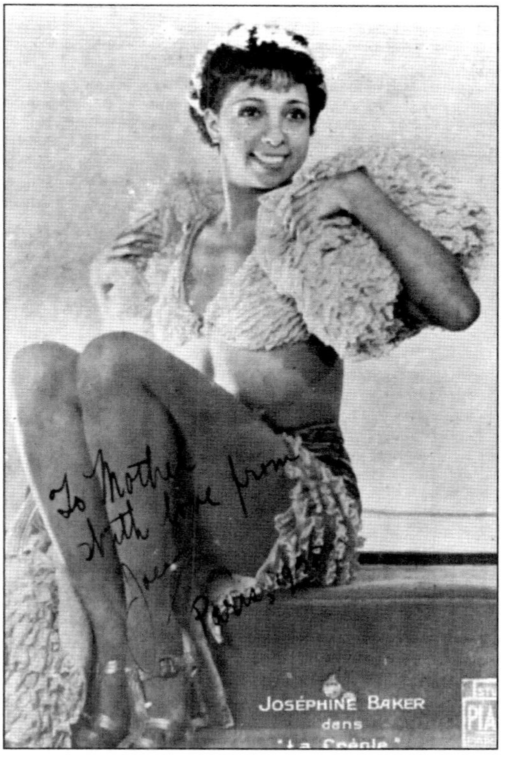


Josephine Baker was born Freda Josephine McDonald in 1906 at the Female Hospital. At age 13, she wed, but she was underage, and the marriage was illegal. She went on to marry four times legally. She kept the name Baker from her second husband. At age 17, she was on Broadway and appeared at the Cotton Club in Harlem. By the age of 25, she was living in Paris and became a French citizen in 1936. She died in Paris in 1975. (Missouri History Museum.)

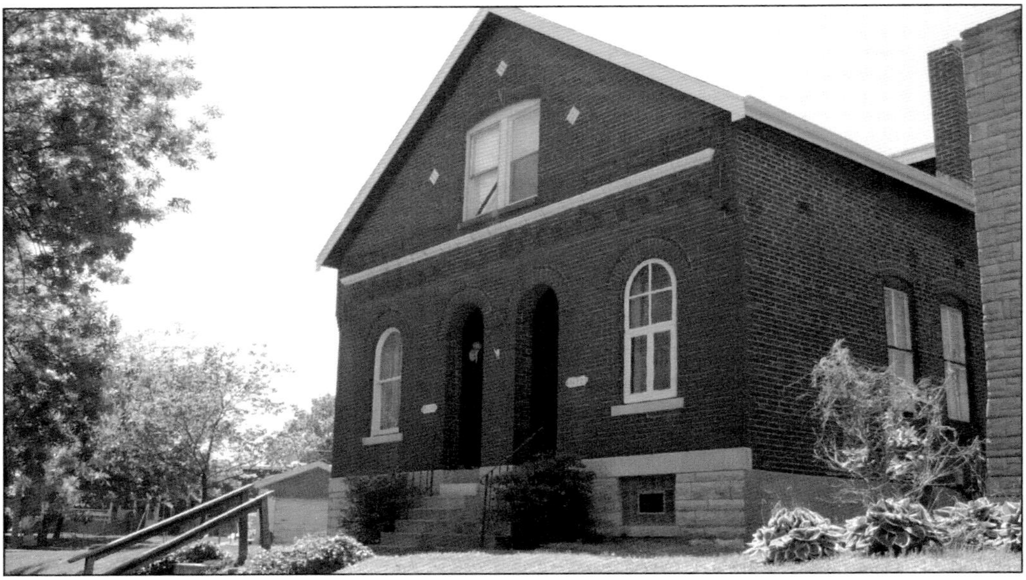

The two-family home (site D11) at 5630–5632 Reber Place was built by Henry Wahoff in 1901 for $1,800. Wahoff was a carpenter who built houses and lived at 5611 Reber Place. The 1920 city directory lists residents as Jacob and Lillian Helgoth and Harry Helgoth. Jacob was a printer, and Harry was a molder. In 1930, Jacob is listed at 5630 Reber Place, and John Kreutz was in 5632 Reber Place. In 1940, Michael Miano lived at 5630 Reber Place, and Michael Demarco was in 5632 Reber Place. (Photograph by Janice Markham.)

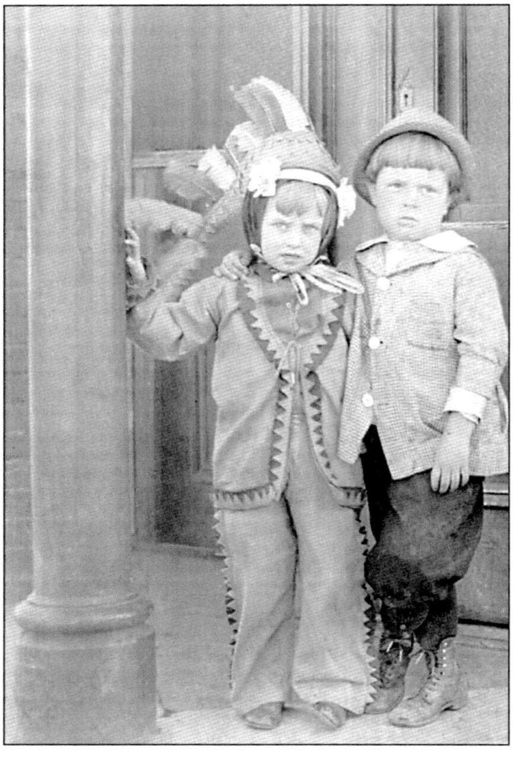

Here Bernice and Ed Owens are photographed in costumes. There were several children in the neighborhood that they could play with. Ed lived on Reber Place, and Bernice lived nearby on Southwest Avenue. In 1910 in the 5600 block of Reber Place, families with young children included the Wahoffs, Ernstmanns, Metzs, and Ranschs. In the 5600 block of Southwest Avenue, families with young children included the Lamprechts, Krases, Sparrers, Cliftons, and Osboures. (Owens family collection.)

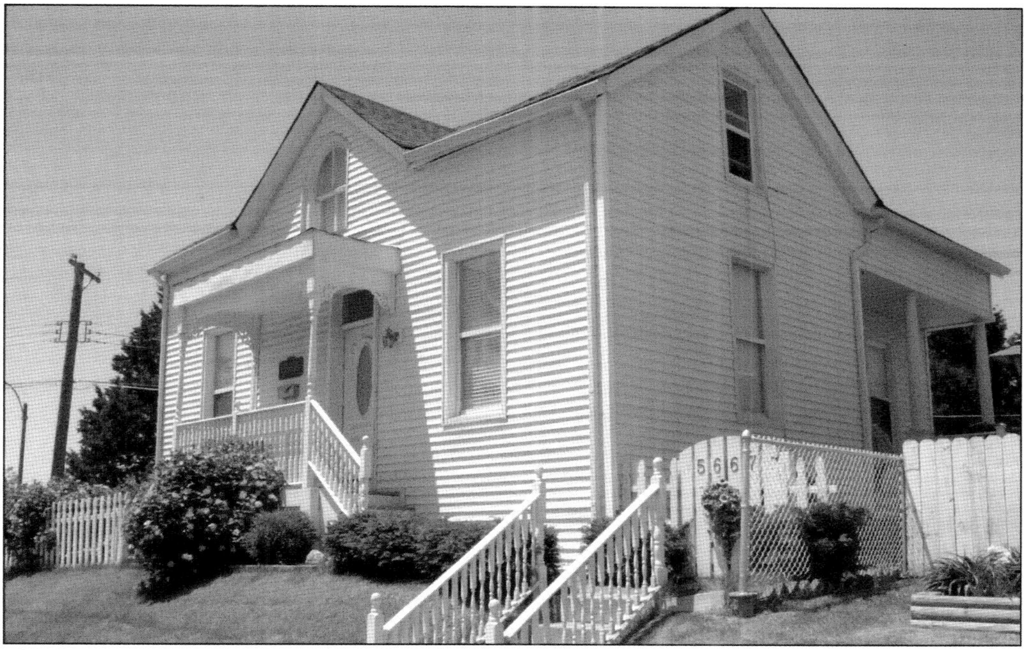


The house on the hill (site D12) at 5667 Southwest Avenue was rented to Winifred Berrigan in 1910. The census records list Winifred as a widow from Ireland. Living with her were her children Bridget and James Berrigan, another daughter, Catherine Maher, and grandson Paul Maher. Winifred also had a nine-year-old boarder, Nellie McMahon. Bridget and Catherine were seamstresses. By 1920, another widow, Emma Burgoltry, and her sons George and William lived there. (Photograph by Janice Markham.)

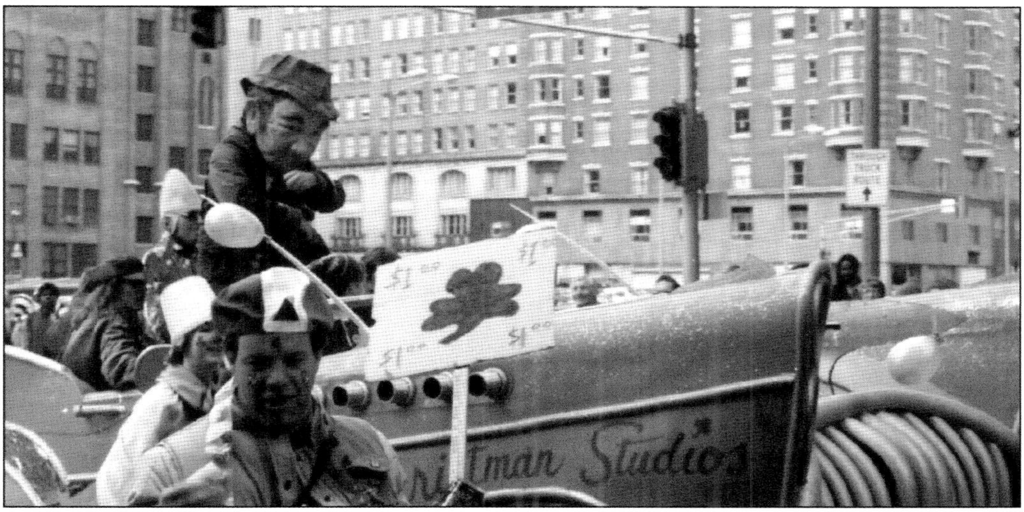

St. Patrick's Day is celebrated in a downtown parade. Most of the Southwest Garden's early residents were of German, Italian, and Irish descent. In 1925, the Fairmount Democratic Club, made up of players from the Southwest Garden and the Hill, signed up to play in the St. Louis Municipal Soccer League. Most of the players on the team were Irish. That year, they won the league championship. John P. English, who lived at 5716 Southwest Avenue, was on the team. (Operation Brightside.)

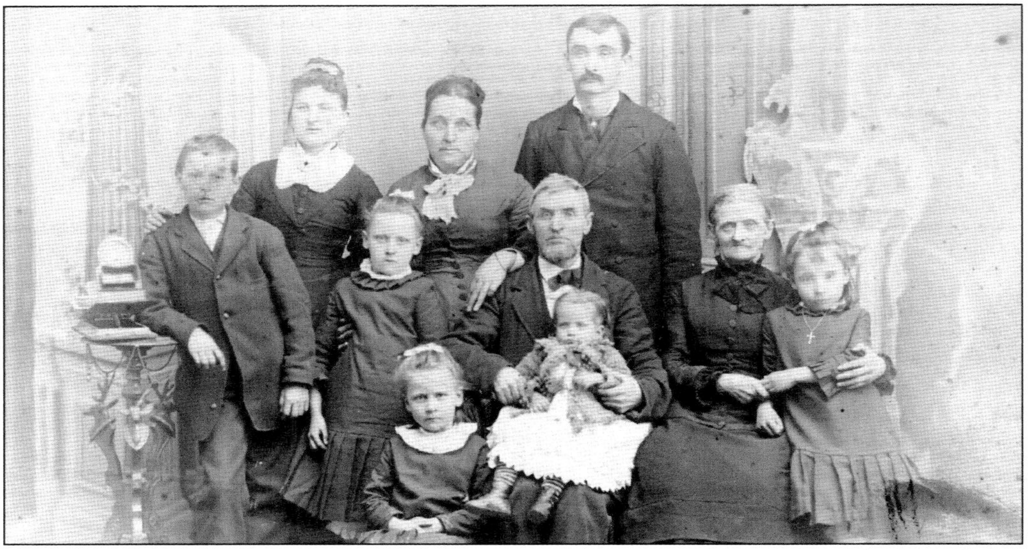

The former Fleming and English family homestead (site D13) on the 5700 block of Southwest Avenue is gone; the house that sits at 5716 Southwest Avenue took the place of the frame houses. Pictured around 1880, the Fleming family includes, from left to right, (first row) Kate (girl sitting); (second row) Eddie, Ellie, an unidentified man holding Alice, Mary, and Margaret; (third row) Annie, Julia, and John. Annie married John T. English and had six children: Julia, John, Edward, Arthur, Francis X., and Henry. (Mary Ann English Winkelmann and Marella Hardesty Baird collection.)

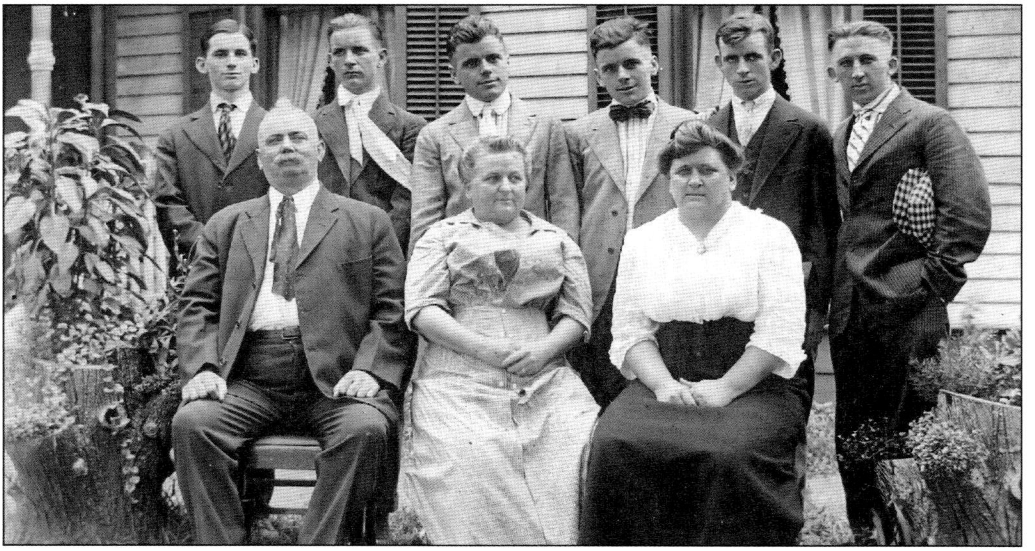

The English family poses in front of the old house at 5716 Southwest Avenue around 1920. From left to right are (first row) John T. and Annie English and unidentified; (second row) Arthur, Henry, Edward, John, and Francis X. English and Fred Hardesty. In 1910, the census records list the residents of 5716 Southwest Avenue as John T. and Annie, their children, John, Edward, Arthur, Francis X., and Henry, sisters-in-law Kathryn and Alice Fleming, and boarders Frank Jones and James McKormack. (Mary Ann English Winkelmann and Marella Hardesty Baird collection.)

Francis X. English is pictured around 1900. In 1910, he was 12. In the 1920 city directory, he is listed as a clerk residing at 5708 Southwest Avenue. Julia Fleming, the mother of Annie, purchased half the block, and they built the family home and three or four other small houses that were rented out. In 1920, the English family appears at 5708 and 5714 (or 5716) Southwest Avenue. (Mary Ann English Winkelmann and Marella Hardesty Baird collection.)

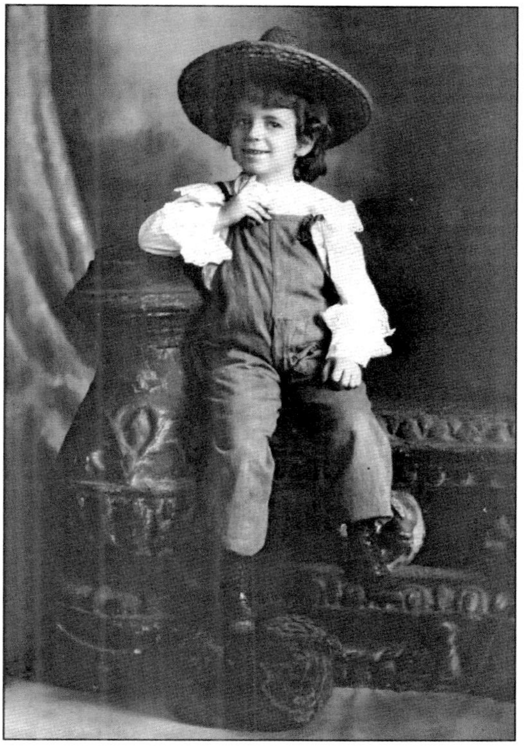

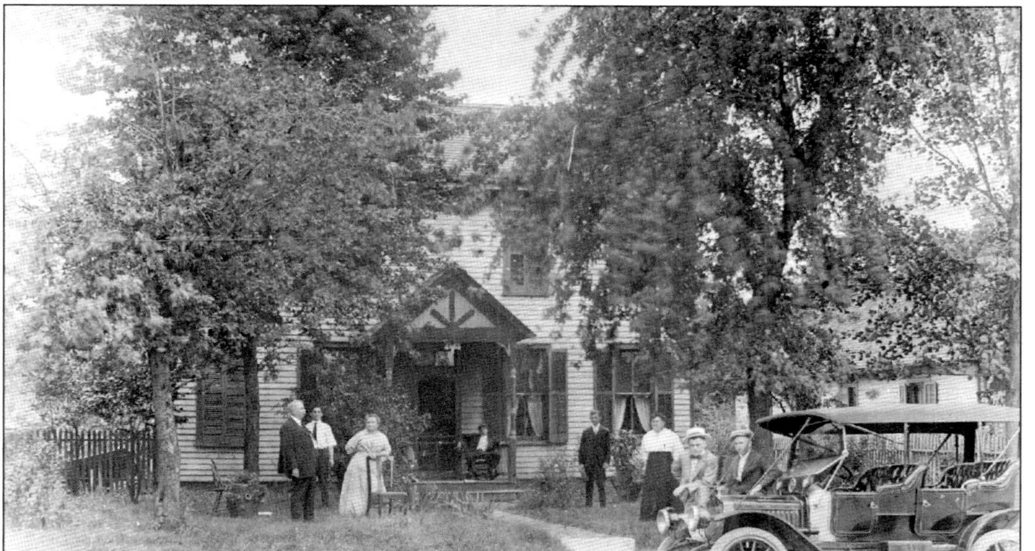

The English and Hardesty families gather at 5716 Southwest Avenue around 1920. John P. English was the recorder of deeds from 1935 to 1943. He died on October 2, 1972, when he was 78. He was survived by his wife, Ruth, daughter Faith Nooney, and brothers Arthur and Henry English. (Mary Ann English Winkelmann and Marella Hardesty Baird collection.)

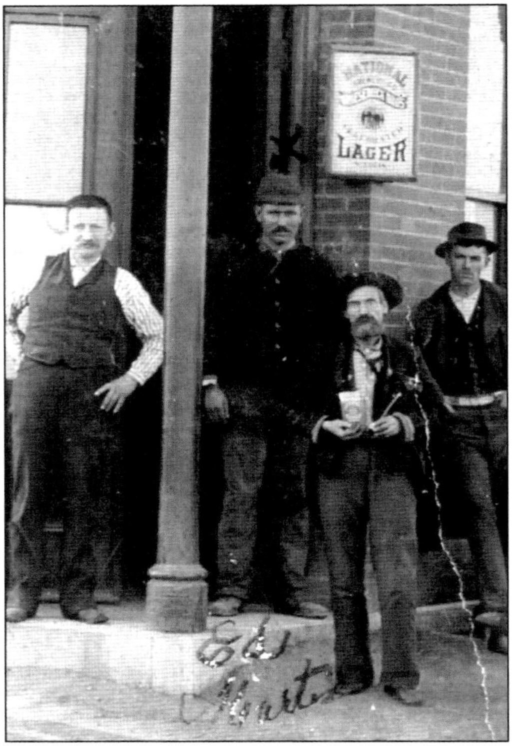


Friends gather at the corner tavern (site D14) at 5800 Southwest Avenue around 1900. Ed Martin is the gentleman with the *x* over his head. The others are unidentified. The kitchen was added in 1893 for P. Bevois for $300. In 1914, the Hyde Park Brewery built a shed, and by 1920, the city directory lists "Frank Owens, drinks" at this address. Mike Badalamenti bought the place in 1984 and established his business, Mr. B's Bar and Grill. (Mike Badalamenti collection.)

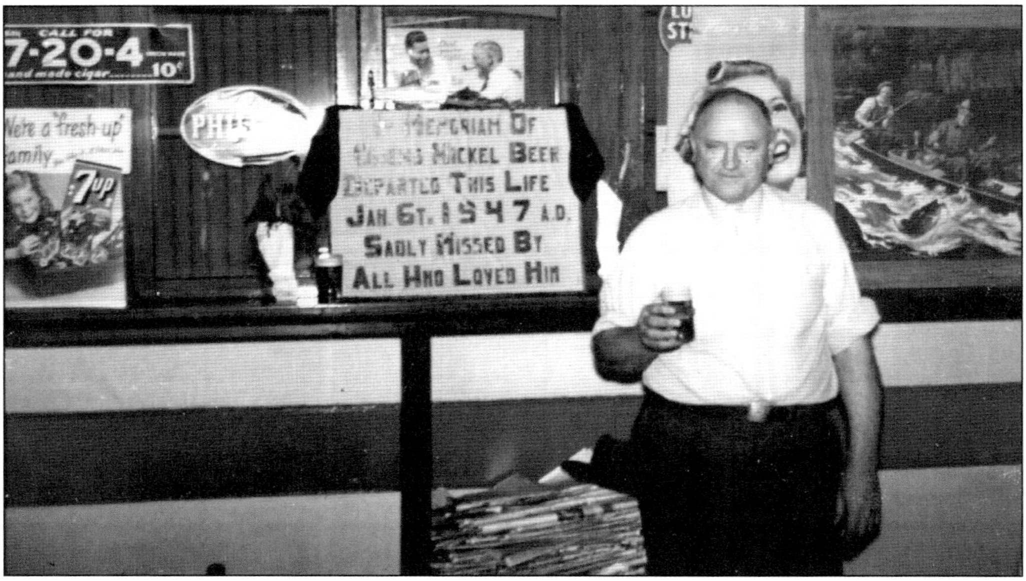


No more nickel beer. Henry "Dude" Owens, owner of Owen's Place, mourns the death of the 5¢ beer. Frank Owens is listed as the owner in the 1920 and 1930 city directories, and the 1940 directory lists "Henry Owens, liquors" at this address. In 1920, across the street at 5801–5803 Southwest Avenue was the Bethlehem Evangelical Bible School. In 1930, it was the location for Blue Ridge Mercantile, and by 1940, it was a grocery and a clothing cleaner. (Owens family collection.)

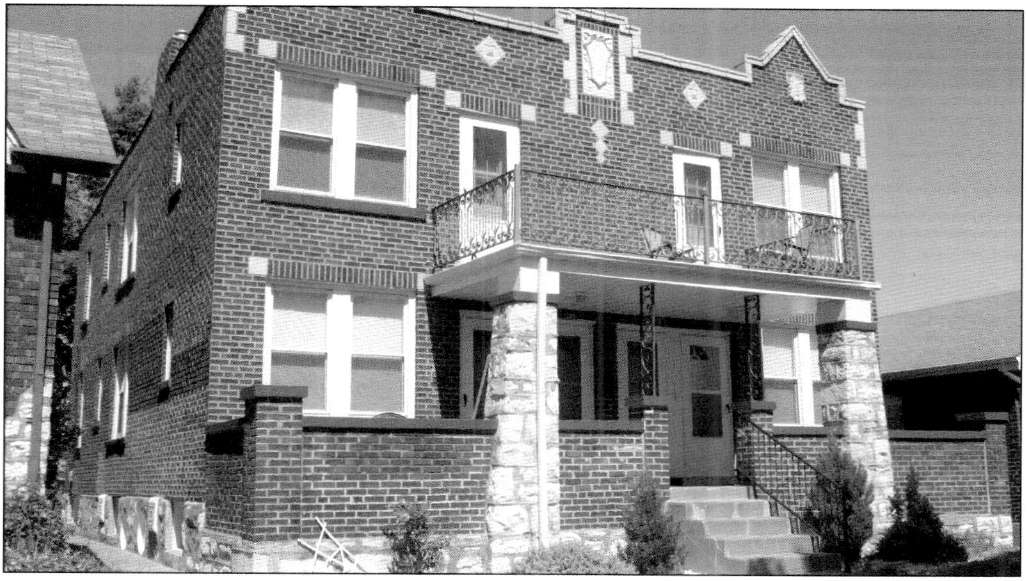

The four-family home (site D15) at 2817 Fifty-ninth Street was built for $10,000. A building permit was issued on May 14, 1929, to the owner listed as Becker. The permit was for a brick two-story, four-tenement structure. The units were rented to the working class. The residents included a claims investigator, a widow, and a salesman. In 1952, resident James T. Clarke was the accountant for the Clarke and Gable Company, opticians at 522 North Grand Boulevard. (Photograph by Janice Markham.)

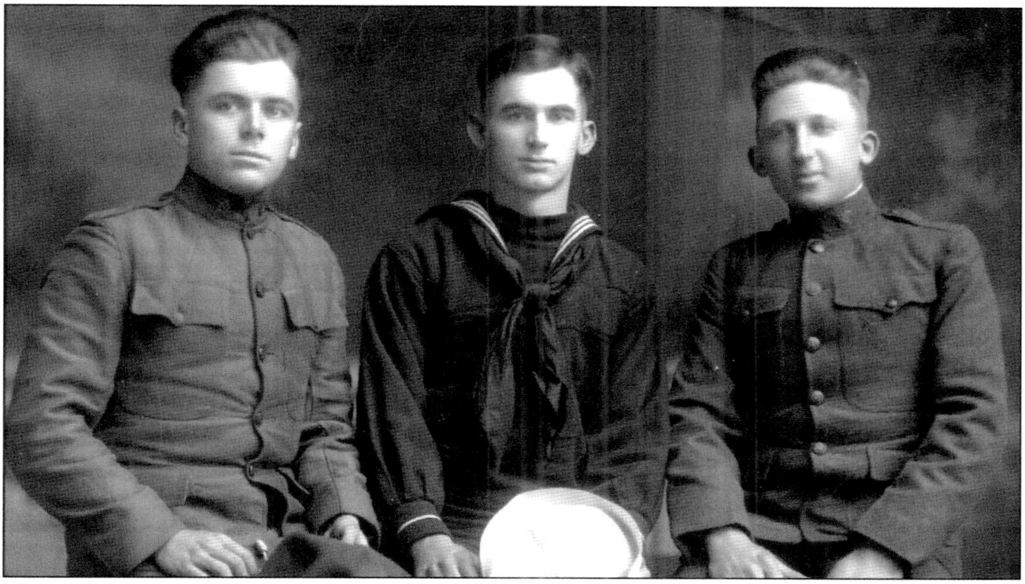

The Southwest Garden has a large stock of two- and four-family dwellings built after World War I and World War II to provide housing for soldiers returning to their community. These young men enlisted during World War I and lived in the neighborhood. From left to right are John P. English, Arthur English, and Fred Hardesty. The photograph was taken by well-known St. Louis photographers the Gerhard Sisters. (Mary Ann English Winkelmann and Marella Hardesty Baird collection.)

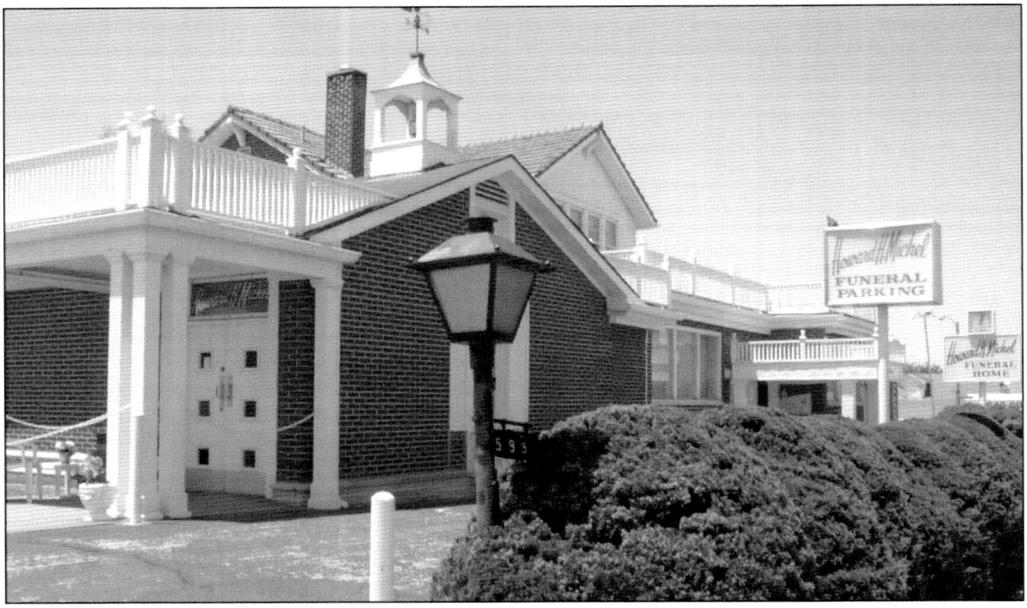


The Howard Michel Funeral Home (site D16) at 5930 Southwest Avenue is listed in the 1955 city directory. In the 1800s, the owner was John Johnson, and there is a trail of building permits uncovering the history. In 1889, two dwellings and a feed store were built. In 1897 and 1898, two more structures were built. In 1903 and 1905, a stable and a henhouse followed. By 1920, J. F. and Margaret Green were the residents. (Photograph by Janice Markham.)

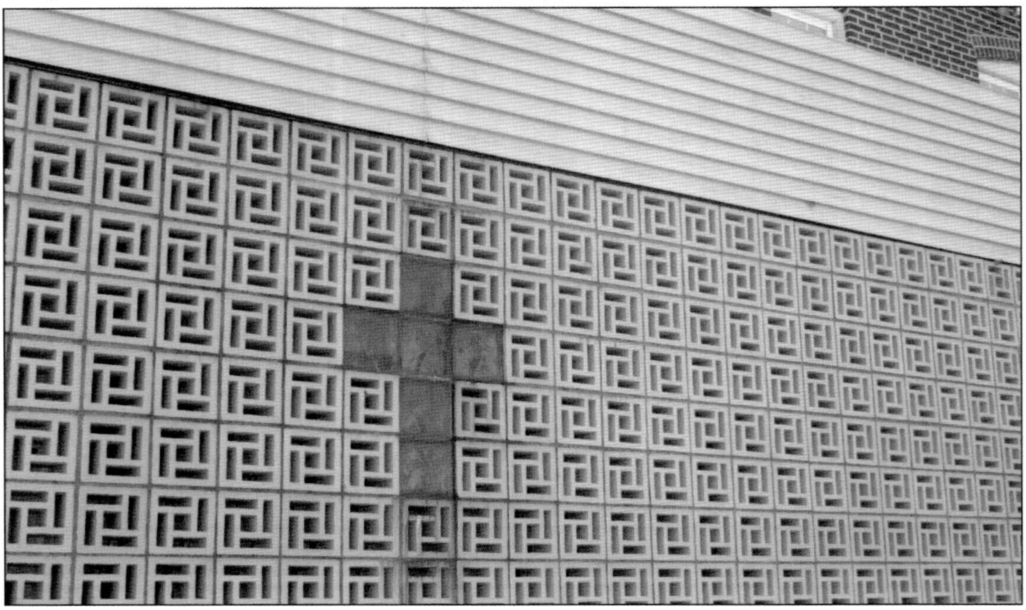

The structure with the rooftop peering behind the cross at Howard Michel Funeral Home was built in 1927. In the 1930 city directory, the address is listed as the office and home of Dr. Horace F. Cleveland. In 1942, the doctor was still there. The Michels became the owners in the 1950s. In 1975, there was an addition built by the Emmernegger Construction Company. (Photograph by Janice Markham.)

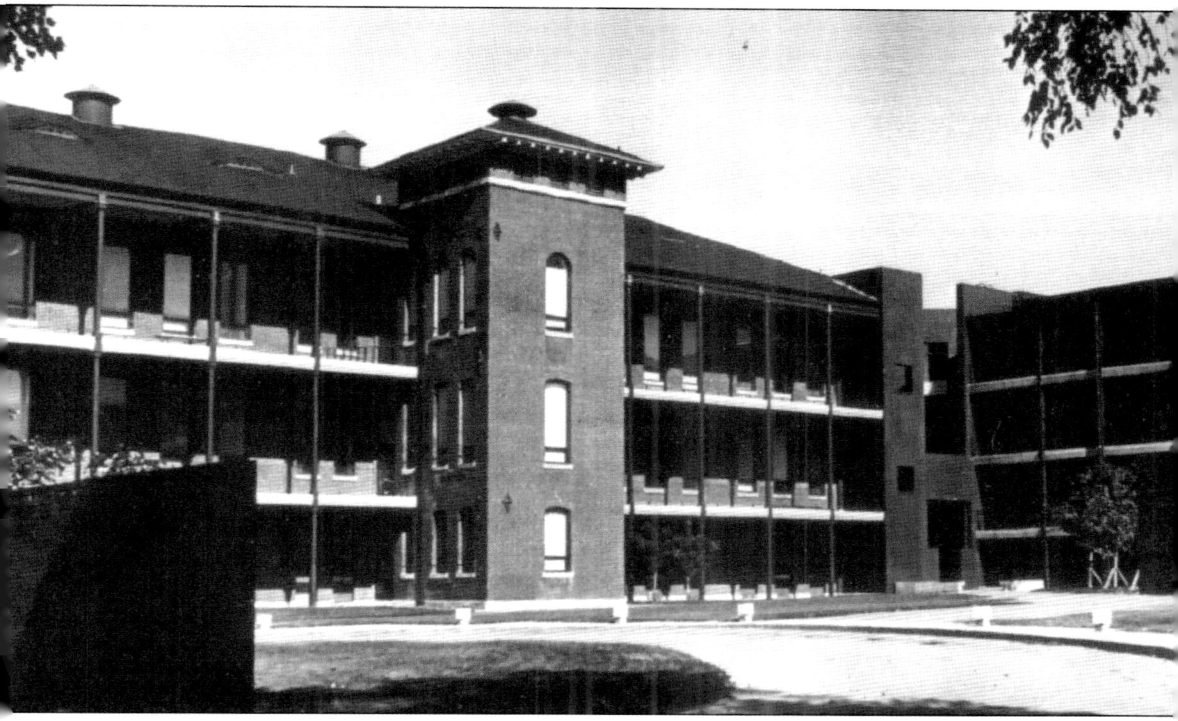

One Campbell Plaza (site D17) at Fifty-ninth and Arsenal Streets has its history, which was researched by Laura Lodewyck, on display in the main lobby. This photograph of the complex, taken around 1972, registers abandonment. The complex that was purchased in 1996 by some of the partners that make up CDG Engineers Architects Planners opened in 1872. The St. Louis County Poorhouse was the official name, but it was unofficially known as the poor farm. In the 136 years after its opening, the poor farm went through many changes. When the poorhouse opened, it was part of St. Louis County. In 1876, it was taken over by the City of St. Louis. In 1888 when C. W. Orear wrote *Commercial and Architectural St. Louis*, this is what he had to say about the premises: "City Poor House and Farm is near the Insane Asylum. An extensive and expensive building of four stories, built of brick and stone to accommodate half a thousand of people." (Richard D. Lodewyck, CDG Engineers Architects Planners.)

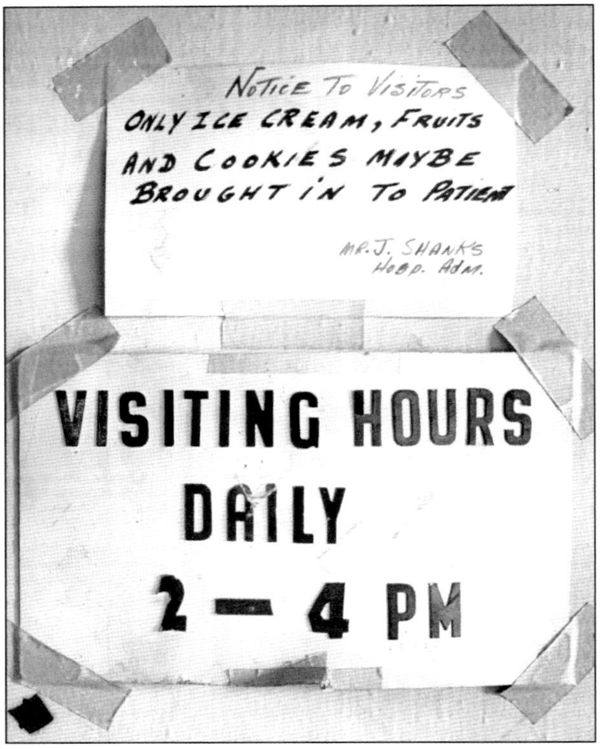


The patients are gone, and only the sign remains. In 1910, the city poorhouse became the city infirmary, and in 1952, it became the Chronic Hospital. The destitute patients were sick, injured, battling incurable diseases such as tuberculosis and insanity, or dying. In 1968, the Chronic Hospital closed. It applied for Medicare, but because the complex was in such bad shape, it did not qualify. (Richard D. Lodewyck, CDG Engineers Architects Planners.)

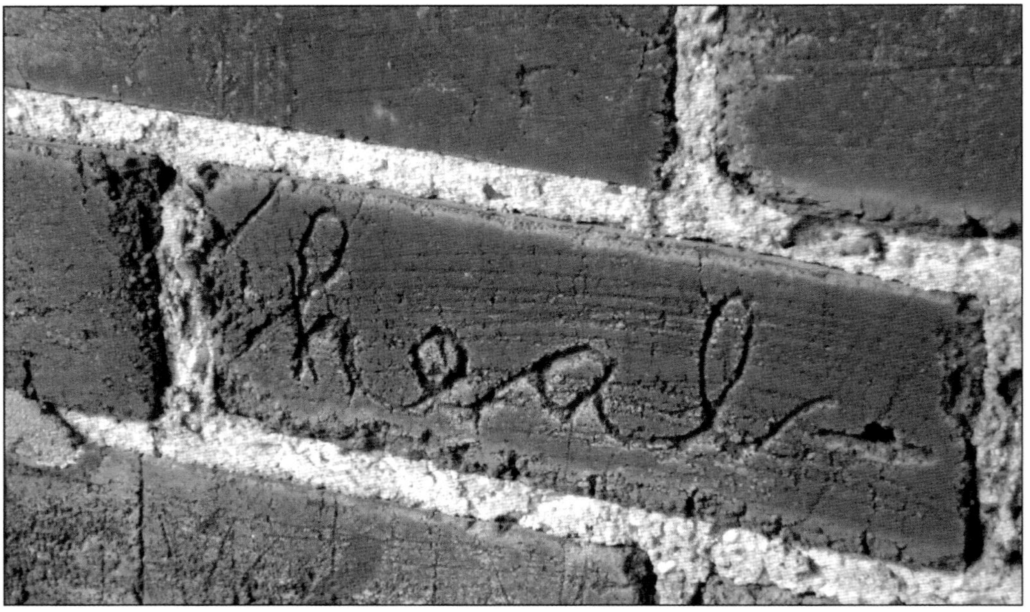


There is no way of knowing what year a patient's hopes to heal were etched on this brick. The exterior walls of the complex hold messages in words, others are marks, perhaps counting the days until patients got out. The complex did have some healing in 1996 when it was purchased by CDG Engineers Architects Planners, which specializes in materials management. Its offices are located here. (Richard D. Lodewyck, CDG Engineers Architects Planners.)

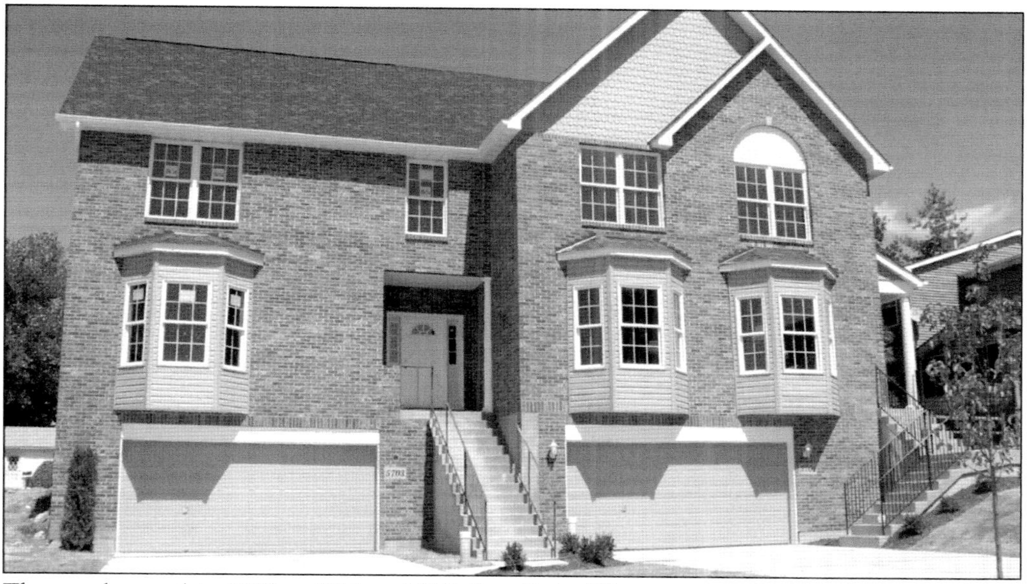

The new homes (site D18) at 5719 and 5721 Parc Ridge Way are part of Parc Ridge Estates. They range from single-family villa-style homes to attached town houses. They sell from $315,000 to $900,000. This development is projected to bring in an investment of more than $18 million to the City of St. Louis and was 25 percent presold before a display home was built. The groundbreaking took place in October 2005, and the development is anticipated to be completed by 2009. (Benckendorf collection.)

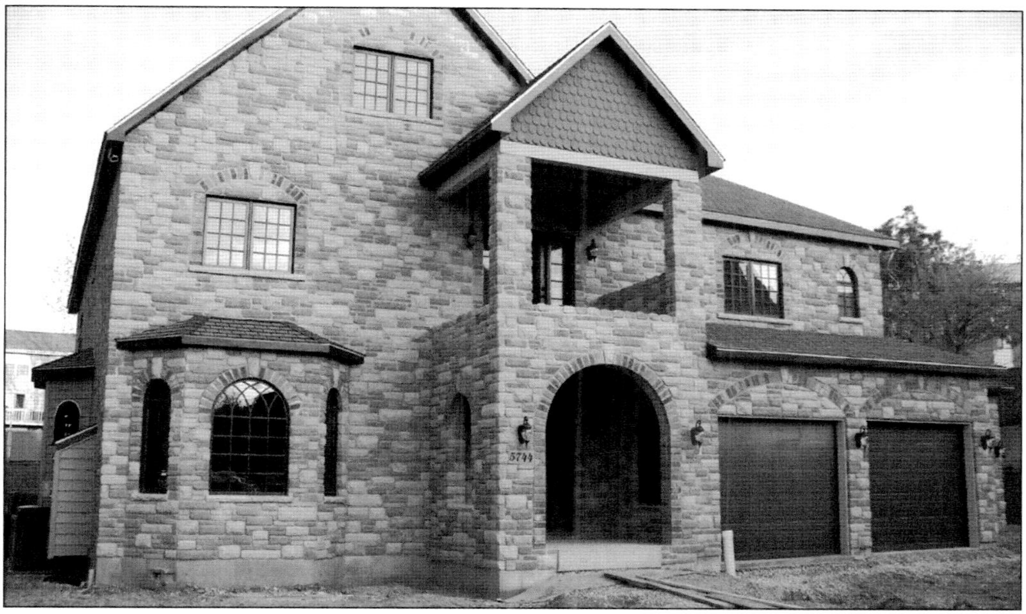

A new home at 5744 Vera Court is one of the 52 single-family homes planned for Parc Ridge Estates. This area was not residential previously. There were no streets or utilities to support housing. The City of St. Louis worked closely with the developers to make Parc Ridge Estates a reality. This development is very close to the Hill, the Italian area of St. Louis. The name Parc comes from *parco*, the Italian word for park. (Benckendorf collection.)

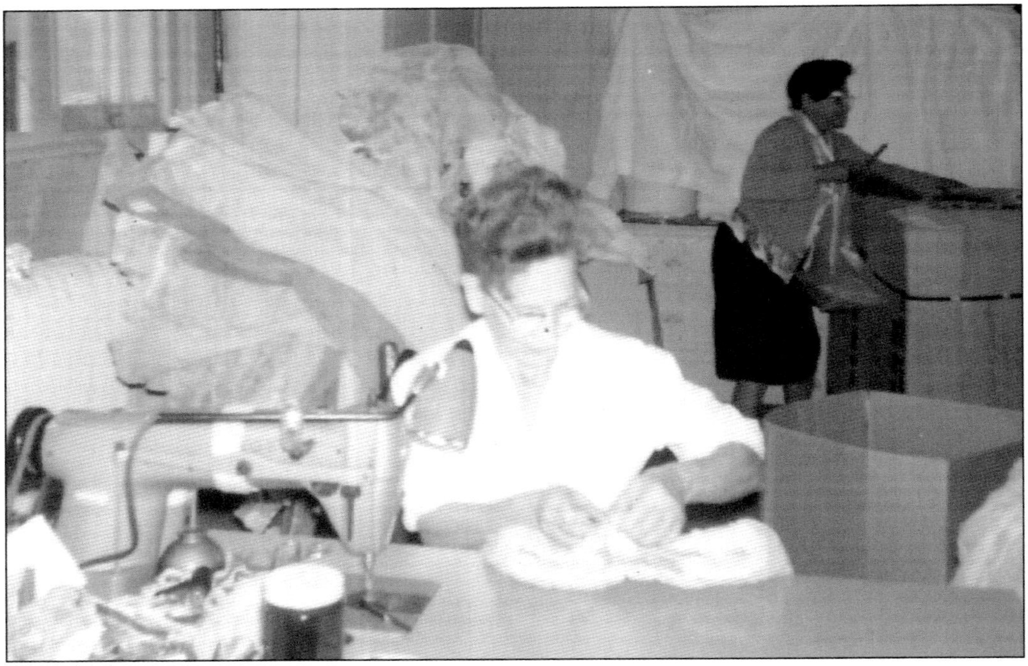

May Schreiber, sitting, and an unidentified lady are at work in the Isolation Hospital laundry. Schreiber lived at 5581 Connecticut Street, a short distance from the hospital. The Schreibers were some of the first residents of the hastily built houses called "cracker boxes" on the street. There was a housing shortage after World War II, and returning servicemen and their families needed homes. Schreiber lived in her house until 1995 when she moved to a nursing home. (Schreiber family collection.)

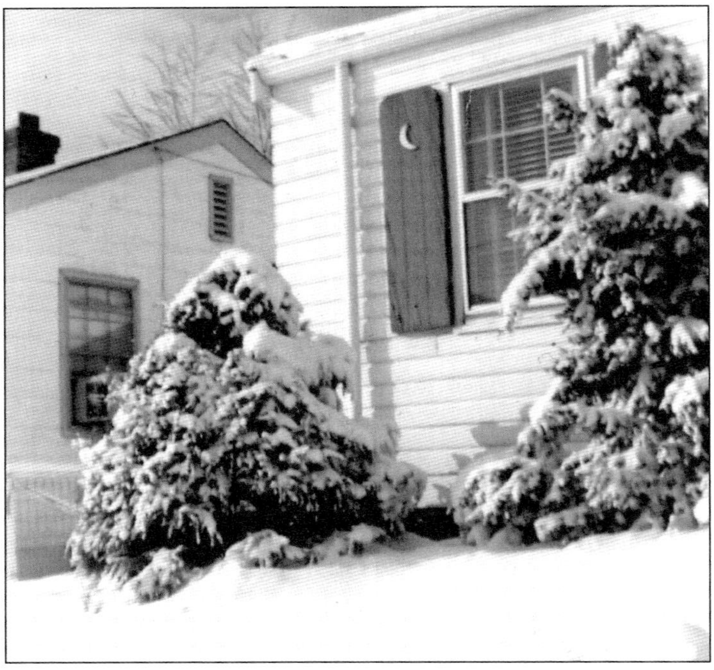

In back of Parc Ridge Estates, there are rows of one-story single-family homes built in the 1940s. The residents of Connecticut Street were working-class people who raised their families and still lived in these homes that were built to meet the demand of soldiers returning from war. Today Parc Ridge Estates homes are meeting the demands of present times—new high-end urban housing. (Schreiber family collection.)

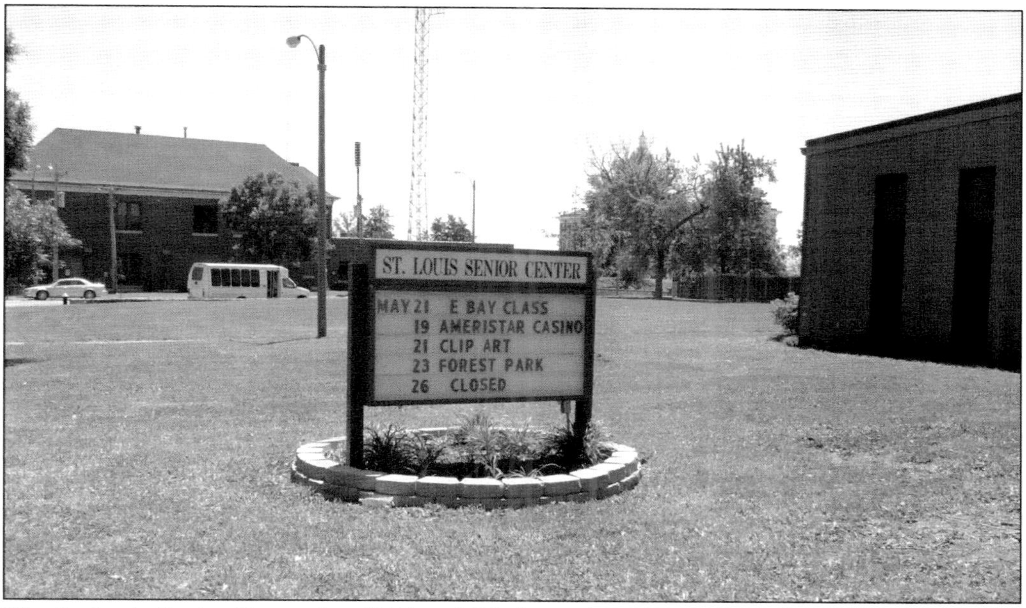


The St. Louis Senior Center (site D19) at 5602 Arsenal Street is a busy place where seniors can keep active by taking classes and visiting city attractions. In the 1920 city directory, the Isolation Hospital for Children and the Infectious Disease Hospital are listed at this address. In 1930, it is listed as the Isolation Hospital. By 1955, it became the St. Louis Chronic Hospital, and in 1965, it is listed as Washington University Medical Center. (Photograph by Janice Markham.)

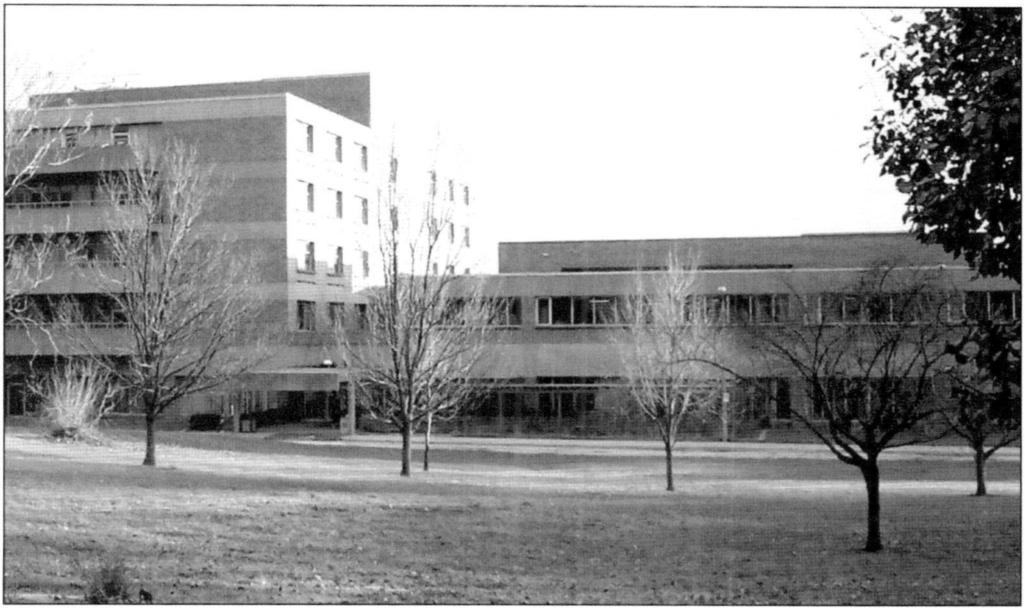

The Truman Restorative Center was a 220-bed nursing home that opened in 1967 and closed its doors in 2003. Developers Mark and Laura Benckendorf, the owners of the 5700 Property, LLC, bought the land in 2004. The Benckendorfs bought an additional parcel of land adjoining 5700 Arsenal Street for residential development. The two parcels total 8.76 acres. The old nursing home was demolished to make room for Parc Ridge Estates. (Benckendorf collection.)

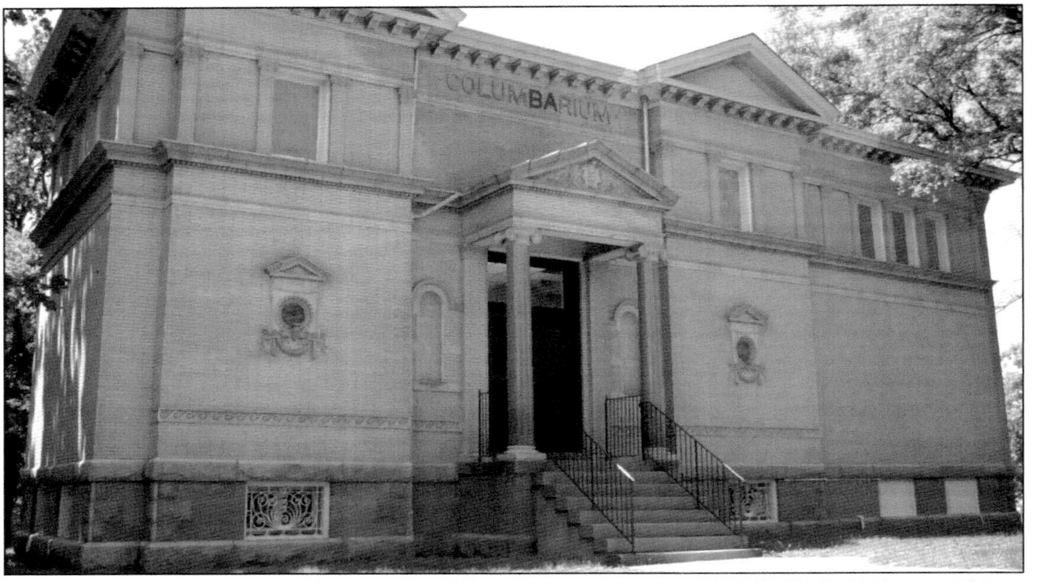


The Columbarium (site D20) at 3211 Sublette Avenue is part of Valhallas's Hillcrest Abbey. Designed by architect Otto Wilhelmi, one of the founders and originators of the Missouri Crematory Association, it was built in 1895. In the 1920 city directory, custodian L. J. Schreiber is also listed here. The Seifert Dairy was next to the property. In 1930, the Blackmer and Post Pipe Company, owners of mines, is listed across the street at 3222 Sublette Avenue. (Photograph by Janice Markham.)

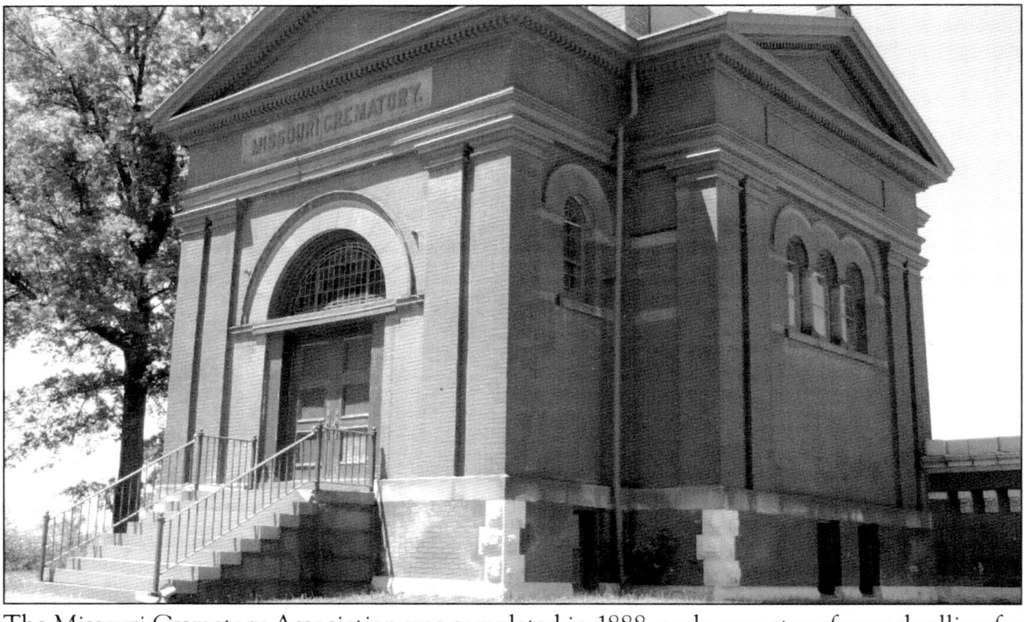


The Missouri Crematory Association was completed in 1888, and a one-story frame dwelling for $800 was built the same year. In 1915, outlaw Frank James was cremated here. Frank's brother was the infamous Jesse James. In 1866, the James brothers and cousin George Clifford Wymore robbed a bank in Liberty. Wymore was killed, but the James brothers got away. They went on to become part of the James-Younger gang. Jesse was killed in 1882. (Photograph by Janice Markham.)

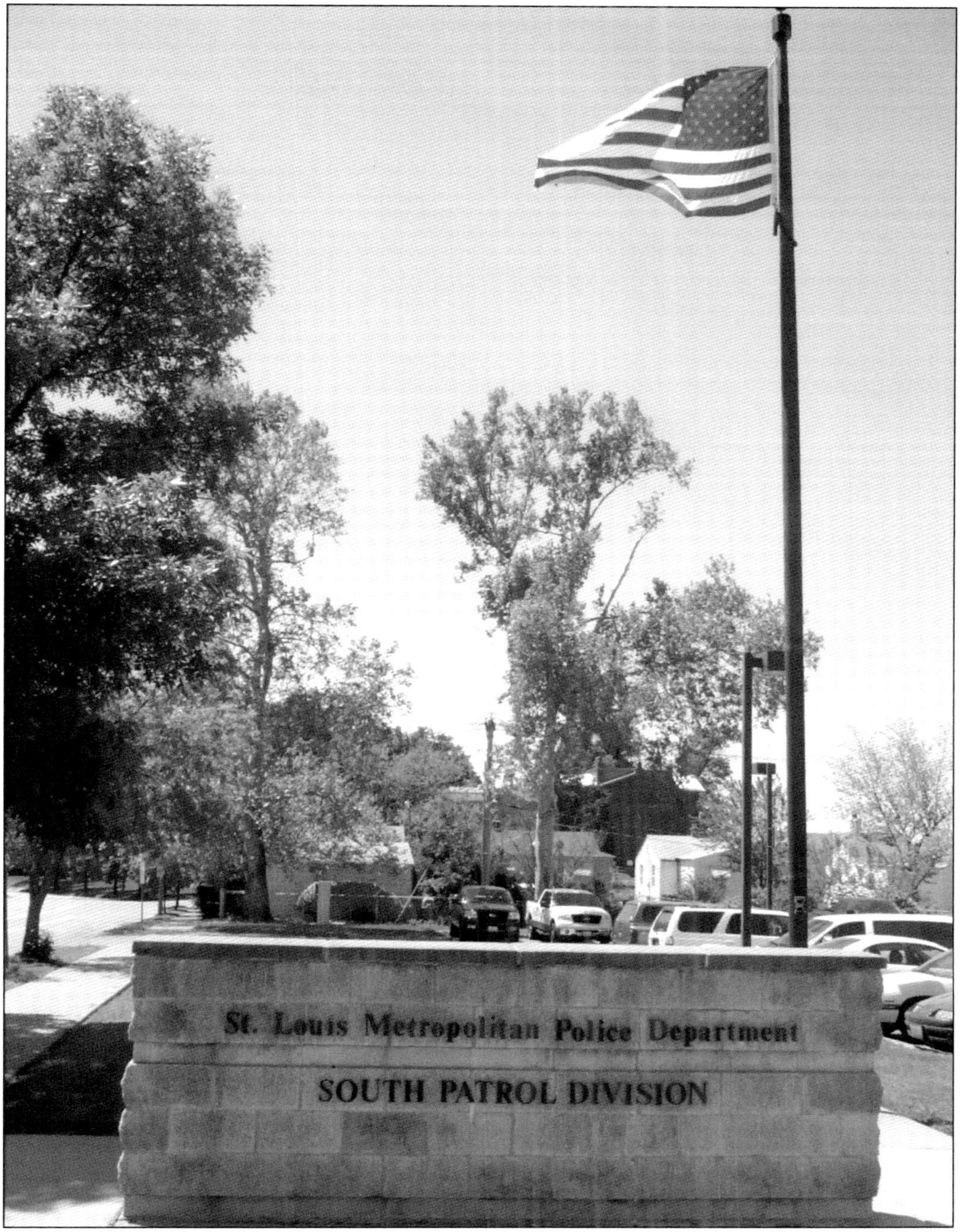


The St. Louis Metropolitan Police Department, South Patrol Division, at 3157 Sublette Avenue was the site of a ceremony to mark the 55th anniversary of the attempted Southwest Bank robbery on April 24, 2008. Former officer Melburn F. Stein was recognized for his heroic actions during the robbery for saving a hostage by shooting one of the robbers. Stein was never given formal recognition until he attended afternoon roll call at the station. (Photograph by Janice Markham.)

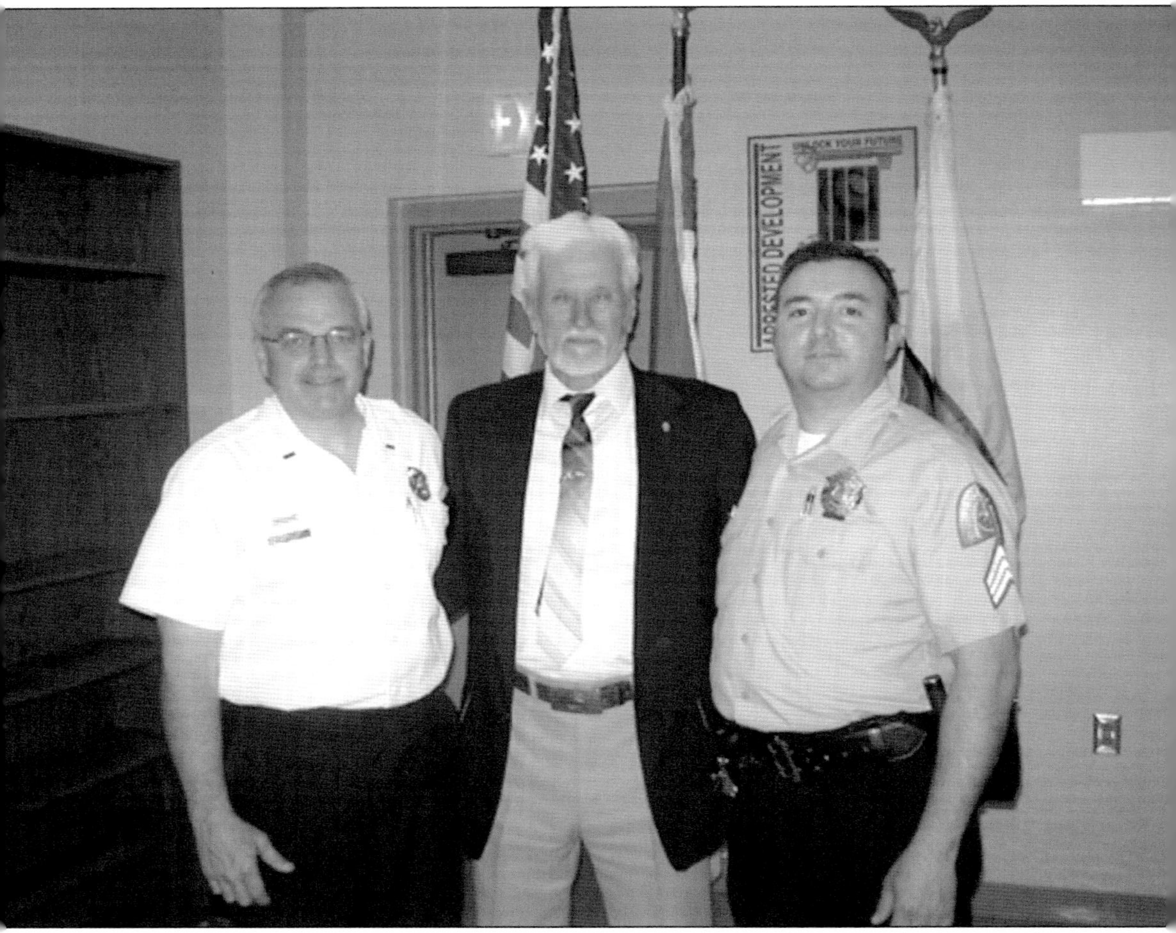

Kim Bell, writer for the *St. Louis Post-Dispatch*, wrote the article on April 25, 2008, "Bravery Never Gets Old," to mark the anniversary of the bank robbery. Lt. Dan Coll called Melburn F. Stein, age 94, an inspiration to young officers. Coll and Sgt. John Vollman, collectors and historians of police history, organized the ceremony. Marking the celebration are, from left to right, Coll, Stein, and Vollman. Stein's wife, Mavis, and Ed Berra, a representative of Southwest Bank, were also there. (Sgt. John Vollman collection.)

# BIBLIOGRAPHY

Amsler, Kevin. *Final Resting Place, the Lives and Deaths of Famous St. Louisans*. St. Louis: Virginia Publishing, 1997.

Casey, Marie A. *Schnucks 60 Years of Commitment to Our Customers, Associates and Communities*. St. Louis: Casey Communications and Schnuck Markets, 1999.

exhibits.slpl.org/mayors/

Hannon, Robert E. *St. Louis: Its Neighborhoods and Neighbors, Landmarks and Milestones*. St. Louis: St. Louis Regional Commerce and Growth Association, 1986.

McAlester, Virginia and Lee. *A Field Guide to American Houses*. New York: Alfred A. Knopf, 2003.

Southwest Garden Neighborhood Association. *Home and Garden Improvement Tour*. May 20, 2007.

———. *Home and Garden Improvement Tour*. June 26, 2005.

Wright, John A. *Discovering African-American St. Louis: A Guide to Historic Sites*. St. Louis: Missouri Historical Society Press and St. Louis Public Library, 1994.

www.familysearch.org

www.mobot.org

www.saucecafe.com

www.southwestgarden.org

www.stlcin.misouri.org

www.usgennet.org

# ACROSS AMERICA, PEOPLE ARE DISCOVERING SOMETHING WONDERFUL. *THEIR HERITAGE.*

Arcadia Publishing is the leading local history publisher in the United States. With more than 3,000 titles in print and hundreds of new titles released every year, Arcadia has extensive specialized experience chronicling the history of communities and celebrating America's hidden stories, bringing to life the people, places, and events from the past. To discover the history of other communities across the nation, please visit:

## www.arcadiapublishing.com

Customized search tools allow you to find regional history books about the town where you grew up, the cities where your friends and family live, the town where your parents met, or even that retirement spot you've been dreaming about.

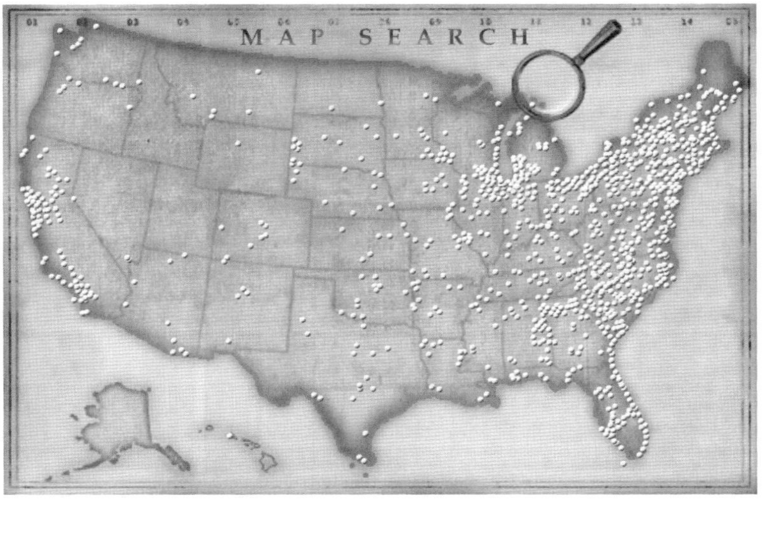